TONY GLENVILLE

New Icons of Fashion Illustration

LAURENCE KING PUBLISHING

LAURENCE KING

Published in 2013 by
Laurence King Publishing Ltd
361–373 City Road
London EC1V 1LR

email: enquiries@laurenceking.com
www.laurenceking.com

A catalogue record for this book is available
from the British Library.

ISBN: 978-1-78067-104-8

Design: Praline
Picture research: Claire Gouldstone
Commissioning editor: Helen Rochester
Senior editor: Sophie Wise
Printed in China

Front cover and endpapers: Jason Brooks, *Lipstick*, 2011.
Back cover: Sara Singh for Estée Lauder, 2008.
Cover and endpapers design: Charlotte Bolton

Facing page: Bil Donovan, *Oscars Red Carpet,
February 2011, Vanity Fair Italia*, 2011.

Dedication page: Cédric Rivrain, *Lara in Balenciaga*, 2007.

I would like to dedicate this book to
my parents, Joan and Leslie, and to Auntie Rose.
Thank you for planting all the creative
seeds that eventually grew into this book.

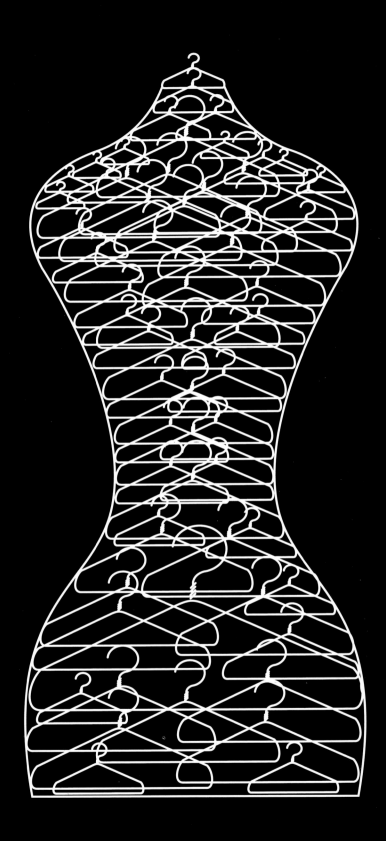

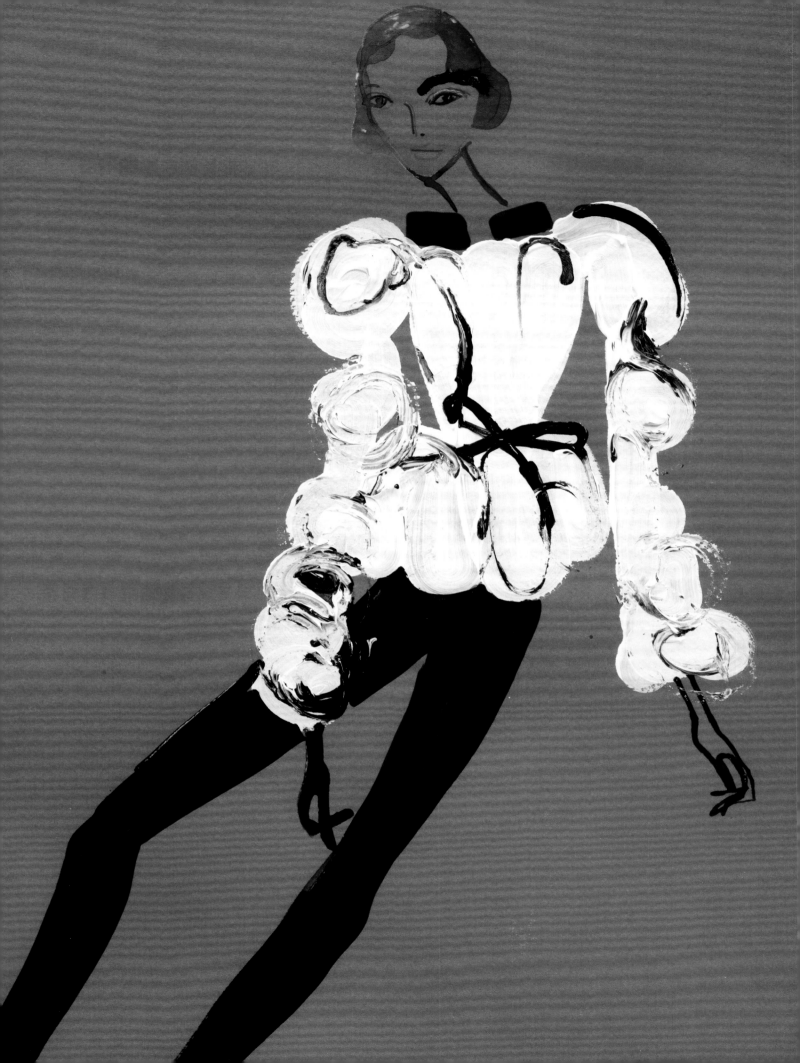

INTRODUCTION

The art of the contemporary fashion illustrator can be seen as defying the times – an anachronism in this age of the digital photograph, instant internet communication and technology-driven creative processes. Even when computer software is used as a tool, the idea of forging a career as a fashion illustrator today seems highly unrealistic. Yet in spite of this, or possibly even because of this, from the Mediterranean to Scandinavia, from the UK to the USA, highly accomplished and highly successful fashion illustrators are working away.

After the Second World War it seemed as if fashion illustration would be relegated to becoming a historic craft. It was seen increasingly as either an oddity that broke the mould or a still much-needed filler for newspapers or advertisers that had smaller budgets and were unable to afford a costly shoot. In *An Introduction to Fashion Illustration*, published in 1980, Madeleine Ginsberg closes with the words: 'The era of the fashion artist came to an end in 1939, for the post-war years have belonged to the artist–photographer, not the illustrator.' But some thirty years after this bold statement was made, fashion illustration might be described as enjoying a renaissance, not just in Paris or London, but across the world.

Perhaps this is because capturing the ephemeral world of fashion creates a document of our society and the times in which we live. Often the seemingly inconsequential drawings and portraits of fashion illustrators tell us more about our values and lifestyle choices than the posed, edited and re-touched images of photo shoots. Fashion illustration is, by its very nature, of-the-moment. The characters in Jordi Labanda's illustrations, for example, speak to us of the latest style fetishes, from the clothes that the figures wear through to their body language.

It is also true that we are currently rediscovering craft and technique and seeking to preserve skills – such as drawing from life at speed – that were in danger of disappearing. Fashion illustration is an art based simply on the skill of the hand and the eye. The delicacy of the line in an image by Cédric Rivrain, for instance, reminds us of this. The hand of the illustrator demonstrates both the timeless craft of illustration and the follies and fancies of the current mode. With his sharp observations and graphic lines, Piet Paris provides another fine example of this, confirming that fashion illustration is and always has been about a great deal more than a pretty drawing of a pretty dress.

The enduring art of illustrating fashion has been explored in many forms, from exhibitions to books. Many of these publications and showcases have been about artists of the past, however. While they demonstrate that the artists who stand the test of time are both those who use the recording of fashion as part of a larger picture and those who focus on the illustration of fashion as an end within itself, there is little available on today's artists of tomorrow. This compendium seeks to fill that gap and celebrate fashion illustration's renaissance.

Tellingly, it is at the height of our interest in multimedia and cross-media communication that our interest in fashion illustration has become much more widespread. From department stores to jewellers, all the major fashion businesses are investing in the art of the illustrator and realizing there are myriad styles for the drawn image, from polished technical effects that only the computer can achieve to traditional pencil or watercolour delicacy. Major fashion stores across the globe surprise us by using, say, Tanya Ling for their campaign as opposed to the glossy images of photographic studios.

Today, while fashion illustrators continue in their traditional role of recording and observing – communicating through line the essence of a season – they also have much broader horizons. These include advertising campaigns, of course, but also designs for accessories, such as bags, and even china plates – and this by illustrators as diverse as Julie Verhoeven, David Downton or Jeffrey Fulvimari. Moreover, as technology rides roughshod across craft in many domains, fashion illustration is reinventing itself through the application of technology, albeit in tandem with more traditional drawing skills. Indeed, Richard Haines's swift hand-drawn lines are posted on-line in a matter of minutes.

Above all else, however, there remains the joy and wonder of watching an illustrator put drawing instrument to paper and capture, in a few brief seconds, the line and form of the model, the pose and the movement of the garments.

Page 8
Carlos Aponte, *Form*, 2007.

Page 10
Tanya Ling, *Burberry* A/W 11, 2011.

Facing page
David Downton, *Love YSL*, 2010.

Following page
Piet Paris, Backdrop for Viktor & Rolf S/S 11 collection, 2011.

CARLOS APONTE

A bold, graphic line characterizes the work of Carlos Aponte. Even when his imagery is comparatively soft there is a clarity and confidence to his approach. His statements are strong and rely on elimination of the superfluous, and this in turn depends on a thorough understanding of the subject and faultless execution. A solid technical foundation is the hallmark of many fashion illustrators; the importance of the editorial eye cannot be underestimated, and bold omissions demand supreme assurance. Aponte has a great feel for the sweeping line within his work, turning the brogue detailing of a classic shoe into the spiralling flight of an insect, the flow of an arm during exercise into a fan of colours or transforming a linear map of New York into the swinging outline of a dress. Thus his strong lines are fluid rather than aggressive, attracting observers rather than challenging them.

Often, graphic boldness has a hard or static edge to it, but Aponte has an absolute understanding of how clothes move; in his latest works the figures are imbued with implied movement through the use of painterly lines. While his output is totally contemporary, Aponte also draws on the heritage of the bold communicators of the twentieth century who had a linear and graphic approach too; he is firmly a modernist yet there is a timeless quality to his work. His sense of balance within a layout, his control of colour – often monochromatic – and his use of pure line can be seen to great advantage in his menswear fashion drawings. These pinpoint a specific look and genre but retain a universal appeal.

It is interesting to note that although right up until the early twentieth century there was extreme control in the line of most fashion illustration, dictated mainly by the quality and modes of reproduction (Étienne Drian always excepted), later fashion illustrators such as René Bouché or Eric display more freedom of line and show the physical marks of the pen or brush clearly within their work. Now we have returned to clarity of line, not always due to the use of technology and computers in the creation of the image, but often through the actual mark making – perhaps more related in fashion illustration terms to the work of René Gruau. Aponte's desire to sharpen the image has led him to work on new techniques for creating the line beyond straightforward drawing, for example introducing 'tape lines' that are flat and hard-edged yet at the same time capable of being manipulated into his repertoire of styles.

Seated Model, Gilbert & Lewis, 2011.

Bold tonal planes of blue are accented with red in the fabric pattern of the matching shorts and shirt in this cropped image.

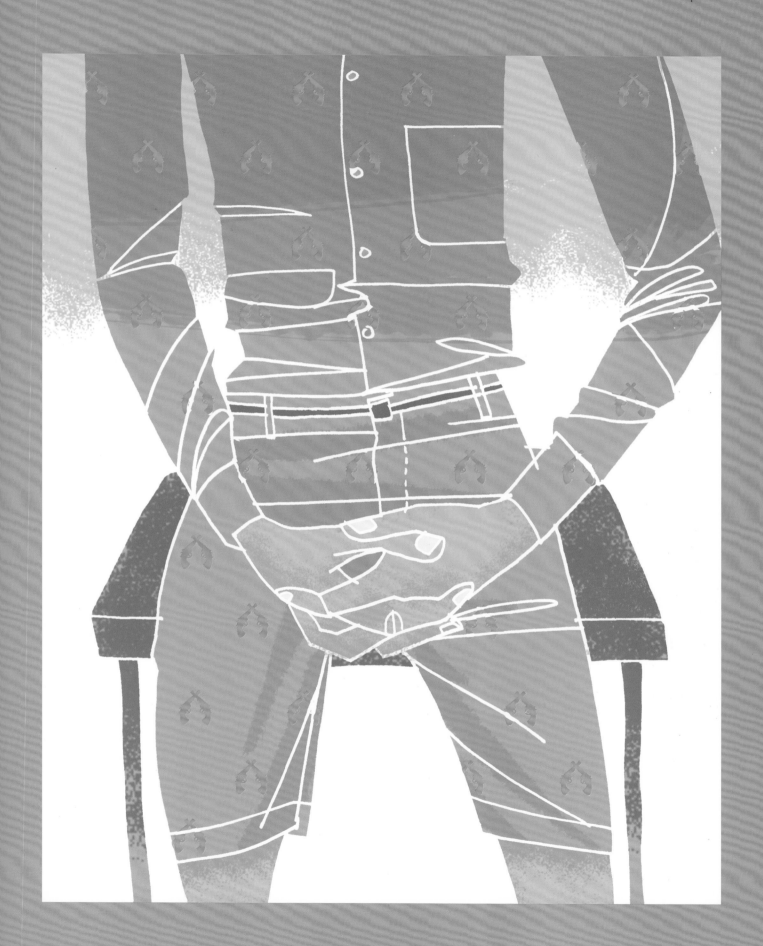

Left and bottom left
Black & White I & II,
Gianfranco Ferré, 2013.

Below
Untitled, Visionaire, 1993.

Aponte crafts tape into graphic
lines, communicating a strong
feeling for silhouette as well
as movement.

Where and when were you born and where do you live now?
I was born in New York but grew up in Puerto Rico, where I have spent most of my life. Now I live in downtown Jersey City, a few minutes away from downtown New York. I have the best of both worlds: the excitement of the city and a quiet and beautiful working retreat.

Any particular childhood influences?
My first influence was Marvel superheroes, then it became classic films from Hollywood. But my biggest influence was the way of thinking of fashion illustrator Antonio Lopez, whom I met a few years before he passed away. I attended his last drawing seminar in Altos de Chavón. He taught me to always try something new, to experiment. He became my mentor and big brother; we both shared the same cultural background so it was easy to relate to him. He strongly encouraged me to come to New York.

What is your earliest drawing memory?
One of my earliest drawing memories was doing a Miss Universe contest with my own drawings of women with crazy costumes. They were all done with notebook paper, pencil and Crayola.

What was your first professional work?
I did some images for a hotel promoting a fashion show in Puerto Rico. I wanted to make sure they got excited so I presented them with a lot of ideas – I spoiled them – and after that first assignment they expected as many ideas as before.

Do you have a preferred medium?
I don't have a preference. I love to hand draw but I always like to try something different.

Do you work in silence or with background music / radio?
I like to play music. I like to create a soundtrack for a job, like a film – what's the storyline, what's the mood?… Sometimes I work without music. It all depends on the project.

What would be your ideal commission?
Any campaign with a daring and visionary art director.

Are you a slow and careful or quick and speedy draughtsman?
I'm pretty fast, but whatever I do with the artwork has to feel fresh.

Do you keep a sketchbook?
Yes, I always keep a sketchbook where I put down ideas, sometimes even short stories. Some of these visual ideas end up in a commissioned job or my portfolio.

How would you describe your work?
In constant search and evolution, just like fashion.

Above
Untitled, Christian Dior, 2003.

Right
Untitled, 2010.

As with his tape illustrations, Aponte embraces Arte Povera, using humble media – in this case corrugated card creates a textured A-line dress.

José & David, Gilbert & Lewis, 2011.

Simple clothing is communicated using body language and a heightened sense of proportion.

Below
Scarf, Gilbert & Lewis, 2011.

Grooming requires careful styling to work as an illustration. Here glasses, a bandana and a carefully coiffed preppy hairstyle get the message across loud and clear.

Untitled, Gilbert & Lewis, 2011.

The pose used by the illustrator is all-important: these relaxed images show menswear as worn by real people in a real world.

TINA BERNING

Tina Berning has a very original approach to fashion illustration, both in terms of technique and results; however there is a faint echo of another illustrator in her work – Constantin Guys, who drew in the nineteenth century. The use of monochromatic wash, the interaction between the subject and the viewer, the careful observation of the subject allied with an off-kilter individualism are truly special within her work. Also, although in other ways her work is very unlike that of contemporary fashion artist Hippolyte Romain, Berning likewise fills the page with fashion 'types', recording their expressions and the look of that moment.

Berning has a layered approach to much of her work, surprising the viewer with an abstract panel, or a pattern seemingly unrelated to the main image. There is a wonderfully disconcerting quality to the final image, and her work with photographs takes this to another level. In this way she is able to create a multi-layered fantasy that draws the observer into the world of her imagination. Berning is both communicator and creator, showing us her particular vision of the clothing. Like Diana Vreeland, she forces us to believe that this is the real thing – her strength of vision convinces us that the hair was this wild, that the bow was this big… It is not a question of 'artistic licence' – a much-abused term loved by those who cannot draw well – but a characteristic of her work that the drawing must tell the tale she wants us to see. The results are superbly worked and are often portraits in their own right as much as they are fashion illustrations.

Alongside all of this is the ability to draw almost anything she is commissioned to draw, from a series of women about the house for an architectural publication through to Soviet leaders. The hallmark of the great fashion illustrator is, as always, this basic essential, to be able to draw anything the client commissions, but also to have a specialist understanding of fashion as an extra fillip to the portfolio. Berning's work displays a range of techniques, a range of subjects and a range of moods; her portfolio offers a challenge to all those wishing to enter this world of illustration simply to draw fashion. Her mantra – 'a drawing a day keeps the doctor away' – demonstrates her work ethic: keep drawing. It also implies that one should keep drawing all kinds of subjects. From *The New York Times* to a vast range of European publications, her individual and exciting work is in demand, proving that such dedicated practice yields results.

Twiggy, *A Guide to Looking and Feeling Fabulous Over Forty*, Penguin Books, 2008.

Contrasting the boldness of the fashion with soft rounds of colour, Berning shows us the bow-tied blouse, longer-line waistcoat and box-pleated skirt in a modern yet romantic image.

Suzy Menkes, The New York Times, 2007.

This portrait of fashion writer extraordinaire Suzy Menkes, complete with her famous hairstyle, conveys her personality exactly. The blurred depiction of the fashion imparts a timeless quality to the image.

Where and when were you born and where do you live now?
Born in Braunschweig (or 'Brunswick', a town near Hannover) in 1969, I grew up in West Germany and moved to Berlin ten years ago. My sister and father now live next door and Berlin has become my hometown.

Any particular childhood influences?
I grew up with the FAZ magazine, the weekly supplement of my father's newspaper (the *Frankfurter Allgemeine Zeitung*). My sisters and I fought about who would get it first to cut out the beautiful photos. I was the youngest so I had to settle for with the remains – the illustrations – and they were wonderful. Heinz Edelmann, famous for his art direction on *Yellow Submarine*, contributed at least twice a month; Hans Hillmann, Paola Paglia, Brad Holland, just to name a few, were also regular contributors. I did not know that these pictures were called illustrations but I knew that this was what I wanted to do always.

What is your earliest drawing memory?
As a small child I would draw on everything as soon as I got hold of a pencil. This was especially true of our walls, so my mother painted a whole wall with chalkboard paint, on which I was supposed to draw – and I did. Now my daughter starts drawing on everything as soon as she gets hold of a pencil – especially the walls...

What was your first professional work?
The first illustrations I sold were drawings for bakery paper bags. One of these bags, originally produced in 1992, is still being produced – a copyright disaster for me!

Do you have a preferred medium?
Venetian glass quilts and ink.

Do you work in silence or with background music/radio?
There is a magic music choice that has been following me for a long time, that will always help me get into the mood and concentrate. It's like a mantra. When I am doing all-day stuff I listen to the radio (the news channel).

What would be your ideal commission?
Any commission that shows respect for the artist's work as well as the artist's respect for the content is a good commission. Combined with a challenging subject, it is ideal.

Are you a slow and careful or quick and speedy draughtsman?
I take my time in thinking about things, preparing and planning. The execution is mostly fast. When it is not fast, I am stuck and then it can take a long time...

Do you keep a sketchbook?
Together with friends I have a sketch blog (Bilderklub.de) that we have been filling for the last seven years, sometimes a lot, sometimes less. The times I do it daily are definitely the best periods creativity-wise. A sketchbook, or anything that keeps you evoking and following your inspiration day by day, is essential for sustaining creative work.

How would you describe your work?
Drawing is learning to look properly and I try my best to look properly, mostly at human beings.

Do you research your subjects? How do you research?
For research, the internet is of course always an option – especially random abstract searches that can lead to very interesting results. But of course I can't work without my collection of fleamarket treasures: photobooks like *Women in Paris* from 1965, or a compendium of collector cards of film stars from the 40s – and the list grows, from Sunday to Sunday.

How does your personal work relate to your professional output?
Doing both illustration and exhibition work, I love to switch between commissioned and non-commissioned art. I am very thankful for the fact that I am confronted, through my illustration work, with mostly time-relevant subjects and these flow automatically into my personal work.

Anything else you wish to tell the reader?
I always love to share my grandmother's credo, which she had in old-fashioned handwritten type in a little frame on her wall: *Liebe lacht doch*. Love laughs nonetheless.

Above
Vanessa & Johnny, Süddeutsche Zeitung, 2011.

A famous couple who are always wonderfully dressed but not necessarily fashionable, Johnny Depp and Vanessa Paradis are shown here complementing each other's style perfectly.

Right
Rustic, 'Fashiontrends', Branche und Business Fachverlag, 2010.

The dark herringbone tweed and furry winter scarf are accented by rich onyx green and ruby red, demonstrating the styling that strong fashion illustration requires.

Left

Darlinghurst Strasse, Riot Magazine, 2006.

By combining the architectural curves of a Balenciaga cape with the graphic pleats of a Pierrot ruff, linked by Harlequin diamonds, Berning brings commedia dell'arte to fashion.

Below

Romantic, 'Fashiontrends', Branche und Business Fachverlag, 2010.

The exquisite detailed drawing of the floral decoration and the delicate handling of the ruffled and bloused dress here is contrasted by the throw-away nonchalance of the background drawing.

Above
Androgyn, 'Fashiontrends',
Branche und Business Fachverlag,
2010.

An aviatrix flying through a
night sky: her dark leather cap
and jacket are played off against
the strong colours of the make-up
and background.

Right
Konfektion, 'Fashiontrends',
Branche und Business Fachverlag,
2010.

The painterly space here contrasts
with the intricate work on the
clothing and allows breathing
space. Within this space an ethereal
bird seems poised for flight.

JASON BROOKS

The ability to create a 'type' – an iconic interpretation of a character, which becomes the personification of a specific time or even a brand – through fashion illustration is well documented. The Arrow Collar Man, the Gibson Girl, René Gruau's Dior Woman – all are examples of characters who developed a life of their own. The Jason Brooks girl and her companions inhabit a world that we long to enter, where gloss and glamour reside alongside a seemingly endless good time – be it on a beach or in a bar. We are seduced into believing that this is a real world, so perfectly has Brooks observed every detail. Like an author who knows the back story of his characters, in this case the artist seems to understand every nuance of his invented world.

One element defines and is common to all his work: detailed observation. The basic ability to draw without technology, and the understanding of line and medium underpin the entire output of this artist. There is never any doubt that the rose held by the model will be exactly the right rose, that the tilt of an eyebrow will convey exactly the correct mood. Even recent, sketchier, work implies that all is present and correct. His commissions spread across a wide range of clients and products, and from early newspaper work through to major campaigns Brooks has brought the same rigour to everything he has touched.

Colour has always played a key role in Brooks's work, with a sharp use of contemporary colour balance in many of his images. Reflecting trends while retaining a personal identity and signature style is always a challenge for a fashion illustrator. Concerns of longevity also enter into the perceived stylishness of a fashion image, be it illustration or photograph. However, Brooks remains totally in control – whether in his glossy digital images or in his simple line drawings – by distilling the essence of what he wishes to say. He exemplifies the need for the professional, full-time fashion illustrator to adapt and move on, yet retains the integrity and strength of his personal vision. A combination of solid, basic skills alongside a desire to embrace technology is reflected in the references in his work. His best-known work is perhaps closer to the great poster and cartoon artists of the twentieth century than to fashion illustrators such as Eric or René Gruau, demonstrating how he has reinvigorated the art of fashion illustration for today.

Model Walking, Pink, 2008.

Smiling directly at the viewer, this long-legged elegante strides confidently across the page in her killer heels. The bold strokes of the artist leave much unsaid and yet tell us everything we need to know.

Where and when were you born and where do you live now?
I was born in London on 23 February 1969 and I now live and have my studio in Brighton, England. Here I have space for all my books and art materials and can really focus on my work.

Any particular childhood influences?
I was insatiable in my desire to make pictures from an early age and my parents were always kind and encouraging. One of my strongest early influences was a trip to Tuscany, when I was six. It was my first experience of looking at large-scale paintings and sculptures of the human figure. I particularly remember standing in front of Paolo Uccello's painting *The Battle of San Romano* in the Uffizi Gallery in Florence and being completely overwhelmed. At that age I particularly loved drawing battle scenes; I think it was because I could attempt to draw figures in all sorts of poses, and they also contained their own sub-narratives. I also used to draw my family and visitors to our house.

What is your earliest drawing memory?
I remember being around two-and-a-half or three and drawing a large head and shoulders in red crayon on a piece of paper, I guess around A1 size. It felt bigger than I was. When I had finished what I strongly remember is the grown-ups' reaction of surprise because I had included details like eyelashes and eyebrows and added hands with fingers on either side of the figure. This was the first time that a drawing I had made brought me unexpected attention and praise.

What was your first professional work?
My first paid illustration work was in my early teens. I used to send drawings to all sorts of windsurfing companies and magazines and sometimes they would publish them and send me £25 or £50, which felt like an absolute fortune at the time. I also drew maps as a teenager that were put on rollers for printing into school exercise books – the company that produced them used to send me royalty cheques twice a year for many years.

My first real break came when I was 22, at Saint Martins College of Art, when British *Vogue* published an illustrated story about New Orleans across five or six pages. That was really exciting and lead to a whole string of wonderful commissions from *Vogue* throughout my time at college.

Left
Fragment, 2011.

Sleek coiffure, arched brow and red lipstick convey a Paris allure, heightened by the strict collared jacket. The band of exotic fabric provides a touch of the oriental.

Below
Lipstick, for Fashion Illustration Gallery, London, 2011.

In a nod to René Gruau and Le Rouge Baiser, Brooks gives us a quadruple red mouth with a tip-tilted curl of seduction.

Do you have a preferred medium?
Drawing on paper is still the foundation of everything I do but the medium I spend the most time using is Photoshop on an Apple Mac. I'm convinced that if illustrators like René Gruau or Antonio [Lopez] were around today they would be using computers extensively because so many of the effects they used – like blocks of hard-edged colour, gradients, coloured films, typography and collage; effects I also tried to create before computers arrived – are now so much easier to work with and manipulate.

Do you work in silence or with background music / radio?
If I'm working on the concept drawings that are the very beginning of a project I prefer it to be as quiet as possible so that I can really, really focus on what I am doing without any distraction or outside influence. The rest of the time though I like to listen to music or radio programmes.

What would be your ideal commission?
I have always wanted to create a series of really stylish illustrated travel books, like sketchbooks illustrating cities around the world. I would also love the freedom to create completely my own artwork, paintings, drawings and sculptures for, say, two years and have a gallery show after that time. I'd like to direct movies or create the title sequence to a James Bond movie in collaboration with David Lynch or Tom Ford. I'd love the opportunity to design and realize a really wide range of products for my own brand. Anything in collaboration with Madonna, Steven Spielberg, Ridley Scott or Karl Lagerfeld would be more than interesting – I could go on…

Are you a slow and careful or quick and speedy draughtsman?
My favourite way to draw is quite swiftly from life, having the person or object in front of me. This is the kind of drawing I have learnt from travelling or when I need to get an idea or composition onto paper quite quickly. Some of my all-time favourite drawings, like Picasso's Vollard Suite etchings, or David Hockney's Rotring portraits using one decisive line, have been an inspiration nearly all my life. Commercially the style I use most takes a lot longer and involves many layers of drawing and colouring over the original quick line drawing that has been scanned in.

Do you keep a sketchbook?
Yes, I love sketchbooks, I have boxes full of them going back many years. My sketchbooks these days tend to be more functional than they have been in earlier periods of my life, as I'm so busy with commercial projects and I tend to write more as well as draw in them.

How would you describe your work?
In five words I would say figurative, idealized, glamorous, sexy and optimistic.

Do you research your subjects? How do you research?
I find research essential and in a general sense it's an ongoing process. I have a small library covering many aspects of art and design at my studio to call upon. Sometimes I assemble a stack of books on a particular theme that will help to inspire me and put me in the right frame of mind – I find it's important to make visual connections and draw on different sources to do my best work. If it's something I need quickly I also use the internet.

How does your personal work relate to your professional output?
My personal work gives me a chance to experiment and develop new styles, ideas and directions. Ideally I like to work on a series of images. At the moment my professional work is a bit more glossy and highly finished, whereas my personal work is heading in a direction that references more traditional media such as drawing and screen-printing. Having time to create personal work definitely enhances my professional output.

Inspired by Antonio Berardi, 2008.

A sense of proportion is an essential skill for a fashion illustrator. Here, the soft, rounded fullness of the coat is contrasted perfectly with the sleek hairstyle and skinny legs to emphasize the model's silhouette.

Right
Capri, 2010.

There is a hint of the past in this graphic image in which the broad stripes, carefully arranged silhouette and the relaxed swim-suited siren are all viewed from above.

Below
Martini Glasses, 2005.

In every one of the illustrations featured on these shot glasses, a glass is being raised. Bold colour with black and clear make strong graphic shapes and a definite style statement.

VISIT
Capri

Facing page
Balenciaga S/S 10, 2010.

This illustration shows every detail from eye colour to shoes yet in an unconventional pose exactly right for the style of Balenciaga designer Nicolas Ghesquière.

Balenciaga
Spring
Summer
2016

Jean Paul Gaultier

Nina Ricci

Marni

Louis Vuitton

Justin Brooks November 2007

Facing page and below
Fashion drawings, Autumn/Winter 2007.

Brooks has invented his own model: almond-eyed and confident, she is constantly on the move and wears fashion with nonchalance and total assurance.

CECILIA CARLSTEDT

First impressions can be totally misleading and with Cecilia Carlstedt this is certainly true. Her work has a magical quality, which does not reveal itself at first glance. In her portfolio there are many examples that demonstrate her technique of taking a figure and partially representing it in a simple, bold and recognizable manner while at the same time allowing it to blur into abstraction. Such graphic boldness is balanced by the exquisite drafting of the model's face, hair and hands, while the shadowed silhouette tells the observer a great deal about the personality and attitude of the subject. The inherent contrast within Carlstedt's work is between a style that seems to emulate steel engravings of the nineteenth century and a certain abstractionism that resists any nostalgia or retro impressions. Each illustration hints at a richer story that exists beyond the single moment captured in the image.

There is a narrative quality to Carlstedt's work. The feeling of movement adds to this cinematic impression, as though there were an unheard musical soundtrack to the imagery, propelling it along. The images are in the great tradition of fashion illustration with their storytelling quality, using the medium to convey more than the simple factual representation of a garment. Antonio Lopez comes to mind as a comparison – he used real models and actresses posing for him to draw from life. Carlstedt deploys an extraordinary variety of poses and positioning within her work, from close-up portrait in repose to on-location activity. She uses her illustrative skills to tell many different stories – a sexy story, a holiday story, a romantic story – there is always a narrative and a specific atmosphere associated with her fashion illustrations. It is particularly interesting to note the colour palette of the work, which reflects a specific Scandinavian sensibility within a controlled spectrum. There is a specific soft face-powder shade, which transcends season or fashion, to which she faithfully returns, and for which she finds a myriad of uses. Of course bold colour is used, but rarely.

All these elements combine to give the work of Cecilia Carlstedt that 'something special' that both the client and the viewer are searching for – original work with personality and presence, which is not necessarily attention-grabbing but nevertheless makes us stop and look and think.

Green, Black, Pink for 'Visual Poetry', Gallery Hanahou, 2011.

In eliminating the superfluous, Carlstedt delineates the chic of this image. Huge skill and panache – and often many attempts – are required for the balance to be as perfect as it is here.

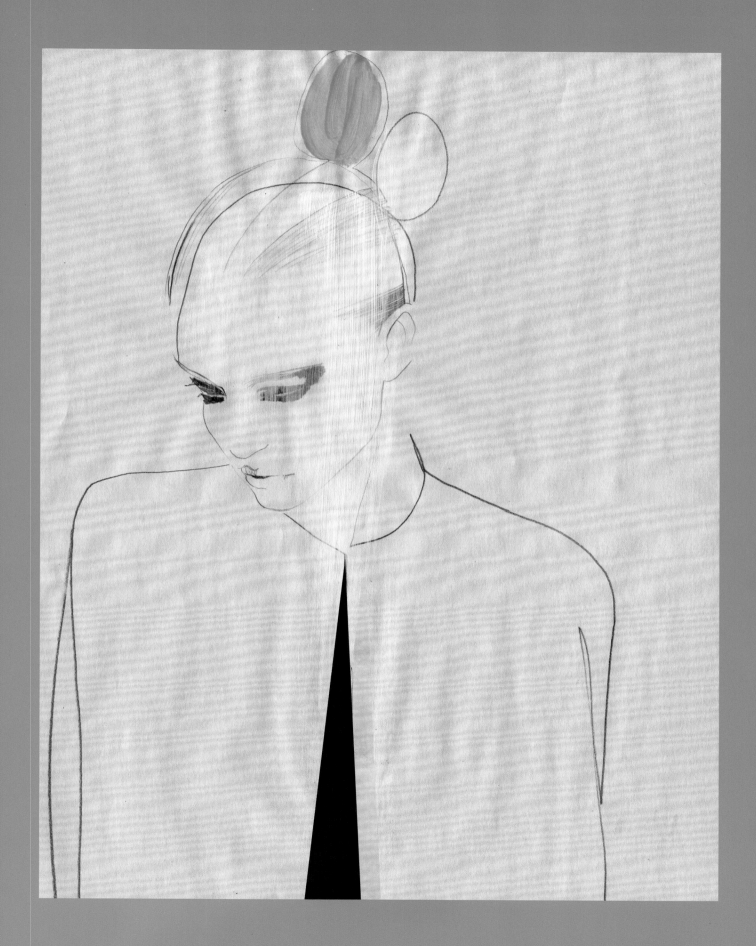

Facing page and above
Untitled, 2011.

White against black conjures up an almost a nostalgic feel here, with soft washes and feathery brush strokes. These images evoke vintage cinema, thanks to the skilled handling of monochromatic lines and spaces.

Bold and confident brushstrokes against a soft watery background are highlighted withthe deep colour of the earring. It is impossible for photography to emulate this kind of fashion illustration.

Below
Martini Gold Russia, Martini Collection VERO, 2011.

The classic dark eyes–crimson lips cosmetic image is updated here by being viewed through a trellised fan of cutwork. The eyes stare directly at the viewer and the veil only heightens the mouth's impact.

Where and when were you born and where do you live now?
I was born in 1977 in Stockholm and that's the city I'm back living in again after some years abroad.

Any particular childhood influences?
My mum is also an illustrator so her encouragement has always influenced me.

What is your earliest drawing memory?
Drawing a little round lady at six years old. She had very detailed clothing – a coat with a large collar filled with embroidery. I remember being very proud of this drawing.

What was your first professional work?
A fashion illustration commission for Swedish *Elle*, illustrating the current [at the time] English trend.

Do you have a preferred medium?
Pencil mixed with ink and various paints.

Do you work in silence or with background music/radio?
Almost always music.

What would be your ideal commission?
To freely interpret a cutting-edge fashion label.

Are you a slow and careful or quick and speedy draughtsman?
I'm pretty speedy.

Do you keep a sketchbook?
I used to, but sadly I never seem to have one around when I want to get something down so end up with hundreds of loose notes dotted everywhere and not often found again.

How would you describe your work?
Eclectic, experimental and essentially linked to the world of fashion.

Do you research your subjects? How do you research?
Depending on what I research I use the usual channels like the internet, buying lots and lots of magazines, books and just anything that catches my interest.

How does your personal work relate to your professional output?
It's usually pieces that I have experimented with for me personally that later end up inspiring professional commissions.

H&M Fashion Against AIDS, 2011.

The graphic word-print and easy shape of the all-in-one (left) could so easily make for an unattractive image, yet due to the skilful balance of the drawn shadow and the slightly softened technique used for the lettering, this model looks relaxed and stylish. The fashionable word-based print on the top (above) is made the focus of this illustration using the balance of soft monochrome with colour.

JEAN-PHILIPPE DELHOMME

The boundary between fashion illustration and the social observation found in cartoons is often blurred. Tongue-in-cheek approaches to the fashions of the day have coloured the work of illustrators since the British caricaturists James Gillray and Thomas Rowlandson in the eighteenth century. In the nineteenth century the great cartoonist and illustrator Sem (Georges Goursat) viewed fashion as a tool to point out the characteristics of those he drew. More than a century later but in much the same way, Jean-Philippe Delhomme pins down fashion 'types'. In an interview he once said, 'People might get it or they may not. It's amusing for those who get it, and they are not unpleased that others don't.'

After he finished school, Delhomme studied animation at L'Ecole nationale supérieure des Arts Décoratifs in Paris, graduating in 1985. His first fashion illustrations were published in British *Vogue* and soon afterwards his work appeared in a collection of publications including *Vogue Nippon*, *Vogue Paris* and *House & Garden*. In 1987 he created for French *Glamour* the series 'Polaroids de Jeunes Filles' – pictures that viewed a specific section of society with a wry sense of humour. By the early nineties his style was internationally recognized and his gouache illustrations with witty captions were used by Barneys New York for their seasonal advertising campaign, as well as for billboards and animated adverts. That the creative directors at Barneys, Ronnie Cooke Newhouse and Glenn O'Brien chose to replace photography with illustration says much for Delhomme's ability to communicate both an affection for and a humorous approach to the terminally stylish and aspirational world of modern society. This world featured again in his 2009–10 campaign for the Mark Hotel in Manhattan with billboards and, once more, animation. Back in Paris, Le Bon Marché, which has been part of the LVMH group since 2000, commissioned Delhomme to not only provide the concepts and illustrations for their advertising but also the script.

Delhomme has had exhibitions in New York, Paris and Tokyo and a collection of his work entitled *The Cultivated Life* was published by Rizzoli in 2009. His blog, 'The Unknown Hipster', details the comings and goings of the world according to Delhomme, and his oblique slant on the sophisticated world of the fashionable continues to enchant viewers everywhere.

Andy Warhol and Jean-Michel Basquiat at Indochine, 2010.

Warhol and Basquiat gaze back at the viewer across the luncheon table, their black and grey jackets balanced by their black and silver hair, silhouetted against the palm background. This striking image sums up the skill required to communicate with both style and humour.

Below
Behind the Scenes, Pennyblack, 2011.

Coordination and colour balance is carefully created by a fashion designer; an illustrator must then decide on the location and the colour of the setting to show the garments to their best advantage. Here, the grey-blue steps hold these two models in perfect harmony.

Facing page
Vivienne Westwood, *Muse* magazine, 2009.

This fearless fashion portrait is quite simply the distillation of Vivienne Westwood for all time. The unnatural red hair, the draped tartan and scattered badges, all underlined by the bold pose, offer us the definitive Westwood.

Where and when were you born and where do you live now?
I was born in a Paris suburb in 1959. I live in Paris, but often go to New York where I have a studio.

Any particular childhood influences?
I used to see my father, a surgeon, paint landscapes in his free time. My grandfather was a painter (and a creative director at Lancôme in the fifties and sixties). The first piece of modern art I remember seeing as a child was a Fernand Léger in an art book for children. Then Impressionist paintings from the museum in Saint Tropez, and the Calder mobiles at the Fondation Maeght in Saint-Paul-de-Vence. And cartoons, good or bad, from various magazines.

What is your earliest drawing memory?
A family picnic scene under a tree, where the main element was a Citroën 2CV, or maybe it was a Renault 4L, drawn with coloured pencil, when I was six years old. My schoolteacher was so in awe she carried it all around the school.

What was your first professional work?
Small black and white cartoons for a French music mag called *Rock & Folk* in the early eighties.

Do you have a preferred medium?
Gouache, coloured pencils.

Do you work in silence or with background music/radio?
Music always: jazz, electronic, soul, rock; I like to listen to a wide variety of music in a single day, for changing moods. My favourite radio show to keep up with a tough deadline is Gilles Peterson on BBC Radio 1.

What would be your ideal commission?
Working for people who inspire me.

Are you a slow and careful or quick and speedy draughtsman?
I can sometimes work very fast, but in fact, there's no rule, only the right state of mind matters.

Do you keep a sketchbook?
I do different sketchbooks at times, when travelling, or simply looking from my studio window. And I love to do portraits of family or friends. Painting or drawing from life are the most interesting things to me, and I do this whenever I have the time.

How would you describe your work?
To me it's like the way one writes by hand: would you describe your handwriting? Or the way you walk?

Do you research your subjects? How do you research?
If I'm interested in a place or a certain group of people, I go there, try to experience it, do sketches and take pictures. I then combine my sketches and pictures for inspiration or as references. But sometimes I do all my research using magazines, books and the internet.

How does your personal work relate to your professional output?
There are no boundaries; the professional output should be nothing else but personal work.

Anything else you wish to tell the reader?
Most important is to keep being inspired, and moving. Going from one medium to the other. And being driven by your personal projects, no matter what.

Jean-Philippe Delhomme **45**

Left and below
Behind the Scenes, Pennyblack,
2011 and *Rehearsal at Valentino*,
2003.

In these images Delhomme takes
us behind the scenes of a shoot and
a fitting. In the image featuring the
Italian designer, Mr Valentino is
shown accompanied or 'assisted'
by his pugs. The tightly controlled
colour palette adds enormously
to the strength of the images.

Facing page
Christian Lacroix, *Madame Figaro*,
2003.

As Christian Lacroix pensively
chews the frame of his spectacles,
the model stands immobile in
Lacroix's haute couture salon
in the heart of Paris's Faubourg
St Honoré. This illustration reveals
the creative process and the
relationship between the model
and designer.

Above
'Man, did you ever think of doing jazz album covers?' Advert for Maison Kitsuné, 2011.

In her red hunting jacket and white jeans the elegant model looks amused by her portraitist and his friend who seem to be channelling a more abstract approach to the image. La vie de château as seen by Picasso perhaps?

Right
'Didn't I tell you? This dress has to be worn with a horse?' Los Angeles Times Magazine, 2011.

Lady Godiva in a bias satin evening dress posed in the living room may seem a strange conceit but in the 1930s, Penelope Chetwode, wife of poet John Betjeman, frequently took her horse into the house.

'You should have told me you'd
be wearing your Viktor & Rolf.
I bought the Porsche', Los Angeles
Times Magazine, 2010.

Is the man aghast at the idea of
fitting this evening dress into his
car or simply its sheer scale?

BIL DONOVAN

Bil Donovan's strength of technique and confident approach to his work is evidenced by the sheer insouciance with which his pen or brush speeds across the page. Confidence, skill and a passion for the power of fashion illustration as a communication tool are apparent in his every move. There is also an element of wit in his portrayal of many of the characters within the business, whether they are models or mavens. To take illustrating the foibles of the fashion business too seriously would be to leave no room for what Ernestine Carter once memorably called 'tongue in chic'.

The visibility of pen or brush marks has always characterized fashion illustration, demonstrating to the observer the craft behind the line. In fashion illustration terms Donovan is a direct descendant of the greats of the past; he carries forward the especially American qualities found in the illustrations of Kenneth Paul Block or Joe Eula of the twentieth century: freedom and movement. There is a lightness of touch that corresponds to the styles of Claire McCardell, Halston or Calvin Klein; no superfluous clutter, urban chic and a timeless, pared-down look to the page. His work reflects the American attitude that style must not impede and that ease is as important as statement. Donovan makes the world of stylishness look easy. He understands that many observers don't want to see the hard work and techniques that underpin his work; they want to feel that a great illustrator simply 'dashes off a drawing' – in other words, they want to be seduced by the images.

Today's fashion illustrators have taken the crafts and gifts of their predecessors and mixed them into a neat, nonchalant contemporary style. Even when fashion dictates ball gowns or suits the look is less studied than it was in the past. Donovan adjusts his techniques and the way he communicates fashion accordingly. There are nods to the golden days of haute couture but these are merely acknowledgements of the past, and in no way overpower his imagery. Brush, pencil and pen, ink and watercolour remain staples of the fashion illustrator's repertoire and Donovan is a classicist with total mastery of these tools. Every retro fashion trend that appears is a reminder that for some this is a revisiting and for others it is totally new. So in fashion illustration the need to reference past styles and techniques without ever becoming a pastiche is essential. Donovan is a superb exponent of this attitude and approach to fashion illustration, balancing on the tightrope between heritage and modernism.

Shower, 2009.

This standing figure in a classic Hellenic pose is accented by the column of water from the shower, heightening the classical allusion. The surrounding space allows the viewer to concentrate on the figure.

Where and when were you born and where do you live now?
In 1956, South Philadelphia, an Irish-Italian Catholic blue-collar working-class neighbourhood. Today, I reside in the East Village, a bohemian crossroads in downtown New York City.

Any particular childhood influences?
Old movies. I was entranced by the glamour, style and beauty portrayed through the exaggerated lens of Hollywood films and mesmerized by the movement of flowing gowns. My epiphany moment was Audrey Hepburn filling the screen with beauty, grace, style and elegance in the movie *Sabrina*. She epitomizes the ideal of fashion illustration. A passion was born to capture that moment forever not on a dress form or with a camera but on paper with pencil or crayon.

What is your earliest drawing memory?
Marilyn Monroe. In the classic film *Niagara*, Marilyn wears an off-the-shoulder skintight red dress and gold hoop earrings, a potent combination of sex and glamour. I tried to emulate that image over and over, through clumsy attempts with a crayon and paper, much to the consternation of my father, Duke Donovan, who was a welder and at one time an amateur middleweight boxer… The next day he attempted to teach me how to box, much to my consternation.

What was your first professional work?
An advertisement for a gay bar, The Barefoot Boy, where I was a waiter at night while attending the Fashion Institute of Technology by day. I still have it in a sketchbook.

Do you have a preferred medium?
Brush and ink, oil stick, graphite and gesso on paper, wood or canvas.

Do you work in silence or with background music/radio?
Music shuffled from an iPod with an eclectic mix from Billie Holiday to Philip Glass.

What would be your ideal commission?
An animation! I would love to use the nature of movement to bring to life the spirit, elegance and stylization associated with the genre of fashion illustration. I love the character of line and how it communicates so much with so little, especially in fashion drawing. To animate those flowing lines and movement has never been done, as in my imagination… The possibilities are exciting and endless.

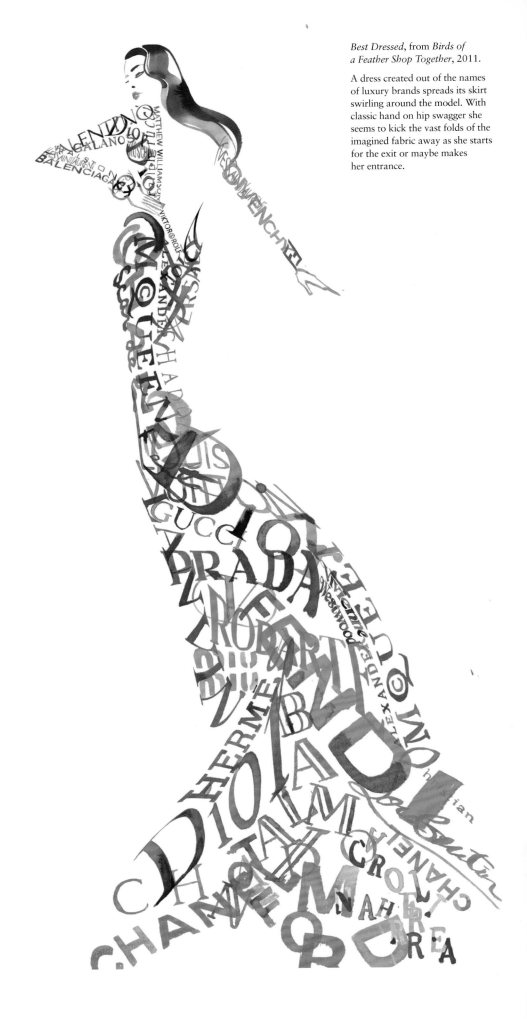

Best Dressed, from *Birds of a Feather Shop Together*, 2011.

A dress created out of the names of luxury brands spreads its skirt swirling around the model. With classic hand on hip swagger she seems to kick the vast folds of the imagined fabric away as she starts for the exit or maybe makes her entrance.

Are you a slow and careful or quick and speedy draughtsman?
I'm slow when I go too fast and fast when I am going too slow... Intuition rules. As much as I like accident and chance there has to be a visual unity to the work.

Do you keep a sketchbook?
Always. It is a constant companion since 1978. Sketchbooks are the heart and soul of my work.

How would you describe your work?
Chic understated elegance with a nod to spirit.

Do you research your subjects? How do you research?
Thoroughly, totally and obsessively. I have a a degree in Fine Art and it was drilled into us that any decision we made concerning the work should impact on the content, a premise I use when doing a commission. I read, research the web and become a detective in searching out facts or fiction. I illustrated a book on the legendary costume designer, Edith Head, titled *The Dress Doctor: Prescriptions for Style from A to Z.* I read every biography and article, searched the web and located and interviewed a former assistant to gain insight into the legend. It is important to do your homework; it layers the work with a subtle content.

How does your personal work relate to your professional output?
I have a fascination with the figure, and although my fine art is driven by personal experiences and my professional work is driven by stylization and selectivity, the common denominator is the figure.

Anything else you wish to tell the reader?
In order to succeed you have to be willing to fail. Passion is the driving force of success. As an aspiring artist, my passion outweighed my technical skills. I indulged my passion through classes, constant drawing in my sketchbook, studying, practising, exploring and perfecting my ability and craft. I still do.

Amy, 2011 and *Red Chic*, 2011.

Simple columns of colour such as these require confidence and understanding of the principles of elegance. Viewed slightly from below, to elongate the silhouette, these examples demonstrate the importance of getting the angle and balance of the hip line correct.

Bil Donovan 53

Left
Doppelganger, 2011.

The holiday atmosphere is palpable in this fashion image. Swaying palms provide a frieze for a background, black and white swimsuits are contrasted against bronze-toned flesh and the hair of the models is drawn back off the face.

Below
Chado, Ralph Rucci couture collection, 2011.

Eleven garments shown on their hangers create the effect of a mural, the entire image relying on perfect colour balance so as not to appear cluttered. Each garment is distinct as well as working as part of the collection through the application of colour, weight and texture.

Top left
Thirteen Ghosts, 2007.

Donovan ditches the inessential to
get to the core of the message: shape.
The stance emphasizes the boldness
of the image.

Above
Crossroads of the World, 2011.

A photograph could never
convey Times Square the way
this illustration does. The sky is
left blank and the focus is on the
extraordinary accumulation
of colour and graphic signage.

Left
Muse, 2011.

Captured at exactly the moment
the model sways towards us, this
illustration communicates the
power of the arching silhouette
with an easy grace.

DONOVAN

Left
Diva, *Elle*, 2011.

Bubbles or balloons surround this model in her black strapless dress, accessorized with chandelier earrings and her black hair swept back into a low bun. There is a hint of the Spanish flamenco about her.

Facing page
Tomo-Glam for 'Visual Poetry', Gallery Hanahou, 2010.

Fashion illustration sometimes offers the opportunity to convey a fashion message in bolder terms than even photography can achieve. Here Donovan shows us gravity-defying postiches of hair, or possibly tulle or even feathers, balanced above a haughty face.

DAVID DOWNTON

Towards the end of the twentieth century fashion illustration had become a rare sight but since the late nineties several fashion illustrators have re-entered the world of glossy magazines and advertising, sometimes even making it onto the covers. Downton is among this select group and his work reflects the craft of his predecessors in a totally contemporary way.

David Downton combines two of the great characteristics of fashion illustrators: an extraordinary ability to eliminate line and a love of beautiful women. When drawing a model – say Catherine Deneuve or Amanda Harlech – his pen swiftly imparts the salient features to paper with no wasted flourishes. He clearly establishes a rapport with his subject, his semi-abstract line capturing the character of the model as well as communicating the particular garment she might be wearing. The elimination of extraneous detail and reliance on line recalls work by Eric or René Gruau yet without a hint of pastiche.

Downton uses several different techniques, from an initial pencil sketch through to collage, paper-cut work, gouache and coloured inks and even the common felt-tip pen. It is this array of media, combined with technical wizardry, that brings such vividness to his rendering of a taffeta ball gown or gem-encrusted chandelier earrings. He understands how paper weight, colour balance and even typography contribute to the final outcome. His sense of space and proportion, allied to an in-depth understanding of the structure of the human body and the swing of a skirt, gives a unique strength to his work.

The artistry and observational techniques that Downton brings to his work are reflected in the diversity of his clients and the commissions he undertakes. Portraits, advertising campaigns, editorial and limited-edition portfolio work are all part of his extensive repertoire. His work is just as likely to be hanging on the walls of a boutique hotel as it is to appear in a fashion publication. His contacts within the highest echelons of the fashion world enable him to work with some of the most exquisite clothing and sought-after models.

In this age of the digitally produced image, the heavily retouched and the mechanically reproduced, it is exciting to discover that there is still room for the traditional craft of fashion illustration. Downton has a following from Sydney to New York, which goes to prove that however mechanized the world becomes, people are still astonished by the simple art of being able to take a pencil and draw in pure line.

Erin O'Connor, Dior Couture, 2002.

The extraordinary often attracts the extraordinary. In this case, model Erin O'Connor poses in the Stephen Jones headdress created for a Christian Dior catwalk show designed by John Galliano. This is pure fantasy in terms of wearability but offers the sensational pleasure of knowing there are people, including Downton, capable of creating such a visual.

ᵍnt
Belle de Jour DVD cover, Criterion Collection, 2011.

Cinema and fashion have a strong link and nowhere more so than in France. Catherine Deneuve wore Yves Saint Laurent both off screen and on, so a fashion illustrator creating a DVD cover showing Deneuve in one of her great screen roles is the perfect pairing.

Below
La Dolce Vita, 2008.

Fellini used clothes as part of his storytelling; even just a hint of the black strapless dress worn by Anita Ekberg in the Trevi fountain in *La Dolce Vita* conjures up the entire scene.

Where and when were you born and where do you live now?
I was born in Kent, in 1959. Today I live in East Sussex about 10 miles from Brighton, where I have a studio.

Any particular childhood influences?
I grew up in a household that was pretty unconcerned with fashion or style. My family was a sporting family; my brother played cricket for England. My earliest influences were all from the cinema. I lived at the cinema; Hammer films when I could get in, 'Carry On' and James Bond – the things you might expect of someone growing up in the sixties.

What is your earliest drawing memory?
I was always drawing. As a child, my idea of a treat was a big sheet of white paper, which I bought from WHSmith every Saturday. I used to copy film posters from the newspaper using an HB pencil. It would take a whole day. My parents worried that I was not socialized enough. I remember saying that I saw my friends all week at school, which was enough.

What was your first professional work?
I started out first as a general illustrator, taking on whatever jobs came along, learning as I went. I considered myself to be 'successful' (by which I mean I was working more or less every day), but I was bored and frustrated at my lack of direction. I developed the self-employed mentality of 'wagging my tail when the phone rang'. I don't think there was any subject I didn't tackle. I did a long stint in romantic fiction, worked for educational press, cook books, wine labels; I even did a sex manual, which was a high point of sorts! From time to time, I got a fashion commission, but I certainly didn't consider myself a 'fashion illustrator' – that came much later.

Do you have a preferred medium?
My working method changes depending on the brief or my mood or what I want to get from the finished result. I use watercolour or gouache for small-scale pieces. If I need flat saturated colour, I use cut paper collage and then apply line using an acetate overlay. Fluidity, capturing a sense of the moment, layout and use of space are all-important elements, but most important of all is strong drawing. The great thing is you can't be too good at drawing. And although, unfortunately, your reach may exceed your grasp, hope does spring eternal…

Do you work in silence or with background music/radio?
I can go for stretches working in silence then I get hooked on Radio 4, which has been my education – I know a little about a lot. Then I listen to the music Jo, my assistant, has put on my iPod. I love it because I never know what's coming. It might be *The Best of Bond*, or Bob Dylan or Montserrat Caballé; often it's someone I haven't heard of. Sometimes I can't switch it off fast enough!

What would be your ideal commission?
Drawing the cast of *Mad Men* on set, in LA and writing the copy to go with it.

Are you a slow and careful or quick and speedy draughtsman?
Both. I aim for a controlled spontaneity. A lot of my work involves elimination of detail. I like to leave 'a breathing space' in a drawing, which allows the eye to fill in the gap. But in order to leave something out, first you have to put it in, or at least understand how everything works. I do dozens of drawings on layout paper, taking the best from each one as I go. When the drawing looks right I start to eliminate, to deconstruct if you like. My mantra is to keep working until it looks effortless.

Do you keep a sketchbook?
Yes, in a drawer to my eternal shame! I don't do nearly enough work in sketchbooks, which is ironic because I find other people's fascinating. The only time I really use a sketchbook is when I am sitting around waiting for a fashion show to begin. Sometimes if I am eating alone in a restaurant I like to draw the other diners. I think it makes me look interesting rather than lonely…

How would you describe your work?
I try not to describe it. I think we become very hung up on the notion of style. In my experience you don't find a style, it finds you, eventually. It is something you develop, work with and modify. The worst thing is when it comes to dominate your thinking and approach. But I did like the way Ian R. Webb of *Elle* once described it as 'Contemporary Nostalgia'. That pretty well sums up what I'm trying to achieve.

Do you research your subjects? How do you research?
Sometimes it's necessary, sometimes not. As with everything, it depends on the job. I recently did the cover for the re-release of *Belle de Jour* on DVD. 'Research' was

watching the film through twice and looking through the YSL archives (YSL did the costumes and the brief was to give a fashion slant to the image of Catherine Deneuve) – all of which was a pleasure, of course.

How does your personal work relate to your professional output?
A commissioned piece of work is only half mine. I do the best I can within the confines of the brief and all the factors that go into making the job a success. The most important thing is that the client is happy; if I can't always produce exactly the piece I would like, I accept that. It is part of what being a commercial artist means. For my personal projects, I'm prepared to open a vein. I work and work and rework them, and as the only person that needs to be happy is me, it can be a long process.

Anything else you wish to tell the reader?
Who knew that 40 years after the 'death of fashion illustration' it would be undergoing such a revival of interest? The depth and breadth of talent today is extraordinary. The truth is that we will always need artists to record and interpret a designer's work. It's a symbiotic relationship; one art form describing another.

Cate Blanchett, Vogue Australia 50th anniversary cover, 2009.

An illustrated cover – a rarity in the 21st century – for the *Vogue* Australia 50th anniversary issue featuring Australian actress Cate Blanchett. Even rarer is the fact that there were actually four alternative covers, all illustrated by Downton.

Dior Couture, 2009.

The skill, art and instinct
required to eliminate within
a fashion illustration is a feat
of magic that can perhaps never
be taught. Here, the bold lines
of the hat and broad striped
top are balanced by a model
whose hair and face are only
lightly sketched.

Above
Erin O'Connor, Valentino Couture, 2003.

The luxury of drawing from a model is enhanced when that model is one of the supers of the last few decades. Erin O'Connor has posed for Downton many times and his speed at sketching her every move is honed to fine art, demonstrated here as she revolves across the page in a vivid slash of red Valentino.

Left
Absolut Classics Timeless Cocktails Edition, *Acne Paper*, 2010.

Luxuriating against her El Morocco-style zebra background, this elegant model is portrayed entirely in a world of black and white, except, of course, for the vivid green of the olives in her martini.

PETRA DUFKOVA

Petra Dufkova is a perfect example of a fashion illustrator whose professional range is broad and diverse, and yet whose most popular style and work are unrepresentative of this breadth of techniques and approaches. Her exquisite, romantic portraits, often with a floral, fairy-like element to them, are superbly accomplished. The almost *Midsummer Night's Dream* quality to them appeals to a huge number of people, who often purloin these particular images for blogs and websites. However this is only a part of Dufkova's work; her fashion illustrations away from this specific style are in the great tradition of Jean Pages or René Bouët-Willaumez, with their tight observation of fabric and form yet freedom of line – often resulting in a web of extended lines forming an almost abstract aura around the garment and its wearer.

Her starting point of total technical control and knowledge of figure drawing enables Dufkova to 'spiral off' in a drawing, adding her own particular spin. She is hell-bent on showing the observer her vision through the medium of fashion illustration, and she succeeds triumphantly. The woman wearing the clothes is clearly seen, her body language echoing the form and flow of the garment. This is reminiscent of classic fashion illustration from the mid-twentieth century, yet Dufkova's work has nothing retro about it; it is totally original and reflects the fashion of the moment. She has an excellent understanding of clothes and a superb sense of the body within those clothes. Above all, her illustrations have a surprising strength but with no hint of heaviness or trying too hard; there is nothing overworked about the finished results.

Dufkova's body of work demonstrates the range necessary to become a successful fashion illustrator; she can produce anything from an illustration of musical notes to a cocktail dress or a straight portrait – offering a range of styles, techniques and moods. She focuses on demonstrating the truth of a subject through illustration, be it a jar of cream or a celebrity.

Untitled, 2008.

Puppet-like on her strings, this model is shown sideways to the viewer, thus exaggerating the chopped-up proportions of the clothing. The line varies in weight from all-but-invisible to dense black, preventing the image from becoming purely a silhouette and conveying the 3-D qualities of the figure.

Where and when were you born and where do you live now?
I was born in the Czech Republic, but now I live in Munich, Germany.

Any particular childhood influences?
As a child I possessed many children's books and storybooks with wonderful illustrations, which I looked at all the time, and I've ever since tried to draw my own interpretation of fairy tales. The biggest influence on my career was my education at art and design school.

What is your earliest drawing memory?
A lot of fairy tales – castles, woods and many imaginary animals.

What was your first professional work?
I illustrated a book for small children.

Do you have a preferred medium?
My favourite drawing medium is watercolour, especially gouache. My drawing style starts with traditional techniques and from there I make new effects in combination with other drawing media such as ink or lacquer.

Do you work in silence or with background music/radio?
Mostly I listen to music.

What would be your ideal commission?
Fashion illustrations for *Vogue* magazine.

Are you a slow and careful or quick and speedy draughtsman?
I think I'm not too slow, but always careful.

Do you keep a sketchbook?
Rather than a sketchbook I keep 'inspiration' books, where I have not only sketches, but also photos, cuttings from magazines, cards, fabrics and so on. All the beautiful things that I find during research.

How would you describe your work?
My illustrations are a combination of traditional methods and a modern feminine look, with a focus on fashion, beauty and lifestyle. All the images have a 'fashion feeling', although I don't work only for fashion companies.

Do you research your subjects? How do you research?
Before I start work I search many sources of inspiration: I look at books and magazines, listen to inspiring music, walk in the streets with a camera and take pictures of beautiful people and things…

Anything else you wish to tell the reader?
I love the freedom and creativity that I have as a freelance illustrator. And I do my work with passion and enjoyment. I think that's the best way to be successful.

Facing page
Music, 2011.

The use of the single word 'free', flowing into the musical staves as they wind ribbon-like across the page, conveys the spirit of the unheard notes swelling out of the drawing.

Left
Zodiac 'Sagitarius', 2008.

By contrasting the rich autumnal colour palette of the make-up with a black-haired model and related textured background, Dufkova throws the cosmetics used into a much stronger role.

Below
Beauty, 2010.

The rich Manhattan feeling of this cosmetics still life is achieved by relating the image to the New York skyline. Even the lit metallic stem of the nail polish bottle resembles the spire of the Chrysler Building.

Left
Untitled, 2010.

By inference of colour balance we know the hair of this model is white blonde and we can feel the weight and flow of the dress. We can also tell her left knee is half way through a stride. But the story behind the image is what each individual observer invents.

Above
Untitled, 2010.

A seemingly simple portrait but the half smile is enigmatic. Are the eyes also smiling or are they sardonic or even sarcastic?

Facing page
Untitled, Stella McCartney A/W 11, 2011.

This wonderful illustration shows off the rich textured ribbing of the fabric with grace.

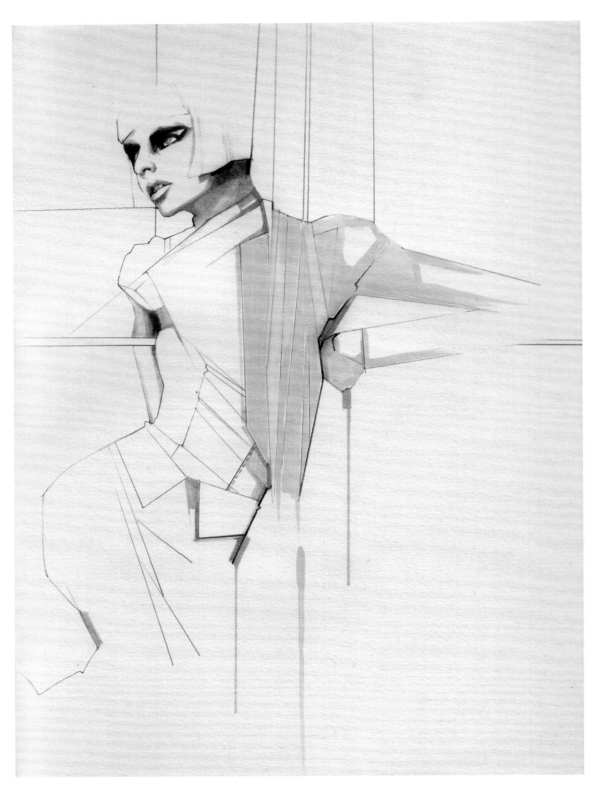

Untitled, 2008.

There is a mathematical precision to this image where the geometry of the lines and the sharp hairstyle combine to make the figure all angles. The angle of the model's head is just off profile and, with her heavy eye make-up, supports the diagonal line of the image perfectly.

Above
Untitled, Iben Høj, 2011.

As she gazes skywards, this model also shows off the soft folds of her smock-style top with its gently curved yoke.

Above right
Zodiac 'Taurus', 2008.

The sultry pout of the deep crimson mouth and the almost geisha-style eye make-up are shown emerging from abstract flowers in a *Midsummer Night's Dream* image of a fashion Titania.

Right
Untitled, 2009.

In spite of the denseness of the colour, this illustration clearly shows the petal-like layers of the dress and its tendril-style tie. The opaque darkness of the model's long bob hairstyle is a perfect balance to the dress in the soft yet structured shape it creates.

GARY FERNÁNDEZ

Creating a magical world where anything is possible is part of the charm of fashion illustration. The work of Gary Fernández enters the realms of *Alice in Wonderland*, Federico Fellini and possibly even Aubrey Beardsley in order to convey the impossible as reality.

Hair is draped as fabric, weightless models may be suspended in mid-air simply by holding a parasol, or stripes can swirl from a giant-sized bauble right around the bubble-shaped skirt of a mannequin. As Lewis Carroll put it, 'Why, sometimes I've believed as many as six impossible things before breakfast.' The imagination Fernández brings to his work implies that each image may have sprung from a larger story, perhaps an animation or a series recounting a fashion fable; indeed he does often create a visual narrative through a set of images.

Fernández's machines for creating elegance are extraordinary and the gravity-defying invention of his landscapes secures him a special position in the world of style. Yet his imagination can be harnessed for such relatively prosaic applications as portraying store interiors, or advertising products, among a range of outcomes and applications; his fantasies can come down to earth as a commercial proposition.

The interesting thing about fashion illustrators like Gary Fernández is how they turn a totally personal vision into a reality for others to share. Like Richard Gray, yet in a very different manner, he uses illustration as an intense tool of communication that ties a ribbon around a bundle of elements to create a cohesive whole.

His fashion and style illustrations are timeless in their mood; they are not faithful depictions of the season's hot item, rather their intent is to surprise and engage the viewer. Many of the images seem to suggest music – jazz is hugely important to Fernández – and they appear to correspond to his desire to awaken more than just the visual sense.

Fernández has international experience and appeal. There will be some who find his blinding visions unpalatable, while others appreciate this great gift of fashion illustration – the ability to let personal identity shine through in a work. Erté would have saluted his vision, and Fernández's singular inventiveness echoes the great review costumes and bold originality of the Erté journey, from his earliest work through to his later designs for the Casino de Paris and Zizi Jeanmaire. In the end, Fernández offers us his own carefully edited vision of the world, a world in which anything is possible.

Forest-Dress, for *Introduction to Fantastic Girls, Future Landscapes & the Most Beautiful Birds Ever Seen*, 2008.

The trees bend inwards to create a crinoline skirt, the wind stretches the model's hair into a wing, and throughout droplets cascade downwards. All this is perfectly normal in the inventive world of Fernández.

Above left
An Ordinary Day in the Park #2 (Revisted), 2010.

Against a calm blue-grey ground a girl is seemingly hiding musicians under her skirt.

Above right
A Real Good Time (Revisited), 2010.

In another illustration from the same series, a girl ignores two gentlemen – they could be from Verona or be Tweedledum and Tweedledee – who gesture stylishly towards a downpour of decorations.

Where and when were you born and where do you live now?
I was born in November 1980 in Managua, Nicaragua. Now, I've just moved from Madrid, Spain, to Atlanta, Georgia, in the USA.

Any particular childhood influences?
In my childhood I was influenced by my parents' nomadic spirit, becoming a nomad myself today. That gives me a quite wide perspective on and perception of the world that I guess I apply to my work. Lately I have become especially fond of the works of Federico Fellini and Jacques Tati.

What is your earliest drawing memory?
My mother still keeps some of my kindergarten drawings somewhere. What I clearly remember is tracing a painting of the Virgin Mary from an art book when I was nine, which I still have somewhere in a box.

What was your first professional work?
I was tracing logotypes in my hometown, 11 years ago. At that time I was invited to design some T-shirt graphics for a surf T-shirt brand based in the south of Spain. Some time in between then and now, I was working in the design team of a fashion magazine in Madrid, which in some way, I feel, was my first professional work. As a freelance illustrator, my first professional work was a big ad campaign in Spain, back in 2004.

Do you have a preferred medium?
I enjoy very much working with the simplest tools such as pencils, pens and plain basic papers, which is a first level in the work I do. But for me, it's really pleasant to appreciate the finest and detailed work I can only achieve digitally, translated onto fabric, large-scale prints, animations or even three-dimensional objects.

Do you work in silence or with background music/radio?
I mainly work with background music or radio. But lately I'm also enjoying some working days in silence. Just listening to the birds in front of my windows. While working, if I'm not listening to the radio, I'm a jazz enthusiast – the likes of Thelonious Monk, Dizzy Gillespie or John Coltrane…

What would be your ideal commission?
It would be one where I'm asked to make something where you can experience the five senses: you can see it, walk into it, listen to it, touch it and even smell and taste it.

Are you a slow and careful or quick and speedy draughtsman?
My work has two levels of requirement. The first one is done quite fast. It's raw. And the second one, due to the details, requires much more time, and precision.

Do you keep a sketchbook?
Yes, I'm always drawing, sometimes very schematic lines, and taking notes. So I have several notebooks saved that I usually consult to refresh my mind with ideas.

How would you describe your work?
Rhythmic, orchestrated, sensual, full of movement and risky.

Do you research your subjects? How do you research?
Yes, I do. The research consists of just walking the streets, talking to people, visiting antique stores, reading books and also surfing the internet.

How does your personal work relate to your professional output?
I think it has to be very linked, in order to evolve. In most cases, I just translate my personal work into the client's requirements. Sometimes that happens directly, at the request of the client. In other cases, indirectly, when a new approach I discover through my personal work is applied to a project.

Anything else you wish to tell the reader?
If you can see something, that means it exists. Trust in magic.

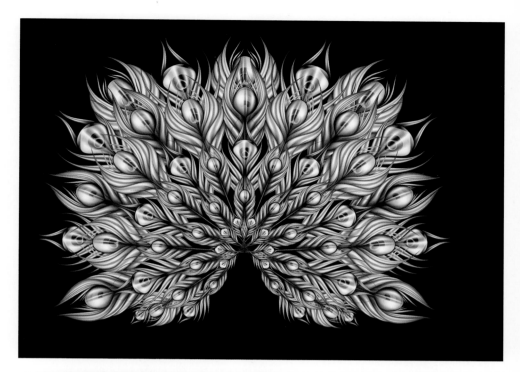

Top
The Metallic Peacock Feathers, Custo Barcelona, 2010.

Soaring away with his imagination, Fernandez reinterprets the peacock feather and fan tail into his own colour palette and arrangement.

Above
Fairwells in a Suitcase, Escala, 2010.

This model's extraordinarily luxuriant hair forms a golden background for the elaborate folds of her huge shawl and matching turban in deep chocolate and violet.

Gary Fernández   75

Facing page
Cloud Girls and *The Pine Cone Girls*, Evans, UK, 2010.

These two images seem like a passing carnival parade we are allowed to witness as the models in their more haute than haute couture gowns and hair twirl past us. The signature droplets seem weightier than usual, with an almost ominous quality.

Above
Slippery Moves, Escala, 2010.

Reminiscent of the extraordinary images of Dalí throwing objects and water across the studio, this beautiful image conveys arrested movement both through the poses and the use of undulating pattern and colour.

Right
Radio-Activity, for *Introduction to Fantastic Girls, Future Landscapes & the Most Beautiful Birds Ever Seen*, 2008.

This image romanticizes technology by visualizing sound through arabesques and tendrils arching from the headphone wires as the hands and face provide a still focus at the centre.

JEFFREY FULVIMARI

Like the Sempé girl or Osbert Lancaster's Maudie Littlehampton, Jeffrey Fulvimari has invented a character – a huge-eyed young lady with bold hair, whatever the style, and usually in a great dress of some design. This creation has been translated into a variety of products, including dresses and china plates, as well as securing him a partnership with Madonna (for *The English Roses*, her children's picture book series). Yet above all Fulvimari is a fashion illustrator whose work is modern, stylish and appeals directly to his audience.

Signature elements recur regularly throughout his work, such as the naming of his ladies. Fulvimari's subjects are most definitely young 'ladies'; they may be resolutely up to date but the sexy vamp is not what his work is about. His Roberta, Iris or Veronica may flirt and smile but there is a charm about every one of them that is curiously old-fashioned. One of the interesting things about many fashion illustrators is this ability to invent a specific viewpoint, forming a recognizable 'core' to their work. Fulvimari employs a very specific colour palette; a total reflection of the mood and image he is communicating – there is never anything overstated and it is predominantly feminine. This is a girl's world where men do not feature and real life is suspended while they go about their business of looking well turned-out and appealing.

Charm is a curiously absent quality from much in fashion but Fulvimari manages to retain it across his entire oeuvre – he communicates a real affection for his creations and the world they inhabit. It is this ability to imagine and then create an original character that sets the true fashion illustrator apart from those who simply record fashion. Far from factual reportage, Fulvimari is perhaps closest in fashion illustration terms to the delightful early nineteenth-century *Lady's Companion* illustrators of Regency modes and manners. Perhaps in more modern terms his creations echo those 'perfect young ladies' of the 1954 musical *The Boy Friend*... Either reflect the timeless appeal inherent in his work. Jeffrey Fulvimari succeeds in delighting the observer seemingly without effort, making light of the undoubted skill required to achieve this.

Untitled, 2010.

Her face entirely concealed by her extravagantly feathered Merry Widow hat, this diva in a strapless dress and draped stole is created by a series of broad black strokes. The image is timeless in its glamorous appeal and classic fashion elements.

Where and when were you born and where do you live now?
I am from Akron, Ohio, and presently live in Woodstock, New York. I lived for most of my life in Manhattan and went to college there. But I can only relax and be inspired near the mountains and the streams. Akron was a great place to grow up in – there is a lot of music and creativity there, and tons of people in New York come from there.

Any particular childhood influences?
I was really influenced by cartoonists, Charles Shultz mostly. I love the warm, simple feeling of his drawings.

What is your earliest drawing memory?
I remember my mum teaching me to colour inside of the lines in my colouring book when I was two, in front of the black and white TV set.

What was your first professional work?
I was hired by *Interview* magazine to draw a portrait of Julio Iglesias.

Do you have a preferred medium?
Pen on paper.

Do you work in silence or with background music/radio?
Both. Sometimes I overdo it on the music, and love silence.

What would be your ideal commission?
I have no idea, really. I love to see what falls into my lap. I have already done a lot of things that I would consider ideal.

Are you a slow and careful or quick and speedy draughtsman?
Sorry to be so boring, but I would have to answer 'both' here as well. It depends on what is going on in my life at the time.

Do you keep a sketchbook?
Yes, I have since I was 14, but sometimes a lot of time passes in between them.

How would you describe your work?
The work I am most known for is probably my fashion work. I think it's very similar to Japanese painting or calligraphy. It at least looks effortless, but sometimes drawings I do that look like quick doodles take hours, and sometimes the inverse.

Do you research your subjects? How do you research?
Before Google I used to go to used-book stores and buy stacks and stacks of old books. Now, there is Google, which for an illustrator, is the best thing ever invented.

How does your personal work relate to your professional output?
They are usually one and the same... Most of my personal work finds its way into my professional work, either as background patterns or prints, etc.

Untitled, 2010.

Four stylish girls show off their fashion looks, which owe more than a little to social chic icon Babe Paley, in their simplicity and colour palette: a frog-fastened slim-fitted jacket, a streamlined two piece and tonal handbag, a lightweight summer coat and skirt, and a fitted sweater and pencil skirt.

Paulette had it made in the Shade (even when it rained)

SUPER gorgeous

jasmine was one of a kind.

sometimes i like to just do nothing. try it. it's fun

From left to right and top to bottom
Untitled, 2011, 2004, 2011, 2006.

The bold oversized motifs on these dresses cover floral, lace, Art Nouveau and abstract, all heightened by handwritten comments that add to the fun.

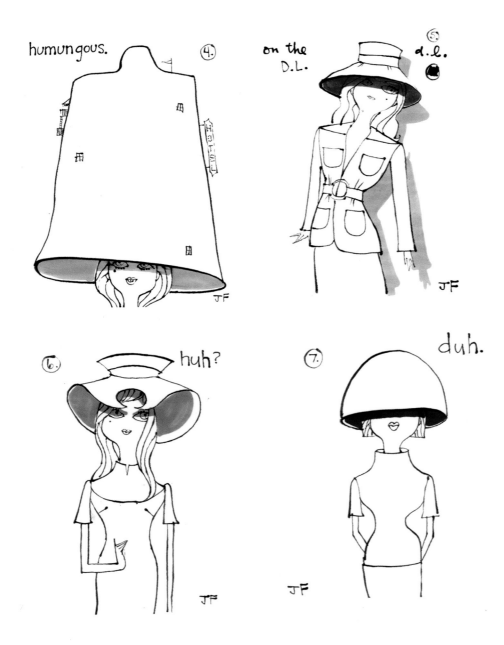

humungous. ④

on the
D.L. ⑤ d.l.

JF

JF

⑥ huh?

⑦ duh.

JF

JF

Facing page
Untitled, 2004.

Here the model is clearly placed
against a background of painterly
casualness reminiscent of the
tourist-inspired fabrics of the
1950s. Her tiny top and shorts
in cherry blossom pattern are
resolutely 21st century though.

Above
Untitled, 2000.

Four girls show millinery taken
to new heights in these witty
depictions of hat shapes that
swamp the models.

Right
Untitled, 2002.

The 1960s spirit of designers Pierre
Cardin and André Courrèges is
channelled through this trio of girls
in their mini dresses and boots.

janice → petra → polly

TOBIE GIDDIO

The rhythm of the strokes that a fashion illustrator makes across the page can determine the mood of the work: consider the contrast in feeling evoked by a delicate watercolour and by a bold slash of brightly coloured marker pen. Tobie Giddio creates a 'soundscape' in her fashion drawings. They have such dramatic flair and extraordinary impact that they might be compared to a full-blown opera. Even in pastel tones or when she employs gentler strokes, there is a true presence to her work.

Giddio's feeling for silhouette contributes to the strength of her illustrations. Whether for Lacroix or McQueen, the women she conjures up take centre stage like the true fashion divas they are. She also displays a very specific eye for colour, turning shades that might look decidedly odd in the hands of less skilled artists into magical renditions of ball gowns or the arch of a heavily made-up eye. The exaggeration of proportion that is traditional in fashion illustration becomes a spectacular feature – with a flourish, the height of a model is extended to accommodate the splendour of the sweep of a sleeve, a sliver of a dress or the cascade of a bustle.

Her combination of boldness and modernity of approach echoes the great graphic lines of the images of Thayaht (Ernesto Michahelles), who specialized – in plates he drew for *Gazette du Bon Ton* in the early twentieth century – in rendering the sweeping bias creations of Madeleine Vionnet. However, borrowing from modern art rather than from the heritage of illustration is what gives Tobie Giddio her individual stamp. As with other successful fashion illustrators, she has a broad range of clients and her work sees many uses, demonstrating the importance of being a commercial artist capable of communicating with the viewer. Yet by retaining her own personal methods and style Giddio plays her part in enhancing the visual language of fashion illustration and its myriad end uses.

Gloire VI, 2004.

Like Brünnhilde in her fiery immolation scene, there is a Wagnerian scale to this image. The bold sweep of the black cape over the shoulder of the layered empire gown has the drama any diva would require.

Left
One Through Eight VIII, 2008.

As though the wing of some exotic bird had affixed itself to a dress, this image has more in common with an Irving Penn photograph of a creation by Balenciaga than anything else.

Below left
One Through Eight VII, 2008.

This silhouette is underpinned by sweeps of colour, emphasizing the line from the head through to the elbow of the collar and sleeves as well as the asymmetric skirt.

Where and when were you born and where do you live now?
I was born on the Jersey Shore. I moved to NYC in 1983 and have never really left.

Any particular childhood influences?
As a child I loved strong female voices, like Barbra Streisand. Singer/songwriters then and now are still a huge inspiration. It is why I approach line in the same way a singer approaches singing or in the way an instrument is played. It's all about varied strength, intonation, clarity… I loved Donna Summer and disco, Led Zeppelin and Elton John. I loved movies like *Eyes of Laura Mars.* The seventies really were the golden age of film for me. I would escape to a makeshift studio in the basement and listen to that music and draw for hours. I would painstakingly copy Richard Avedon photographs with a pencil. My family is Italian so we would visit Florence and Rome and go to the small towns in northern Italy where my grandparents were from. I was always enthralled with the magnificent beauty of the Alps, the great art that came from there. Extraordinary beauty and abundance is from those imprints.

What is your earliest drawing memory?
Being more interested in drawing on the blank inside cover of a colouring book than the drawn pages.

What was your first professional work?
Bergdorf Goodman ads that ran weekly in *The New York Times.* I wanted to do that since I was a teenager. As a kid I would get really excited about getting my *Vogue* in the mail to see those beautiful George Stavrinos full-page illustrated Bergdorf Goodman ads.

Do you have a preferred medium?
Sumi ink and brush and Pantone transparent film. I am now finally getting into working on a computer, scanning my ink drawings in and collaging with my shapes in Illustrator or collaging with photographs I have taken.

Do you work in silence or with background music/radio?
Both. Silence when I am beginning something or composing something new. Once I am in the zone, I will put the music on.

What would be your ideal commission?
Projects that involve collaborating with people whom I highly respect where I love what they do. Projects that create a situation that benefits everyone involved and where the outcome is special.

Are you a slow and careful or quick and speedy draughtsman?
Both. The ink drawings come quickly and spontaneously. The collaging is a slower process as these are built piece by piece. It's all a moving meditation though, whether the process is fast or slow.

Do you keep a sketchbook?
No, but I journal a lot. It's a process of self-enquiry for me. I need to always be very clear about what I want the work to be and to do. Intention is extremely important. Agnes Martin said, 'You have to want the painting… We get what we want.' It saves a lot of time.

How would you describe your work?
Drawing fashion for me is an ongoing exploration, abstraction and expression of inner beauty adorned as outer beauty. It is a language of shapes, colours and forms, ultimately describing who we are. My figures are a representation of the Goddess as she is revealed to me. It is my intention that they touch that aspect that exists in everyone, consciously or not.

Do you research your subjects? How do you research?
I don't do any formal research. In general I am pulling from impressions of what I love and allowing that to flow through my particular filter. It is important for me to constantly look at what is inspiring and beautiful to me. I have my 'go-tos' in the way of heroes, designers, musicians, painters, movies, etc. They remind me of what I am meant to be doing and then I can more easily get to it but I am never looking at anything while I'm drawing. I couldn't do this though unless I had studied anatomy and drawn for many years from life. The structure of the female figure and clothing is ingrained in me like a language at this point.

How does your personal work relate to your professional output?
I have always focused primarily on my personal work and work towards there being little to no separation of the personal and the professional. I make the work and then I have to detach from it. I wait and see how what I have done is utilized and manifests. In my mind the personal is not complete without collaboration. There has to be communication and the imagery needs to be of service on one level or another, which is why I see myself as a fine artist functioning as an illustrator.

Anything else you wish to tell the reader?
It is ultimately my intention to have beautiful drawings be a part of the way we see and appreciate objects, clothing, etc. Art has the potential to uplift an environment or brand and inspire like nothing else. Making drawings in the world at this time is a very special pursuit and not for the faint-hearted. I have been at this for many years now and honestly I have had some wonderful successes and of course there are the disappointments. At the end of the day it is your body of work that has the last word.

Geisha, 2007.

A Madame Butterfly image of a floral kimono topped with a kabuki or geisha wig has a flow of movement through it as though pictured in a Japanese garden.

Tiffany Blue IV, 2007.

Like an exploding chrysanthemum or dahlia perhaps, this ball gown is definitely grand and ready to make an entrance. In the boldness of the image one can almost hear the rustle of the taffeta as the model pauses and arranges the skirt before descending a very grand staircase.

Top
McQueen Rainbow, 2010.

The layers of this skirt open out into a fan-like train in shadowed lilac pink. This dress could only be worn at either Versailles or on the proverbial Red Carpet, where it would certainly be the centre of attention.

Above
Chanel for Amica, 2003.

This siren-like figure is almost abstract yet the head to the right is depicted carefully. The 'confection' on the model's hair and the elaborate make-up have the same quality as an Avedon couture photograph.

RICHARD GRAY

Richard Gray is a modernist in his fashion aesthetic but hints at the ancestry of illustrators such as Alastair (Baron Hans Henning Voigt), Ernst Dryden and even Erté. His illustrations often carry an erotic charge and this is apparent in his recent illustrations of London men – pictures that capture both the sexual and dandy qualities of their subjects in equal measure.

Gray's references and inspirations reflect a lifetime's interest in London style – something he has followed since his early teenage years – with special attention given to those who have caused creative havoc in the city, such as Malcolm McLaren or Michael and Gerlinde Costiff. During his career he has shown amazing versatility, having pastiched René Gruau for the *Independent* newspaper's Haute Couture Report, provided semi-erotic drawings of menswear for *Attitude* magazine and created a monochromatic display for an exhibition at the Victoria and Albert Museum. The painstaking detail within Gray's work, even in a simple pencil sketch, reveals his concern with producing as near perfect a result as possible every time. He has the approach of a miniaturist, with his preferred media being pencil, airbrushing and gouache.

In one sense Gray moves at the highest fashion level, having worked for Alexander McQueen at Givenchy, researched and developed drawn advertising for Vivienne Westwood and collaborated closely with Anna Piaggi on many projects. Seventeen years after their first collaboration, Gray worked with Piaggi again when the V&A paid tribute to her with a unique exhibition in 2006, and Gray calls her a key figure, alongside her late companion, the great vintage fashion collector, Vern Lambert. In another sense, however, Gray is also a working artist with a variety of commissions alongside his current teaching role at the University of Westminster in London.

Aside from recording collections for archives he has worked on many projects with designers, including Boudicca. Gray also illustrated the costumes for the movie *From Hell*, starring Johnny Depp, a task in sympathy with his own sexy-yet-gothic-tinged aesthetic. This direction is also apparent in his work for the lingerie company Agent Provocateur. The films *Eyes of Laura Mars* and *Blade Runner* are cited by him as early sources of inspiration and fit well with his quirky slant on glamour, which often has a theatrical flourish. He creates worlds within his illustrations and his ideal commissions are those that truly capture the imagination of the observer.

Roy, 2010.

Gray focuses our eye from below the model's sideways glance. Is the latter sneering, or possibly suspicious? His choice of classic baseball jacket in brilliant chrome yellow and darkest indigo, with a hint of the dandy about it, suggests that perhaps he is evaluating us.

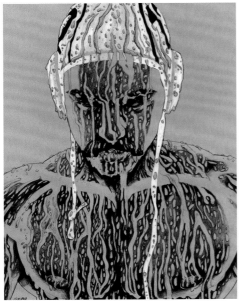

Where and when where you born, and where do you live now?
I was born in Norwich, Norfolk, in 1966, and I now live in London.

Any particular childhood influences?
I had many inspirations as I grew up, but my main childhood influences, the really pivotal ones, were: fashion – Vivienne Westwood's Pirate collection in 1980 and Bodymap's Cat in the Hat collection in 1984; movies – *Eyes of Laura Mars, Blade Runner, All About Eve*; writers – Angela Carter, Thomas Hardy, Philip K. Dick; friends and collaborators – Vivienne Westwood, Anna Piaggi, Vern Lambert, Michael and Gerlinde Costiff, Pepita de Foote; music – Kate Bush.

What is your earliest drawing memory?
I don't really have any specific memories, but drawing was something I always did in any spare moment, as it was always a real pleasure to do.

What was your first professional work?
My first professional work was commissioned by Anna Piaggi for her *Doppie Pagine* in *Vogue Italia*. She had spotted my work while I was a first-year student at Middlesex University. My illustrations had been entered in a memorial competition for Antonio Lopez, and she really liked what I did, so I was invited to meet her in Milan with my portfolio and my first commission for *Vogue Italia* and also for *Vanity* came from that.

Do you have a preferred medium?
Pencil, airbrush and gouache.

Do you work in silence or with background music/radio?
I always work with music; it really helps me get in a creative zone, and block out any outside interruptions or considerations.

What would be your ideal commission?
Something which really captures the imagination.

Are you a slow and careful or quick and speedy draughtsman?
I've got lots of different styles of work, so the speed usually depends on the quality of mark making I want to achieve. My work is usually quite labour intensive, though.

Do you keep a sketchbook?
I don't keep a sketchbook, but I do lots of personal work. I do keep lots of sketchbooks of visual research and very quick sketches of ideas for future illustrations.

How would you describe your work?
The women's pictures are usually, though not always, quite narrative, quite detailed, stylized, often with lots of references to animals, flowers and machinery. The men's illustrations are more straightforward, more stylized portraiture and much more physical.

Do you research your subjects? How do you research?
I always research my subjects, through books, movies, references to art history, art symbolism, music, and any really inspiring cultural references which interest me at that point.

How does your personal work relate to your professional output?
The two inform each other. My work is quite specific, even though the styles vary greatly; there is a common sensibility to it all.

Top
Blue Shirt, 2003.

Delicate technique seems to outline every hair, from skinhead crop through arched eyebrow to classic stubble. The contrast with the sharp blue shirt is carefully judged as the balance of colour to black and white is perfectly weighted.

Above
Wet, 2010.

This lifeguard in his Bondi surf cap has just this second emerged from the waves as the water runs heavily down over him. A split second captured in a painstaking illustration.

Facing page
Miguel Adrover, 2000.

The sheer weight of the bird against the figure of the model makes this image sexually charged even before we note the placing of the arrows and the use of the arousing red for the heart logo and stiletto shoes. The diagonal line of the composition emphasizes how the bird seems to be crushing as well as embracing the girl in her ruffle- sleeved mini dress.

Left

Petra, 2007.

Tweed and knit are rendered with superb technique and made morderm by the exaggeration applied to the total image. The model is annoyed and quizzical and the hand grasping the Venus Flytrap plant has cruel talons.

Below

Flaunt cover, issue 57, 2004.

Like the doll in *The Tales of Hoffman*, this model is an illusion and her puppeteer is the illustrator. Balancing the elements of automaton and mannequin with human qualities, she displays the fashion in a flowery bower.

Facing page

Love, Art Department, Illustration Division, 2008.

The key to this image is a metaphor often used for masculinity: the hard sporty stripes of the helmet and the delicate rose tracery of the tattoos. Gray captures them in this timeless image, which echoes masculine portraits since Tudor and Elizabethan times.

RICHARD HAINES

Richard Haines uses his illustrations to record what he sees in fashionable men about town: street style. Such observational drawing – taking individuals seen on the streets and adapting these figures for a variety of creative outcomes – has been used in fashion illustration since time immemorial. In contemporary fashion terms, blogs – often relying on a cast of street 'characters' for their appeal – and photographic artists like Scott Schuman have developed an eye for fashion as it is worn and turned this into a specialist area.

The interesting point about the swift lines and communication of character conveyed by Haines's drawings is their direct reference to artists such as Holbein, Watteau and Ingres in their preparatory sketches for portraiture. The drawing is chosen as the fastest method of communication, and the edited use of line conveys everything required. Haines's 'sketches' provide clear delineation of the clothing, conveyance of texture and depiction of the body language and attitude of the wearer, and as such comprise finished works. His subjects may be city dandies or simply guys with style, often unaware. Haines records them in a flash, preserving them forever as a series of swift lines and marks that reinforce the craft of fashion illustration yet have a totally modern zing to them. His figures are fully rounded – as if we might bump into them at any moment strolling along the pavement or backstage at a show. Haines's figures are reminiscent of Francis Marshall's sketches – they have a timeless quality and show us the way life was at the precise moment the illustrator picked up his pencil and made the first mark.

Above all, Richard Haines demonstrates the absolute power of fashion illustration: to transform a blank sheet of sketchbook paper into an arresting image in a few brief minutes. There are no tricks, no needless invention; for him the truth is exciting enough, the real has its own strength of message. Such results are almost impossible to achieve without flawless technique, speed and a love of the blank page at your fingertips. Haines upholds the tradition that a fashion illustrator is an observer and a recorder, but first and foremost an artist who just happens to record people and clothes.

Josh Poses with the Perfect Nail Polish, 2010.

In his trench coat worn over classic shirt and trousers, his hand nonchalantly poised on the back of the emerald green director's chair, this model seems to be a man about town relaxing. Closer examination reveals the ruby red varnished nails of the man, reminding us of the old adage that the 'devil is in the detail'.

Where and when were you born and where do you live now?
I was born in Panama on 21 October 1951. My father was an officer in the Navy so we moved around a lot. I've been in New York (Manhattan) since December of 1975, and moved to Brooklyn two years ago. Moving to Brooklyn has pretty much recharged my experience of living in NYC!

Any particular childhood influences?
I think moving around while I was growing up was a huge, great influence. It taught me that there was a much bigger, more interesting world than if I had grown up in one place. When I was 13 we moved to Iceland. I remember my first day of school – all the Icelandic kids were dressed like mods (this was after leaving the very traditional suburbs of Philadelphia) – I was in heaven and my fascination with fashion really kicked in!

What is your earliest drawing memory?
I don't have an exact memory, but I do remember at five all the other boys had World War Two planes and tanks drawn on their notebooks, and I had evening dresses, so I knew something was up!

What was your first professional work?
When I was 15 I got a job drawing an ad for a very posh shop in Alexandria, Virginia (outside Washington, DC). The ad was in the back of *Washingtonian* magazine and naturally it was pretty thrilling. I loved the whole experience of spending time in such a lovely store around beautiful clothes and chic people.

Do you have a preferred medium?
My medium of choice changes and evolves as the work does. Right now I really like using those cheap charcoal pencils that 'refresh' when the string is pulled and the paper peels. I recently bought a jar of India ink and some old-fashioned quill pens, so that's been fun to play around with. I find when I change mediums the line and composition of my work changes a lot, which is exciting and challenging.

Do you work in silence or with background music/radio?
It depends on my mood. I recently bought some lime-green Panasonic headphones so I'm back into listening to music when I draw. I love that feeling of 'being in the moment' when I'm listening to music and drawing but not really thinking of either – everything just flows...

What would be your ideal commission?
There are so many different scenarios that interest me, so this is a tricky question to answer. I love the idea of a store having a signature illustrator, so that would be exciting. And if someone gave me an advance to spend a year travelling and sketching people on the street for a book, I wouldn't say no.

Are you a slow and careful or quick and speedy draughtsman?
This is a good question – I think I'm pretty much known for my speed, so I'd have to say I'm a speedy draughtsman. I love to work really quickly – to capture the moment. I have a lot of admiration for people who work slowly and carefully – I envy that process. But that's not to say I don't put a lot of effort into concentrating on the person, the pose and the clothes, because I do. I just tend to get it on paper quickly.

Do you keep a sketchbook?
I usually keep a few different books going. For most work I use 11 × 14-inch sketchpads, so I usually have a couple of those on my desk. And because I like to sketch people on the streets or in their 'environment' (subway, club, etc.) I have a couple of different smaller sketchbooks on hand. I'm not the most organized person so sometimes I'll forget to carry a book with me and end up sketching on a napkin or back of an envelope but that seems to work to my advantage, so it's all cool!

How would you describe your work?
I think my work is about getting the 'moment' on paper – it's about gesture and speed and immediacy. One thing I think a fashion illustrator can do is tell a story with a few lines and strokes, and let the viewer add their interpretation to the story as well. I love that process. I'm always telling students to edit their drawings, to leave something out and let the viewer engage with it. The first time I saw fashion illustrations was in *The New York Times*, and I was fascinated by how much information could be conveyed with so few lines. I'm still obsessed with that process and looking at different ways of achieving it.

Do you research your subjects? How do you research?
I love to capture some person I see on the train or street – and get that moment – so that involves zero research... But I do feel like I need to 'get into their head' to get them properly. When I do portraits or a series on someone, that involves more time spent with them, studying their face, their body and the way they hold themselves. And a lot of that happens in the give and take of the conversation, so I guess I would have to say it depends on the circumstances.

How does your personal work relate to your professional output?
They both kind of blend together. With my blog I guess the person becomes the professional, so it's difficult to say where one stops and the other starts. I know when I do commission work I listen to what the client says and, assuming we're on the same page, address their needs while staying true to what I do.

Anything else you wish to tell the reader?
I get people contacting me a lot asking me about illustration, the market, what to do, how to do it. I have to say, the constants are practice and hard work. I sketch almost daily, and I think that dedication and effort is what's needed to really get things moving!

Balenciaga Side View, 2011.

A regal gown illustrated on its dress stand is shown from the side to better show off the bustle-effect back. The whole design is silhouetted against a rich blue painterly background.

Facing page
Waiting for a Latte @ Joe's, 2011.

The speed of mark-making is apparent in this fashion portrait, yet the skilled shading of the coat, scarf and trousers shows how different colours and weights of fabric can be achieved in a masterly fashion.

Above
Vanna: Two Sides to Every Story, 2011.

Props can be vital in a fashion illustration. The amount of mirror reflection shown in this drawing is perfectly judged and allows us to see the length of the classic sweater. The mood is preppie yet the chair is Park Avenue grand.

Armorlux
262 MOTT STREET, NEW YORK, NY 10012 USA
+1 212 228 2700
WWW.INTERNATIONALPLAYGROUND.COM
SALES & PR CONTACT
JOHN PIZZOLATO
INTERNATIONAL PLAYGROUND
262 MOTT STREET...
+1 212 228 2700
JOHNNY@SHOPSHOWROOM.US

Fjallraven
262 MOTT STREET...
+1 212 228 2700
WWW.FJALLRAVE...
WWW.INTERNATIO...
SALES & PR CONTACT
JOHN PIZZOLATO
INTERNATIONAL PLAYGROUND
262 MOTT STREET, NEW YORK, NY 10012 USA
+1 212 228 2700
JOHNNY@SHOPSHOWROOM.US
ADD'L SALES
VIRGINIA CRADDOCK
INTERNATIONAL PLAYGROUND
262 MOTT STREET, NEW YORK, NY 10012 USA
+1 212 228 2700
INFO@INTERNATIONALPLAYGROUND.COM

Gorilla USA
888 7TH AVENUE / 12TH FL
NEW YORK, NY 10106
+1 212 354 7071
WWW.GORILLAUSA.COM
SALES CONTACT
CHRIS PEPE
GORILLA USA
888 7TH AVENUE / 12TH FL, NEW YORK, NY 10106
+1 212 354 7071
CHRIS@GORILLAUSA.COM

Haerfe...
... 917 88...
WWW....EST...
R CONTACT
TIM JOO
HAERFEST
410 W. 53RD STREET / #306, ...YORK, NY 10019 USA
+1 917 885 1122
SALES@HAERFEST.US

Ian Velardi
... W. 25TH STREET / STE 4, NEW YORK, NY 10001 USA
+1 917 209 4935
WWW.IANVELARDI.COM
SALES CONTACT
IAN VELARDI
...TER MARCUS GROUP
... 57TH STREET / 6TH FL, NEW YORK, NY 10019 USA
91 209 4935

Pitti Japan
661 N. HARPER AVENUE, STE 201, LOS ANGELES CA
90048 USA
+1 310 614 445...
VISION.FISHER@GMAIL.COM
SALES & CONTACT
LIA FISHER...

Sebago
9341 COURTLAND DRIVE
ROCKFORD, MI 49351 USA
+1 616 866 5500
WWW.SEBAGO.COOM
SALES CONTACT
TOM SIANO
SEBAGO
717 5TH AVENUE / 4TH FL, NEW YORK...
+1 443 618 6698
SEBAGOTOM@EARTHLINK.N...
PR CONTACT
SONYA HARLAND
PIERCE MATTIE PR
...45TH STREET / 3RD FL, NEW ...
+1 212 243 1431
SONYA@PIERCEMATTIE.COM

HAINES

Capsule Brand Addendum, 2011.

Haines draws fashion on real people. Here we see two recognizable types, who care about their appearance but are not posed fashion models. The drawing has been done on the nearest available piece of paper.

JAY
LI

WILL
FROM W

WANT

HAINES

Left
Will from W, 2011.

Avant-garde layers contrast in this fashion illustration against the bespectacled wearer of simple pieces worn with must-have boots.

Below
Mr. Mort @ Pitti, 2011.

A modern bohemian with his hands in his pockets and a narrow jacket, tightly buttoned.

HAINE.

Left
Matthew Thinks, Drinks, 2010.

This pensive man rests in his pristine white shirt and holds his drink carefully in his hand. The entire drawing, on coloured paper, seems imbued with a feeling of summer.

KAREEM ILIYA

The key signatures of fashion illustrators obviously vary from one illustrator to another: with some it is the weight of line, for example, and with others it is the media used. With Kareem Iliya there are two key elements that characterize his work. First, there is the colour palette – a constant in his work, to which he returns again and again. An edited series of shades, encompassing the richness of damson and other wine-stained reds and plums, is combined with the opaque and powdery tones of ochre and mustard. Then there is the atmosphere with which all Iliya's work is imbued. This is a shadowed world of silhouettes and vapour, where his characters and the objects that surround them exist in a realm of ultimate sophistication behind veils and screens.

Iliya is unique in his ability to use softness and semi-transparence built up in layers to create solid form that then fades away again to a mere whisper. This technique enhances all the other elements and yet it never dominates the final outcome. The softness of line combined with almost imperceptible detail demonstrates a control of his chosen mediums and moods, whether the work is straightforward commercial or suggestively ambivalent for special commissions.

The range of clients and subjects covered by Iliya is testament to his versatility, yet he remains absolutely true to his own vision and signature style in his depiction of each individual subject. As with a master storyteller, the images are both romantic and at the same time unconventional, even unsettling, in their approach.

There is a dark streak to the romance in the colour and blurring which counterbalances the beauty of the subject and its impact. Iliya is able to both suggest and depict in extraordinary detail everything from a shoe to a crowded restaurant.

Technically assured in his placing of his subjects, Iliya captures them wonderfully, like flies in amber. It is perhaps in the fleeting second when he has preserved them for all time that there is a suggestion of the work of Odilon Redon or that of the fin-de-siècle artist Alphonse Mucha. Whether the subject be a fragrance or a celebratory image for an accessory, Iliya balances total individualism and modernity with a timelessness that accounts for his success as a fashion illustrator across the world. His shadowed silhouettes and colour application lend desirability to the simplest glass or flower and enhance the quality of the object being observed. It is no wonder that the luxury world calls so often on Iliya's skills to communicate their products.

Personal work of Viktor & Rolf 'jumpsuit', variation from a series for *Madame* magazine, 2003

In the same way as a photograph, fashion illustration can be 'close up'. This is admirably demonstrated here in this watercolour of a multi-collared top. The image focuses on the garment and the face is cast in total featureless shadow.

Where and when were you born and where do you live now?
I was born in Beirut, Lebanon, in 1967. I currently live in Vermont, USA.

Any particular childhood influences?
As cosmopolitan as Beirut was, upon arriving in Texas as a young teen I was immersed in a new culture and quickly learned the important role that clothing played. I began to follow fashion, reading the then extra large-sized *Interview* magazine and *WWD* that were handed down to me from my mother's friends. I went on to study fashion design in college and found that I really enjoyed illustrating the clothes I was designing.

Variation from a series for Saks Fifth Avenue, 2005.

The weightless feathered fronds of this handbag seem to actually move against the background of lightly coloured mist. The bag looks like it might slip from the fingers of the beautifully drawn hand and take flight.

What is your earliest drawing memory?
Maps for an elementary school project – third grade I believe, maybe earlier.

What was your first professional work?
I was commissioned to do the Christmas window illustration for the Romeo Gigli boutique in NYC.

Do you have a preferred medium?
Watercolour and ink on paper.

Do you work in silence or with background music/radio?
I usually start a project in silence or possibly with some low-key music, nothing too engaging or distracting. Then once the project has momentum I like to turn up the volume and have the music be part of the driving force. If it is a slow-moving project with great detail, I might listen to podcasts.

What would be your ideal commission?
Fortunately, I've already had the opportunity to work with incredibly talented people on interesting projects. This inspires me and keeps things interesting.

Are you a slow and careful or quick and speedy draughtsman?
It really depends on the project – I might say slow but I have nothing to compare it to since I have always worked alone. After reflecting on a new project for a couple of days I form a clear vision before I begin to paint.

Do you keep a sketchbook?
Yes.

How would you describe your work?
I don't describe my work.

Do you research your subjects? How do you research?
Less is more. Too much information can overwhelm the creative process. Depending on the project, clients will either provide design-specific information or they request that I create the design.

How does your personal work relate to your professional output?
I have various bodies of personal work. Some are completely unrelated to my commercial work to the point that you would not consider the two to have been created by the same person. Others are really the foundation of my commercial work.

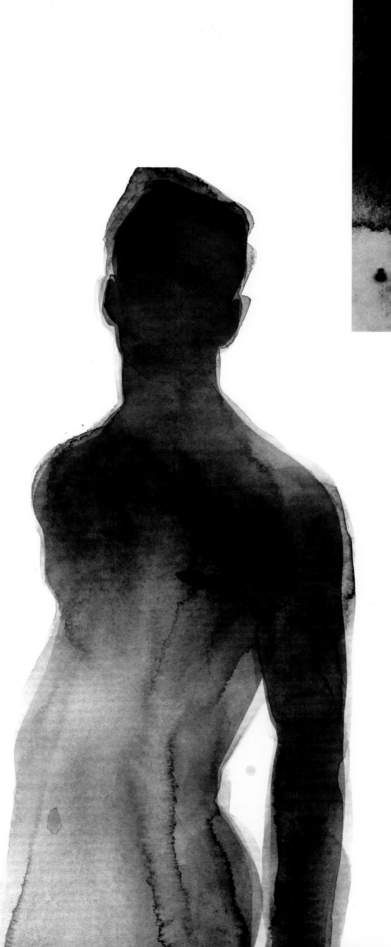

Left
Untitled, 2010

This male torso is built up
of layers of tone and colour as
a fashion illustration silhouette.

Above
Personal work of Tom Ford
perfume, 2007

This depiction of a fragrance
bottle turns an object into an
object of desire. Although we
cannot smell the scent, this
image evokes a feeling of dark
luxury and the bottle both
emerges from and recedes into
the rich velvety background.

Kareem Iliya   **107**

Left
Sodini Bijoux, *D Magazine/ La Repubblica*, 2010

Like a sunburst revealing only certain details in its glare, this fashion illustration allows us to clearly see the bracelets. We imagine the high-neck corsage and the hairsticks perched in the high bun almost fade to nothing.

Below
Max Mara Occhiali, *D Magazine / La Repubblica*, 2010

The huge volume of hair in this drawing perfectly balances the huge sun shades the model is wearing, counterbalanced by the tiny dark mouth, but it is the single strand of hair, escaping from the bouffant, that lifts the entire image.

Facing page
Untitled, 2009.

Fin-de-siècle courtesan or red carpet diva? This image illuminates the potential of fashion illustration to create extraordinary atmosphere. Silhouetted against blots of watery, misty vapour, this figure drifts towards the horizon with myriad pearls draped across her neck and shoulders.

JORDI LABANDA

Observing social mores and capturing fashion foibles – putting the fashionable under the microscope, in fact – is a task we expect to see realized by fashion illustrators. Jordi Labanda obligingly skewers the fashion crowd as surely as any lepidopterist with his specimens. He treads boldly in the footsteps of George Cruickshank in Victorian times or Sem at the turn of the twentieth century, or contemporary fashion illustration artists such as Gladys Perint Palmer or Jean-Philippe Delhomme.

The images that Labanda creates are totally of the moment, and a cast of instantly recognizable people inhabits his world. He appears to raise a wry eyebrow at his subjects. 'I know them,' he seems to say, 'but I am not fooled by them.' The details are painstakingly, lovingly rendered with a precise knowledge of the milieu and the importance of the current must-have objects. Whether it is a pair of dogs or a wine glass, Labanda identifies the perfect complement to his subject. His people are impeccably groomed and always appropriately attired, reflecting a polished and edited view of a stylish world where nothing is left to chance.

Labanda is equally at home drawing men and women. Like all great fashion illustrators his visual world extends beyond the image on the page, hinting at a complex back story for his characters. Colour and fashion are inextricably intertwined and Labanda's personal palette is specifically modern in its balance and use of shades. He is especially adept at taking tones of one colour – perhaps citrus yellow or café au lait –

and using it with black and white to offer an image that appears highly coloured but is actually tightly edited. This controlled aspect to his work has led to commissions in other disciplines, such as advertising. The high level of finish is akin to *pochoir* – a process of layered stencils – with crisp lines and brilliant colour seen at its best in the *Gazette du Bon Ton*.

One of Labanda's great strengths is that, without resorting to undue cartoonish exaggeration, his drawings are full of humour and wit. Ultimately they make the observer smile – a difficult trick to pull off in fashion illustration while still retaining an element of chic. Only someone who truly understands and loves fashion could nail it so succinctly.

Art Department, Illustration Division, 2011.

The brilliant colour of this fashion illustration explodes off the page both as a statement and with the volcanic eruption behind the black-clad model. Her eyes are shielded from the glare by the blackest of sun specs; the heat sizzles.

Where and when were you born and where do you live now?
I was born in Mercedes, Uruguay in 1968 but I lived in Barcelona from the age of three. At the moment I am living in New York

Any particular childhood influences?
The *Vogue* magazines that my mother brought from Uruguay to Barcelona were very important; I remember that world full of colour and optimism in contrast with a grey and unhappy Spain at the beginning of the seventies, when Franco was in his last years. The television was also very important, things like the cartoons of Hanna-Barbera, classic movie cycles and Disney movies that you could only watch at the cinema.

What is your earliest drawing memory?
A scene of a fox hunt with riders on horses jumping over a stream.

What was your first professional work?
An illustration for the literary supplement of *La Vanguardia*, the most important newspaper in Barcelona, about the marriage of writers Paul Auster and Siri Hustvedt. I still collaborate with the same newspaper.

Do you have a preferred medium?
I feel very comfortable jumping from one medium to another with complete freedom. From the editorial to publicity or to product design.

Do you work in silence or with background music/radio?
If you work as many hours as I do you have time to do everything. To listen to the birds chirping in the garden and to listen to music at full blast. I listen to music from my iTunes library on my computer. I never listen to the radio because it doesn't let me concentrate and I don't like it.

What would be your ideal commission?
That in which creative freedom is valued above everything else. My favourite work is where I forget to eat and sleep because I am having so much fun.

Are you a slow and careful or quick and speedy draughtsman?
I am pretty fast drawer and very meticulous. I think that is a good combination. The drawing is very important to me; until the pencil drawing is perfect I don't start to fill it in with gouache. Sometimes the gouache covers some real tricks done with the pencil.

Do you keep a sketchbook?
I have never used a sketchbook. I always do sketches on sheets of paper; I keep some of them and the others I throw away.

How would you describe your work?
Elegant, ironic, timeless and meticulous.

Do you research your subjects? How do you research?
I like to use books and of course the internet has turned into something essential... It goes so fast that it scares me.

How does your personal work relate to your professional output?
I keep my personal and professional work very separate. I have material that nobody would ever guess was mine; I would rather that not interfere with my professional work.

La Vanguardia, 2009.
Like a 1940s cartoon strip this film noir image of lovers seems to require others to reveal the story; it reads to the viewer as an isolated episode and we want to know more. Fashion illustration as narrative is a powerful tool for communication.

Left

Feria de Abril, poster for Barcelona council, 2007.

The flat planes of colour used for both the model and her background are contrasted with the careful depiction of the roses, both on the fan and in the model's hair. This is a vivid rendition of a señorita with a touch of vintage about it.

Below

Frame for Grand Marnier television advert, 2009.

The heritage of René Gruau adds piquancy to this image. The absence of most of the figures through superb editing leaves us with a kick of legs and a flounce of point d'esprit skirt. Two arms form a strong diagonal as the subject's glass is filled against the boldness of black and red.

Right

Gucci, *Corriere della Sera*, 2005.

The media of fashion illustration in the hands of a master confounds our expectations. Swirls of snow are silhouetted against a brilliant scarlet background, heightening the impact of the monochrome figure wrapped in her white musketeer-collared coat.

Above left

Poster for Adidas shop in
Barcelona, 2006.

Every picture tells a story, so they
say, and this one certainly does.
She may be holding hands with her
skateboarder, but the girl in the
picture is quick to turn to flirt with
the boy walking past. The label
count is also high yet still doesn't
dominate the image.

Above

Vogue Nippon, 2011.

A slice of 21st century lifestyle is
captured: handbags assume a major
role, the seated model has two
mobile phones, and the short skirts
simply couldn't get any shorter.

Above left
Fanzine 137, 2005.

Take a simple ribbon-tied waist on a classic black dress and through the alchemy of fashion illustration make it scroll in the air like a baroque decoration.

Left
Design of a limited-edition jacket, Moncler, 2011.

Showing fashion *in situ* is a matter of imagination combined with some research. But there is no need to go skiing or take models to the slopes to invent a wonderful scene like this; it can all be done from the comfort of the studio.

Facing page
Vogue Nippon, 2010.

Fur-trimmed sheer coat, swing-line skirt, nip-waisted jacket and bold floral coatdress: this image shows three contrasted fashion looks, teams them with standout handbags and places them in front of a crowd. Fashion illustration this complex in construction requires great skill to balance all the components.

Right
Vogue Nippon, 2011.

Karl Lagerfeld is captured in every detail, from his boots to his fingerless gloves. The shades and ponytail, the extra high collar; nothing is missed in this imagined scene of him crossing the road with three designer-clad models.

TANYA LING

Imagine the fashion world as being permanently on show – life as a catwalk, the entire universe led by style. This gives you an idea of the observational viewpoint of Tanya Ling. She has a style that is widely recognizable: a possibly oblique and faintly sardonic, but always kind, view of the fashion world. Her ladies lunch in Chanel, shop in Lanvin and walk the dog in Balenciaga. They reflect the fashion seasons by appearing in furs or chiffons; they sport the latest 'must haves', whether patterned tights or an upswept hairdo. They favour timeless colours such as black and grey and use red as colour punctuation. Above all, in their passion for all things fashionable, they really give the impression of knowing what's hot and what's not and all about style, down to the very tips of their well-manicured (in this week's colour of varnish) fingertips.

The extraordinary contradiction is that Ling's work is as unstudied and free flowing as it is possible to be, with a kind of dégagé air of insouciance that is the complete antithesis of the idea of the uptight fashion slave. Her marks whirl across the page and there is an animation to the illustrations that is in total contrast to the tightly controlled image of the fashion world. Hers are not the blank faces of Botox and fillers (a stereotype straight from the 'shallow' world of fashion), these are women who are animated and communicative, busy and with plenty to say. The individualism of each designer Ling draws for is reflected in the individualism of her characters.

She echoes the approach of Joe Eula in both her panache and her pragmatic attitude to the world she draws; they share a clarity of view.

A notable point about Ling's work is her rendering of, focus on and evident love of hairstyles; no illustration is complete without its bold portrayal of a hairdresser's masterpiece. Her evident relish in rendering each crowning glory brings a particular character to every image. Finally, Ling's fashion illustrations are not sterile reproductions of a garment and the fabric it's made from, but rather skilled commentaries on a specific world, which will be studied in a hundred years by people wanting to find out what women really looked like when wearing the fashions of the day.

Untitled, NARS, 2009.

In a classic fashion illustration portrait, less is defiantly more. Here, Ling extracts in under 20 lines the cool, calm gaze of the fashion model.

Where and when were you born and where do you live now?
I was born in Calcutta, India. I now live in London.

Any particular childhood influences?
The *Mona Lisa* and Paris. My father and my grandfather took me to the Louvre and told me I was going to see the most important and beautiful painting in the world. I sat on my father's shoulders so I could see over the heads of the other viewers and couldn't believe what I saw!

What is your earliest drawing memory?
I remember making drawings of ice skaters and paintings of bright pink and blue blobs.

What was your first professional work?
British *Vogue*, July 1997. I illustrated a page written by Samantha Murray Greenway about Lucien Pellat-Finet. This was soon after the birth of my third child, Evangeline. Before this and soon after leaving Saint Martins, I worked as designer for Christian Lacroix when he was starting up, and then Dorothée Bis.

Do you have a preferred medium?
I use a lot of paint and ink on paper.

Do you work in silence or with background music / radio?
I listen to Radio 3.

What would be your ideal commission?
To illustrate the Book of Proverbs from the Old Testament.

Are you a slow and careful or quick and speedy draughtsman?
Careful and quick.

Do you keep a sketchbook?
Not really, although I have quite a number of sketchbooks in storage crammed with drawings – I almost always now work on loose sheets.

How would you describe your work?
Intuitive.

Do you research your subjects? How do you research?
I spend hours online looking at models and the collections but I wouldn't really call it research – that makes it sound like work – it's just what I'm interested in.

How does your personal work relate to your professional output?
I don't really divide my work into personal and professional because it all comes from the same place.

Anything else you wish to tell the reader?
You're invited to visit tanyaling.com!

White, Viktor & Rolf, 2008.

In this fashion illustration the drawing of the neck ruche and hair of the model swirl into volume at the same time as the lines of the dress and legs counterbalance this weight.

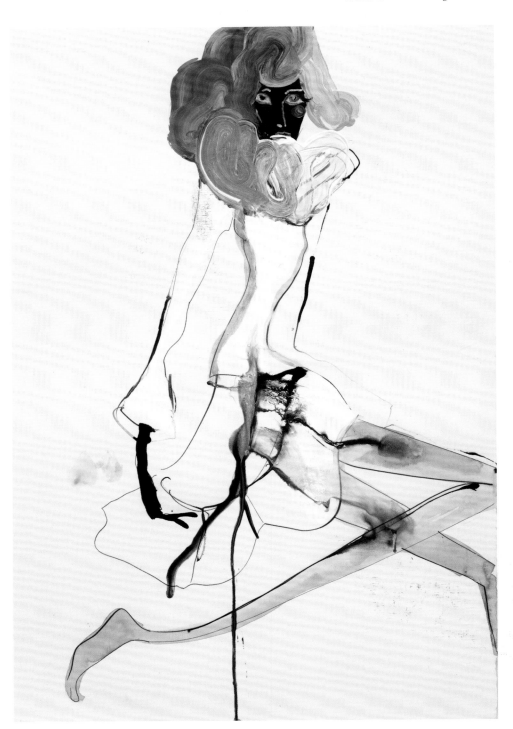

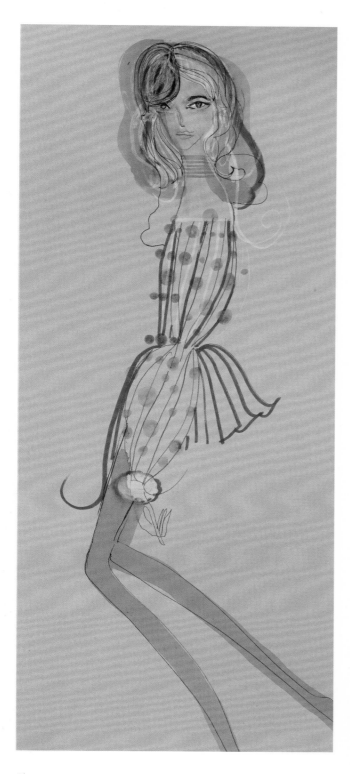

Above
Idea Drawing, 2010.

Flirtatious in this dotty dress, the model kicks her extra-long legs as she flips her hair under her jauntily poised chapeau.

Right
Idea Drawing 19, 2010.

The graphic knits of designers such as Missoni require a sharp use of the medium. Here, the movement of colour down the body is carefully weighted.

Left

Nina Ricci A/W 12, 2012.

In her pale feathery top, this model's ruby lips and darkly kohl-rimmed eyes accentuate the pallor of both her complexion and outfit.

Facing page

Chrisitian Dior A/W 09, 2009.

Frog fastenings give a Russian or military air to this suit with its tightly belted waist and slim lines. The ineffable chic of the wearer is balanced by the unexpected hue of her hair, which imparts a slight air of eccentricity to the portrait.

ZOË MORE O'FERRALL

Character is essential to every drawing created by Zoë More O'Ferrall – it may be a rock star or it may be a cat, even a shoe – but it speaks to the observer. More O'Ferrall relishes every idiosyncratic twist of a subject, from unevenness of teeth to sharpness of claws; her task is to tell us exactly how it is, to 'impale' her subject. Her strength of line enables her to merge graphics and illustration, often combined with lettering. Her subject may be an old building or a hot designer but her work tells us everything we need to know about it without guile or subterfuge. There are elements of surprising line complexity and build-up of technique, yet the final results are strong statements that engage the observer directly.

One might infer a hint of cruelty in More O'Ferrall's microscopic analysis of skin or stance, for instance, but these details are laid down with an authority that negates this and simply presents what she sees as the truth. The styles range from street to portrait, and black and white predominates; colour becomes a real statement. What is especially arresting is her ability to offer close-up, precisely drawn items as well as complex patterned designs, almost in the style of toile de Jouy. The fashion element is matched by a curiosity to investigate all kinds of subjects, from nature to still life.

More O'Ferrall's work evokes careful engravings and woodcuts of the past with its precise lines and clarity of image construction. Some of it recalls the layout of samplers in the clean balance of each element, demonstrating clearly the graphic applications of her work. She offers a style of fashion illustration in opposition to the neo-Romantic styles of past practitioners such as Eric, René Gruau or René Bouché. Her task is to observe and record, and yet the work has real heart and emotion – the outcomes are not mechanical or technical, they are simply drawings that speak for themselves. More O'Ferral's breadth of work is an excellent example of the range required to be a successful fashion illustrator.

Alexa Chung, 2010.

With the matelot striped top, crisp blazer and multiple necklaces there is something quite French about this portrait of Alexa Chung. The softly painted pale blue stripes allow the painstaking detail of the jewellery to show up perfectly.

Kate, 2010.

A fashion individual wears clothes their own way, which is what makes them stand out, but the twist in this fashion portrait is that the illustrator has eliminated the wearer and focused only on the clothes, leaving the viewer guessing about the model.

Where and when were you born and where do you live now?
I was born in London, a Londoner through and through. I've lived south, north, east… and now I'm settled in Notting Hill.

Any particular childhood influences?
From a very early age my parents often found me, pencil in hand, propped up on a stool in the corner of our kitchen, which was renamed 'creative corner'. Travelling has always been a great inspiration for new work; exploring new cities and finding the elements – however big or small – that make up my impression of each place. It's no surprise that architecture is a prominent subject in my work, perhaps as a result of that. Because a lot of my drawings derive from the ordinary and everyday objects in day-to-day life it's hard to be too specific about what influences me; it's fairly continuous.

What is your earliest drawing memory?
Drawing on the walls at home which, unsurprisingly, was not enormously appreciated.

What was your first professional work?
My first professional job was for *Dazed and Confused*. I was asked to create an illustration about the 'Death of Publishing'.

Do you have a preferred medium?
I work primarily in ink and pencil; the only digital contribution comes in after scanning to clean images up and compose or construct them. I'm very much about hand-drawn aesthetics. Often parts of my drawings have started out as mistakes, which is something I think I'd lose in digital imaging. I have a madly expansive collection of pens and seem to have found certain favourites. I'm often sucked into a vortex of stationery shops.

Do you work in silence or with background music/radio?
I like to listen to a mixture of music and the radio while I work. It depends on my mood or the nature of the drawings I'm working on. I usually have Radio 4 on in the background; I pick up snippets and can float in and out of concentration, which is nicely therapeutic.

What would be your ideal commission?
I love that each commission and each brief is different from the last; it's very refreshing to work for a variety of people in a variety of contexts. I loved working for Topshop; the art team there were wonderful and it was a great experience developing their ideas into

visuals. A recent job to illustrate all over every last bit of a piano for Mumford and Sons was lots of fun; a huge amount of work but very refreshing. It would be ideal if I could continue being commissioned in new realms.

Are you a slow and careful or quick and speedy draughtsman?
I'm pretty careful, as there is often a lot of detail in much of what I draw, especially architecture. Thankfully I draw quite quickly – deadlines always feel shorter and shorter but I like working under pressure more than with the luxury of time. Working out of my comfort zone definitely slows things down so it's dependent on the subject.

Do you keep a sketchbook?
Always, I find it's a really important outlet for ideas. It's helpful going through old sketchbooks, finding sources and starting points for new inspiration. Virtually all my commissioned work is drawn in sketchbooks too rather than on loose paper. I like the spatial confinements of a sketchbook.

How would you describe your work?
I've noticed a lot of people come back to the word 'whimsical'. Primarily ink and pencil line illustration with touches of colour, though colour is something I've definitely had to tackle. I used to feel much safer in the confines of black and white but that's developed a lot. Hand-drawn typography has also become a key part of my work, which is ironic given that typography was something that I used to find really quite daunting.

Do you research your subjects? How do you research?
It depends on each job and each subject. Thankfully I can save a lot of time sourcing images online, though with my map illustrations it's usually good to research and explore the areas in person as you get a much better feel of the place. I travel a lot and take endless photographs so I've built up a pretty big catalogue of inspiration and source material. I work in a very literal way rather than from my imagination so the research is fairly key.

How does your personal work relate to your professional output?
I find they're entirely intertwined. It's hard to label it as one or the other. Maybe because of the nature of what I do, work does feel personal. A lot of the ideas and visuals for jobs I'm hired for can originate from personal work and vice versa. It's helpful when you can refer back to previous exploration for new inspiration.

So Last Season, Topshop, 2010.

This witty take on the foibles of fashion implies both that the classic colouring of the bird needs updating, alongside the sad fact that once it is killed and eaten it is, indeed, last season.

Zoë More O'Ferrall **127**

Right
Street Style, 2010

Two lads about town who are dressed to impress are captured in the simplest of drawings where all the focus is on the character of the wearers and the depiction of their outfits.

Below
Rogue Brogue, 2009.

A single colour is used to draw a single shoe perfectly. Everything superfluous has been eliminated.

Below
Karl, 2011.

The intense drawing of the jacket fabric and meticulously drawn hair are balanced by Lagerfeld's hard black tie and spectacles. This is truth unadorned but not a caricature.

Bottom
Flash, Flash, 2009.

The ability of a fashion illustrator to simply draw almost anything is shown here in this charming vignette drawing of a camera.

Right
YSL, 2011.

Capturing the late Yves Saint Laurent in his later years, this fashion portrait shows the essential traits of the designer without tipping over into cartoon.

JENNY MÖRTSELL

Caught as the proverbial flies in amber, Jenny Mörtsell's subjects are seen at a specific split-second in their lives; preserved forever as they go about their business of rubbing an eye or applying make-up. The drama of the moment is captured in a totally different way to how it might be by photography or sketching; it is recorded using a combination of meticulous draughtsmanship, painstaking attention to detail and time-consuming craft.

Mörtsell observes in detail the people of the day who are fashionable in terms of what they wear and who may also work in the fashion world. She draws in the intensive manner of artists such as Horace Vernet or Paul Gavarni from 200 years ago; the ability to fuse the totally traditional with a modern viewpoint is a difficult trick to pull off, but it is one that she achieves successfully. Mörtsell adds a special contemporary twist through careful selection and a refined editorial eye, as well as a predilection for the slightly quirky.

How clothes are actually worn, and how people put them together in particular, is central to Mörtsell's work. The overriding message of her work is the importance of individualism and personal style: her subjects are real people wearing their own clothes in a particular way. They don't dress the way they do because it is the fashion of the season or an editor has told them to. Like a stylist taking seemingly simple pieces and juxtaposing them in unexpected ways to create an original image for a photograph or show, Mörtsell uses skilled editing to produce her images.

Fashion may be seen alongside illustrations of objects, offering a layering of textures; sweaters and vegetables, silky smooth china against a leafy plant or metallic tin against the shell of a crustacean... As in fashion, where, for example, a stripe may be teamed with a check – never the obvious choice. Mörtsell also uses colour so sparingly that it assumes a new significance; a soft mushroom beige, a sharp daffodil yellow are made new by their placement and use in her work.

Men, women and objects are equally represented in her work, and her approach and the quality remains consistent whatever the subject. This combination of labour-intensive illustrative work and an unusual perspective on style creates a unique and timeless record of fashion.

Urban Outfitters, 2010.

Stripes and checks in soft fabrics is an illustration challenge but in this fashion portrait, it looks like the easiest thing in the world. Drawn from life, the soft cardigan and shirt are stylish on this young model, whose gaze is ever so slightly away from the viewer.

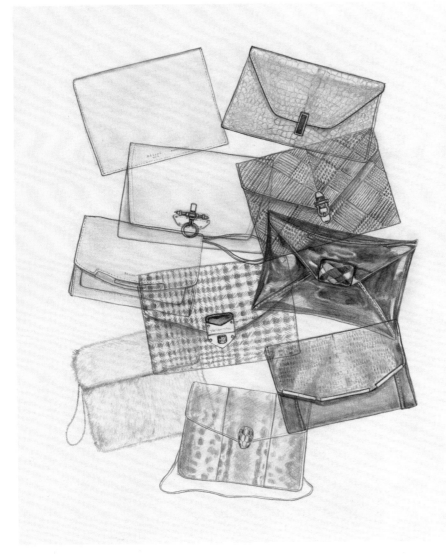

*Where and when were you born and where
do you live now?*
I was born and raised in Stockholm, Sweden.
In 2008 I went to New York to 'try it out'
and I have stayed here since. I'm currently
living in Greenpoint, Brooklyn.

Any particular childhood influences?
Lego, horses, Moomin, Astrid Lindgren
books and all the summers spent at my
family's country house by beautiful Lake
Mälaren in Södermanland.

What is your earliest drawing memory?
Crayolas at kindergarten.

What was your first professional work?
A before-and-after drawing on the subject
of makeovers of girls in films for a Swedish
feminist magazine called *Bang*.

Do you have a preferred medium?
A mechanical 0.5 mm pencil with a rubber
in the end and smooth Bristol paper.

*Do you work in silence or with background
music/radio?*
Always with music or radio documentaries.
This American Life is a favourite! I also
download a lot of DJ mixes from F.E.X
Resident Advisor. I notice that if there are
no breaks in the music I am more disciplined.

What would be your ideal commission?
A portrait of a young Brooke Shields.

*Are you a slow and careful or quick
and speedy draughtsman?*
Very slow and careful.

Do you keep a sketchbook?
No, I never ever do sketches. I always
carry at least two cameras instead.

How would you describe your work?
Photorealistic pencil drawings.

Do you research your subjects? How do you research?
Google image searches and by constantly trying to stay open and interested and listening to what people have to say.

How does your personal work relate to your professional output?
It's not a very big difference except that with my own work I choose the motifs myself. And deadlines and getting approvals makes me have to work in a slightly different way to where I can leave things more open. My personal work is a slower process and because I have the final say and rarely have to change anything it often ends up being more detailed.

Anything else you wish to tell the reader?
Eat your vegetables and keep your promises!

Above
3.1 Phillip Lim, 2009.

This trench swings gently on its hanger, clearly placed on the rail to be drawn. This is a fashion still life of closely observed detail.

Right
Shabba Ranks, *Fader* magazine, 2009.

Deep in thought, the heavily bejewelled hands and ridged haircut of the model offer both a style balance and a style statement.

Left
Rachel Comey, *Liebling* magazine, 2007.

There are many completely different surfaces shown here in intense detail; the hair, the spectacles, the top, the skirt and the shoes. The extraordinary trick is to prevent any of these surfaces from overwhelming the image, giving them all equal weight.

Facing page
Ryan, 2008.

Capturing the moment is a skill at which many fashion illustrators excel. It is exemplified here in this fashion portrait of a long-haired man rubbing his eye.

Caught fiddling with her sleeves, this young woman has slipped her giraffe face mask back to hold her tumbling luxuriant hair. The viewer is almost a voyeur as the model concentrates unaware of the moment captured by the illustrator.

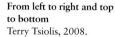
**From left to right and top
to bottom**
Terry Tsiolis, 2008.

Featuring a girl skipping for joy
in her fancy new shoes, this image
is the opposite of our perceived
idea that a fashion illustration
is a static record of clothes.

'Human Behaviour', *Line-A
Journal*, 2010.

Perched on a sawn-off tree trunk,
this Mickey Mouse-eared model
is clearly flaunting her elfin boots
as her prize.

Rodarte, *Liebling* magazine, 2007.

The key to this image is not the
raised skirt but the diagonal line
that extends from the side swept
pony tail across the hip line and
through to the three-quarter view
of the feet.

Christopher Kane, *Liebling*
magazine, 2007.

Hand on hip and gazing straight
at the recorder of this fashion look,
the model seems proud of her
snakeskin print top and frayed,
fringed jeans.

PIET PARIS

When Toulouse-Lautrec drew Jane Avril for *Divan Japonais* in 1893, he preserved the fashion she wore – the silhouette and the styling – forever. Today illustrator Piet Paris builds on the heritage of this particular bold, linear style. Among his prolific illustrations there is a nod to generations of artists whose aim was a stylized line and the elimination of the superfluous. Like all creative work, fashion illustration must walk the line between being fashionable or of-the-moment and the obverse; instantly dated. Paris is resolutely modernist in his work, presenting fashion illustration with a superb edge, and yet its quality of line is also timeless in its references, unconscious though these obviously are. The boldness and precision of his work is married with a sensitivity of balance and form, as well as a very specific colour palette.

Bernard Boutet de Monvel, whose work for the *Gazette du Bon Ton* in the early twentieth century had a strong quality of elimination and space, would have recognized this same rigour in the work of Piet Paris. However, Paris's work is totally up to date in its assimilation of contemporary style and current fashion trends. The images reflect the social mores of today's fashionable society in an understated way, making a firm, sure statement about how Paris views the world of fashion.

Paris's work already has a collectable quality and seems destined not only for publication but also for the gallery. In colour terms he constantly surprises; bold slashes of lavender and citrus with a sharp black line. Somehow, even when he is working with a flat, almost cut-paper line, there is still a three-dimensional quality to the work. Shoes fit feet, dresses look ready to wear and hair seems about to be sprayed to keep it in place. This sleight of hand, combining clarity with total understanding of how to communicate real objects to the viewer, is extraordinary.

Kiss, cover for *Holland Herald*, 2006.

The silhouette of the Eiffel Tower and the flip-hemmed skirt worn by the model seemingly giving it a kiss, are further tied by the horizontal lines of land, grass and jet trail. The 'screen' at the top is slashed by a sky-blue triangle and the vivid red hair of the model's pony tail – true fashion graphics.

Right
Cover illustration for NHK
Symphony Orchestra Tokyo
calendar, 2007.

Colour is used to coordinate
the three figures chopped into
Mondrianesque lines on this
image, with navy and orange
being the common denominators.

Below
Schiaparelli cover illustration for
a shoe special edition of *Vogue
Nippon*, 2003.

In a direct homage to the shoe hat
of Elsa Schiaparelli, Paris celebrates
a shoe issue with this profile
silhouette in marzipan shades.

*NHK Symphony Orchestra,Tokyo
2007/08 Season*

*Where and when were you born and where
do you live now?*
I was born in The Hague, Netherlands.
I'm based in Amsterdam.

Any particular childhood influences?
My upbringing and especially the way my
father introduced me to art and the aesthetics
of fine living made a big impact. My mother's
elegance triggered my interest in fashion.

What is your earliest drawing memory?
I use to draw all the time, even as a young
child. At primary school they couldn't stop
me; I was always aiming to make the
biggest mark.

What was your first professional work?
Just after leaving the art academy in Arnhem
my first job was for Italian *Vanity* – 15
portraits of Italian actresses.

Do you have a preferred medium?
HB pencil.

*Do you work in silence or with background
music / radio?*
I work in silence.

What would be your ideal commission?
Making a series of illustrations for one
commission gives me more room to express
a story and to come up with different
techniques, so in the end these turn out
to be better jobs.

*Are you a slow and careful or quick
and speedy draughtsman?*
Preparatory sketching for one illustration
can take up two days; making the final
illustration is one day.

Do you keep a sketchbook?
No, in my free time and outside of my studio
I never sketch.

How would you describe your work?
As an expression of my lifelong interest
in fashion in all its facets.

*Do you research your subjects? How do
you research?*
In general by searching on the internet,
visiting shows and showrooms, teaching,
museum visits and reading.

*How does your personal work relate
to your professional output?*
I only work on commissions.

Bride for the 'Fashion DNA' exhibition at Rijksmuseum, Amsterdam, 2006.

Victoriana is given a modern twist in this fashion illustration using photographic lace. The image is a fantasy of many historical elements, combined into one bold statement.

Below
'C' for 'Collection', 'Fashion ABC' series, *Het Parool*, 2010.

The young designer kicking her heels in the 'C'-shaped chair is churning out ideas in a wide range of colours, but two pick up the green of her seat and the floor.

Facing page
'H' for 'Haute Couture', 'Fashion ABC' series, *Het Parool*, 2010.

It takes a moment or two to work out that the extravagant seamstress is working on the vast bustled skirt of the model. Notice how Paris links the cotton reel, the bow in the model's hair and the bow shape balanced on the bustle.

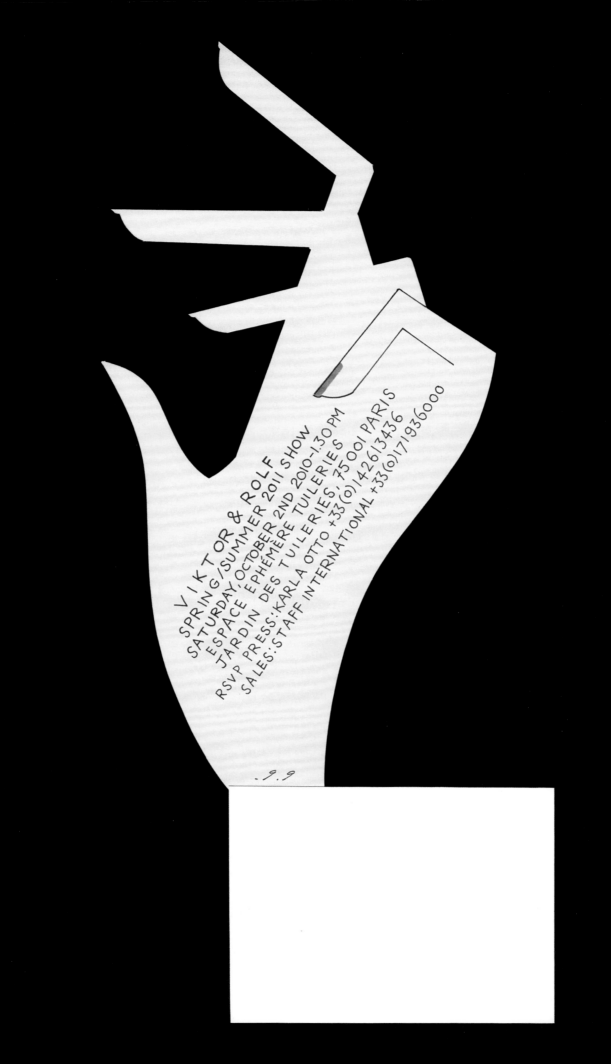

VIKTOR & ROLF
SPRING/SUMMER 2011 SHOW
SATURDAY, OCTOBER 2ND 2010–1.30 PM
ESPACE ÉPHÉMÈRE TUILERIES
JARDIN DES TUILERIES, 75001 PARIS
RSVP PRESS: KARLA OTTO +33(0)142613436
SALES: STAFF INTERNATIONAL +33(0)171936000

Left
Invitation for Viktor & Rolf S/S 11 collection, 2011.

Fashion show invitations are an art form in themselves, from a simple white card to elaborate constructions. Created for Viktor & Rolf, this invitation features a tiny envelope as the cuff.

Above
Backdrop for Viktor & Rolf S/S 11 collection, 2011.

Gigantic fashion illustration images line the backdrop, and even the catwalk, for the Viktor & Rolf fashion show.

STINA PERSSON

Where many fashion illustrators prefer to use monochromatic or restrained shades – perhaps reasoning that unless requested, the season's colours may date an illustration – Stina Persson revels in colour and splashes it with an almost reckless abandon across her work. Yet there is nothing careless about her imagery, and each piece of work makes a carefully considered statement. Like Christian Lacroix, she is confident with colour – to the observer she may seem daring but Persson is simply intent on presenting her flights of fantasy as a creative statement.

Persson's fluid use of media heightens the effect – one colour dribbles into the next – but she always knows when to apply restraint. Her editing both of the image and the palette is scrupulous and instils a confidence in the viewer that an illustration is complete without being overworked. This is especially apparent when she works with other elements, such as paper or photography; like a designer creating a collection, it is all about the final selection of components.

Persson has developed a way of approaching her subjects which incorporates her personal signature yet does not obscure the requirements of the image. Interestingly, she uses black as a colour; sometimes it provides the structure or contours of the image and at other times it is totally absent; other colours are substituted to take on this role with the construction of the image.

Like so many other successful fashion illustrators Persson has the versatility to demonstrate techniques across a range of subjects, making her work commercial. However, whatever the subject, and whether realistic and representational or inventive and fantastical, Persson's work always retains its own personality.

Honey, from the 'Perfectly Flawed' series, 2010.

This model's marmalade hair is swept into an enormous beehive do, and her head is slightly tilted to emphasize its curves. The key element to the image, though, is the hint of geometric pattern in the barely seen clothes, which provide exactly the right, hard contrast to the softness in the rest of the illustration.

Below

Loulou, from the 'Perfectly Flawed' series, 2010.

There is an almost stained-glass quality to the fabric in this fashion illustration. This richness, along with that of the red hair, is balanced by the ghostlike technique used to draw the face.

Where and when were you born and where do you live now?
I was born in 1972 in southern Sweden in a university town called Lund. When I was 18 I moved to Tokyo, and from there to Italy, to finally end up in New York. But when I was expecting my first baby we moved to Stockholm and have lived there ever since.

Any particular childhood influences?
I grew up in Sweden during the seventies, which to me was ideal. It was all about unisex, do-it-yourself and running around in worn-out clogs and torn jeans. It was perfect for an energetic and creative tomboy like I was.

What is your earliest drawing memory?
I remember making a big watercolour drawing of a girl and a boy, which I gave to my father. He took it to the framer and put it up by his bed. My father is no longer but the drawing is still there. Like any kid I gave them drawings all the time, but I really felt special when my father seemed to like that one image so much.

What was your first professional work?
I got a job from a start-up magazine in New York called *Value*. They had this article called 'Picnic Pairs' – well-matched food to bring to a picnic. They wanted an idea (very bad) of a play on words, and asked me to draw pears having a picnic. Which I did. I had to rework it many times as they thought the pears looked suicidal.

Do you have a preferred medium?
Ink, collage, watercolour... But I am constantly looking for new things to combine and collage together.

Do you work in silence or with background music/radio?
When I am alone in the studio I listen to the BBC World Service. I rarely watch TV and this is how I keep in touch with what's going on in the world. When it's too much cricket I change to NPR. Once my studio mate comes in we change to music. Anything from Peggy Lee to Keren Ann, Jorge Ben to Swedish Little Dragon.

What would be your ideal commission?
Some kind of interesting collaboration.

Are you a slow and careful or quick and speedy draughtsman?
Definitely not careful. I work quickly but it takes between one and fifty drawings to get it right. Which sometimes isn't very speedy at all.

Do you keep a sketchbook?
No, and I wish I was the kind of person that did. It looks cool and interesting and I envy them. I have bought loads but just never used them.

How would you describe your work?
It is about finding the right balance between the edgy and the elegant, the raw and the beautiful, to end up with a modern take on illustration.

Do you research your subjects? How do you research?
Flipping through books and old magazines mostly.

How does your personal work relate to your professional output?
I try to always raise the bar and make the work personal even when working with big commercial clients. It's not easy but it's a challenge that intrigues me and makes me sweat.

Above
Liberty, from the 'Perfectly Flawed' series, 2010.

The spirit of the great Alphonse Mucha is evoked in this sinuous Art Nouveau fashion illustration, with tendrils of hair flowing into the fabric of the garment.

Right
For The Heart Truth® Red Dress show, 2010.

Layers of raspberry, fuchsia and deep wine red are built up to create a lush velvety feel to this jacket, contrasted with the lightness of the face and hair as it fades into the collar.

Above
For The Heart Truth® Red Dress
show, 2010.

This dress would fill any catwalk,
as the model strides away, in classic
hands on hips pose. There is an
operatic, perhaps *Tosca*, feeling
to this dramatic image.

Right
Fashion Week Lagos feature for
Arise magazine, 2011.

This group of models demonstrates
that the technical ability to draw a
figure from any angle is an essential
skill for any fashion illustrator.

Catwalk, for the Fashion Business Angola campaign, 2010.

These two models stare at the viewer, confident in their glamour and dressed for success. The colour used by Stina Persson in over-layered geometric shapes heightens rather than obscures the figures, like spotlights.

CÉDRIC RIVRAIN

Delicacy allied to surrealism? This extraordinary description of his work does perhaps best describe the images created by Cédric Rivrain. There is an exquisite refinement of line, and a delicate depiction of the workmanship and craft of designer clothes from such eminent designers as Nicolas Ghesquière at Balenciaga or Martine Sitbon evident in his work. Alongside this is the ability to depict some of the world's great fashion models totally accurately without these images being reduced to the level of insipid street portraiture. Imagine all this and then throw into the creative mix the unexpected juxtapositions and quirky approach of the Surrealists and you come close to appreciating Rivrain's body of work.

To understand the way Rivrain's creative mind works, simply look at how a carefully placed Elastoplast on the drawing of a man's face shifts the image from straightforward to unbalanced. A meticulously drawn depiction of a dress by a great designer may be followed in his portfolio by a pair of eyes staring at the viewer with devilishly arched eyebrows, suggesting – well, that is perhaps best left to the individual observer to decide. What renders the work of Rivrain special is his ability to unnerve the observer and suggest the most elegant of Marquis de Sade excursions or a *Liaisons Dangereuses* world from the past somehow wrenched into the twenty-first century. His inventive depictions of his own original mask-like constructions, often shown on only partially completed drawings of the wearer, are truly haunting.

Underlying all this narrative is painstaking, breathtakingly accomplished technique. Rivrain, put simply, can draw, but his artist's eye and imagination turn this talent into something above and beyond simply recording what he sees. He understands how to faithfully depict and communicate without ever losing his personal signature, even down to how he shows colour – true to the original yet in total harmony with his personal aesthetic. It is also interesting to note the choice of paper on which particular images are created; Rivrain is making specific choices from the very start of the process. The mark of the true fashion illustrator is his ability to take us into a world of his creation as well as the contemporary world of fashion. Rivrain embraces this challenge with his pencil poised like a whip – though perhaps a whip made of feathers supplied by the Parisian House of Lemarié…

Anabela in Maison Martin Margiela, 2007.

Knowing what should be the exact proportion of yellow, through to the delicate modelling of the head is exactly the kind of expertise that is difficult to define. When is a drawing complete? Only the artist will know.

*Where and when were you born and where
do you live now?*
I was born in Limoges, the city of porcelain
in France, in 1977. I now live in Paris.

Any particular childhood influences?
The cartoons I watched, the antique medical
illustrations my father hung on the walls and
the band-aids I collected.

What is your earliest drawing memory?
I don't remember precisely, I guess it was
a cartoon I did not want to end and that
I continued in my own way.

What was your first professional work?
An illustration for *Dazed and Confused*.

Do you have a preferred medium?
Drawing with whatever helps me be precise
in the lines and colouring.

*Do you work in silence or with background
music / radio?*
I always listen to music while I draw.
Sometimes a whole day with the same
song going on and on.

What would be your ideal commission?
One that would give me freedom.

*Are you a slow and careful or quick
and speedy draughtsman?*
Quick and careful, instinctive…

Do you keep a sketchbook?
No I don't do any sketches beforehand.
I always go to the actual drawing straight
away. I stock images, feelings in my head.
And let myself be surprised with what
comes out of it through my hand.

How would you describe your work?
That is not for me to answer. I am too
deep into it. I just hope it is touching.

*Do you research your subjects? How do
you research?*
No I don't really research, I observe a lot
and when something touches me, it always
comes back through a drawing.

*How does your personal work relate
to your professional output?*
It enriches it, and simply makes it
more personal.

Above and above left
Sasha in Balenciaga and *Sasha in Prada*, both 2008.

There is something almost Byzantine about these images. The jewelled and decorated mask pieces, the front-facing poses and the disintegration of each image beyond a certain point are like figures from a fresco. The fashion is, in every instance, absolutely perfectly drawn to the last thread.

Facing page
Sasha in Lanvin, 2008.

The skill of the workrooms that made this dress is honoured by this illustration. Rivrain lovingly records the sheen of the fabric and every exquisite fold the seamstress stitched. The mask and necklace provide a perfect balance through their shapes and lines.

Lanvin, 2011.

Using the same delicate and detailed approach for menswear as for womenswear, Rivrain demonstrates the importance of a strong personal signature style in fashion illustration.

Left
Lanvin, 2010.

The telling point here is the placing of the hands in the low pockets of the outfit, showing the garments' proportions off to perfection and communicating to the viewer how they are supposed to be worn.

Below
Model in Louis Vuitton, 2007.

A conceit imagined by Fragonard or Dalí, this image combines the romance of Leda and the Swan with the knowledge that swans are vicious creatures to make an impossible reality. The style is poetic, with an underlying oddness which is heightened by the model being both naked to the waist and wearing exaggerated shoes.

Cédric Rivrain **159**

SARA SINGH

Sara Singh can take a seemingly simple fashion item and turn it into an object of desire. A cascade of lipsticks, or nail varnish bottles twisting in a spiral become weightless, gorgeous and shimmering as they tumble from her brush. Her work is fashion as aspiration, fashion as pure fashion – with a lightness of touch that prevents any of her drawings becoming arch, twee or even just girly. Her sense of control is apparent in every piece – be it a simple invitation or an illustration of a complex ball gown.

Although Singh uses a rapid touch to create her images there is a strength and poise to her work. Her ball gowns rustle, her killer heels support the weight of the models who wear them and her sushi is almost edible; items are real and solid on the page. The quickness of her mark making comes with an air of confidence; the results are utterly convincing.

Singh combines a graphic line with sensitivity and a complete understanding of how to render the three-dimensional on paper. Instinct and self-awareness colour her work, providing the viewer with the necessary information but with an almost 'throwaway chic' attitude in a compellingly nonchalant approach. Singh employs an especially limited, tone-on-tone colour palette to heighten the lightness of touch and throw focus on the lines – a way of editing the work and ruthlessly eliminating the unnecessary.

Singh can turn her illustrative style to whatever is required: as well as fashion she depicts interiors, food, jewels... Her work follows a direct lineage from twentieth-century artists like Bernard Blossac – her technique seems effortless, yet she has total control over her observational skills and her editorial eye.

Fashion illustration combines meticulous still-life observation with the freedom of life drawing; Sara Singh has mastery of both these aspects. The innate understanding of the construction underlying her subjects is vital to their integrity as illustrations and she allows the viewer to see what she sees. This marriage of flair and solid technical skills is what makes her fashion illustration work so special.

Project for Tiffany & Co., 2006.

The contrast between the painterly freedom of the model, especially the free-flowing hair, offsets the exquisite detailing in the illustrating of the jewellery in this fashion portrait.

Idea for a book cover, 2010.

The sheer weight of the thick, luxuriant hair of the model is contrasted in this drawing with the simplicity of line of the figure. The diagonal line of the image is further extended by the tilt of the head and the dark eyes and lips.

Where and when were you born and where do you live now?
I was born in England in 1967 and grew up in London, Stockholm and Florida. I currently live in New York City.

Any particular childhood influences?
Both parents worked for airlines and we travelled a lot. I was a small voyeur, capturing images of people from all over in the many drawing pads provided by my mother. I remember being 12 and feeling that I should have been born a bit earlier so I could have been a Mod in the sixties.

What is your earliest drawing memory?
I remember being almost five while painting on an easel for the first time. I thought at that moment, 'This is what I will do when I grow up.' I can remember what I was wearing.

What was your first professional work?
Drawing presentations for ad agencies in Sweden. I drew everything from yoghurt containers to Volkswagen beetles.

Do you have a preferred medium?
Inks and brushes and cheap paper (it makes me nervous to work on papers that are too expensive or fancy).

Do you work in silence or with background music/radio?
I work best with music. A job in progress will often have a soundtrack. I play the same music again and again to create a specific mood for the project.

Are you a slow and careful or quick and speedy draughtsman?
Each drawing takes only minutes, but I do many until I get it right. But when I process my drawings in Photoshop I take great care to erase any signs of digital manipulation.

Do you keep a sketchbook?
I think it's a good idea, but I'm a doodler and will quickly fill it up with all sorts of phone doodles and other mindless squiggles.

How would you describe your work?
Fast and fluid lines; feminine, sensual and delicate with a modern attitude. Technically, I like to work with metal nibs and washes of ink.

Do you research your subjects? How do you research?
I scour the internet or look at films, books and magazines.

How does your personal work relate to your professional output?
Naturally my personal work nurtures my professional work. But my professional work often requires me to find a new way to work or solve a problem and this can in turn be used for my own work.

The Diary of Anaïs Nin Volume 1 1931–1934

Eyeshadows, Bloomingdale's, 2010 and *Perfumes*, 2011.

Fashion objects and accessories are shown here demonstrating how the simplest, or even smallest, fashion elements require strong illustrative skills, be it for eyeshadow compacts or scent bottles.

If I were a girl I'd wear a cape every day

Clinique, (slightly altered and text added), 2011.

In this image the model is of minor importance, hence her facelessness, but the contrast between the heavy dark fabric of the cape and the shimmering decoration of the dress says everything the viewer needs to know.

Ascot, 2009.

The perfect balance of this magical image owes a great deal to the drawing of the hand with its immaculate manicure, and the single eye made-up like a bird's tail. The elaborate collage of the headdress and the ruthless elimination of all unnecessary lines completes this tour de force.

Sara Singh **165**

Left
Nina's New Shoes, 2011.

An unusually natural pose and angle allows the fashion illustrator to show us the neat, cropped hairstyle, the soft lines of the jersey dress and the T-strap shoes.

Below
Estée Lauder, 2008.

The strapless feathered gown seems to swirl around the model in this drawing. The contrast between the fronds drifting free and the more solid part of the dress where the lining must be is shown perfectly.

Facing page
Image from a series for Bond 07, New York, 2003.

To be able to draw lingerie without approaching pin-up or creating a contrived situation is a special talent. Here Singh captures a thoroughly modern model in her bra, pants, tights and shoes just at that moment before she finally gets dressed.

Sara Singh   **167**

HIROSHI TANABE

What is that special something that separates the unique fashion illustrator from the crowd? Often it is not an obvious method or style but simply an element that gives every image a quirkiness or strength, as recognizable as the signature found at the bottom of the page.

Hiroshi Tanabe, for example, loves to draw hair, and in almost every single one of his images the hair has this extraordinary life of its own – though there are also other elements that characterize the superbly graphic work of this illustrator.

Tanabe uses colour in a very special way – not limited, but characterized by the juxtaposition of colour to background, and of flat-colour proportion to pure line. His bold use of line also makes him one of the outstanding fashion illustrators of today. The range of images inspired by the world of fashion and style is simply dazzling: eyewear advertising, a punk boy, sixties-style girls, a swift make-up image and an eighteenth-century *bal masqué* are just some of the inspirations to be found in his portfolio.

Tanabe brings to each image a sharp editorial eye, eliminating the superfluous and concentrating on the most essential elements. His use of space, the placing of each element within the image – and perhaps above all, the ability to sum up through key components the absolute essence of the fashion requirements of the image, is amazing. The heritage of Japanese woodcuts has to be acknowledged in the structure of his line, as well as the influence of the great masters of Japanese fashion, such as Junya Watanabe. Across Tanabe's work there is an exciting range of moods, communicated through his confident personal style, be it pop sixties or romantic lightness. He demonstrates how a truly gifted fashion illustrator can successfully combine his own individuality with client requirements and, ultimately, with commercial success.

Hair Catalog, Madame Figaro, 2004.

The perfect coiffure, the perfect manicure and the perfect turquoise droplet – but with the stain on the fingers of the model, the artist creates an imperfect smudge of colour to fascinate the viewer.

Above
Gap, Red Campaign T-Shirt, 2009.

The overlaid repeat images of this prehistoric monster create an impression of movement while the girl astride rides with the wind in her hair. The key is the way her dress of fine pleats echoes the tail flaying behind her.

Right
Labrea T-Shirt, 2003.

Psychedelic graphics are re-examined in this girl's huge hairstyle, formed of layers of tonal colour highlighted with shell pink. The colours are picked up again in the sunglasses and word-decorated trapeze dress.

Where and when were you born and where do you live now?
I was born in Kawasaki, Japan, and moved to Milan, Italy, in 1990 for two years. I have lived in New York since 1992.

Any particular childhood influences?
Japanese TV animations and action heroes – they are very creative. Also my mother was a painter.

What is your earliest drawing memory?
I drew monsters and spaceships just like other kids.

What was your first professional work?
My first job was doing flyers for a nightclub in Milan – for two years from 1990.

Do you have a preferred medium?
Pen and pencil.

Do you work in silence or with background music / radio?
I used to play very loud rock or heavy metal when I was working. But not anymore.

What would be your ideal commission?
Animations.

Are you a slow and careful or quick and speedy draughtsman?
Slow and careful.

Do you keep a sketchbook?
I do some sketches.

How would you describe your work?
Minimal line drawing.

Do you research your subjects? How do you research?
Through books, movies, the internet.

How does your personal work relate to your professional output?
I use the same technique for both but the subject is different. In my personal work there is freedom when it comes to subject. I would like to paint with oil too. And also make objects.

Above
Detail from *Portrait of Sayoko Yamaguchi*, *Achtung* magazine, 2008.

The formality of the drawing of the hair is matched by the fine pleats or ribs of the sleeve emerging at the bottom of this image. The red of the pursed mouth is aimed at the red spot floating away at the top right of the illustration.

Above right
United Bamboo T-Shirt, 2007.

The blur of the empty eye sockets is enhanced by the meticulous detail of the long hair, whose strands form feathery tails.

Right
From *Marie Antoinette* book on film of same title, *Art Days*, 2007.

Ghostly impressions of the 18th century reflect that era's characteristic love of silhouettes and intrigue, as shown in *Les Liaisons Dangereuses*.

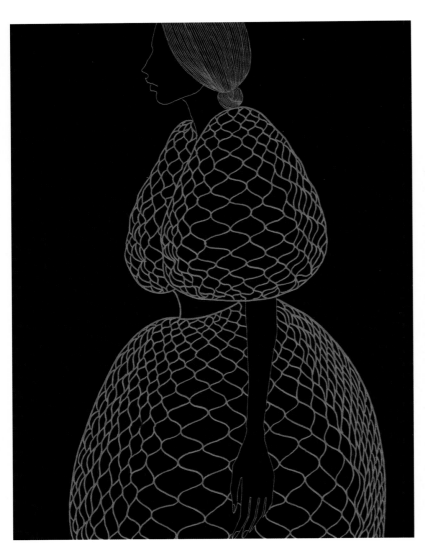

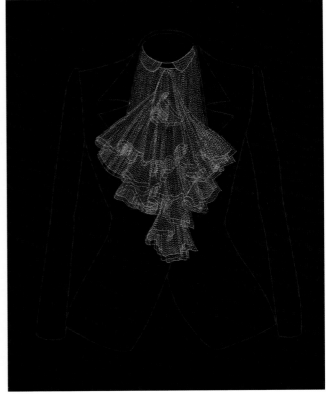

Above
Junya Watanabe A/W 00, *NOVA*,
2000.

The lightness of this garment is
suggested by the weightless drawing
of the intricate construction. The
garment seems ready to collapse like
the folding lanterns that inspired it.

Above right
Irene (Cocktail Suit circa 1950),
S Magazine, 2009.

All the focus of this illustration
is on the elaborate fichu cascading
down the front from a tiny neat
collar. The outlines of the rigid
structure of the tailored jacket
provide the perfect foil.

Right
Detail from *Portrait of Oliver
Kahn, Sepp* magazine, 2008.

Drawn detached from any hint
of anatomy, this perfect bob in
the style of Vidal Sassoon assumes
an unreal quality, especially when
repeated across the page.

Marc Jacobs A/W 95, DUNE
Magazine.

Tanabe takes a quirky view of this
girl in her neat plaid dress walking
her dog. The viewer is left to
wonder what the dog is doing and
where it might be going on its long
chain lead as it exits the frame.

Right
Hermès S/S 97, *Blue Mode*, 1998.

The repeat image here represents
the unfolding of a symmetrical
paper-cut of a body in black
silhouette. The hems link into each
other on the figures, emphasizing
the arc formed by the pose and the
curving construction of the dress.

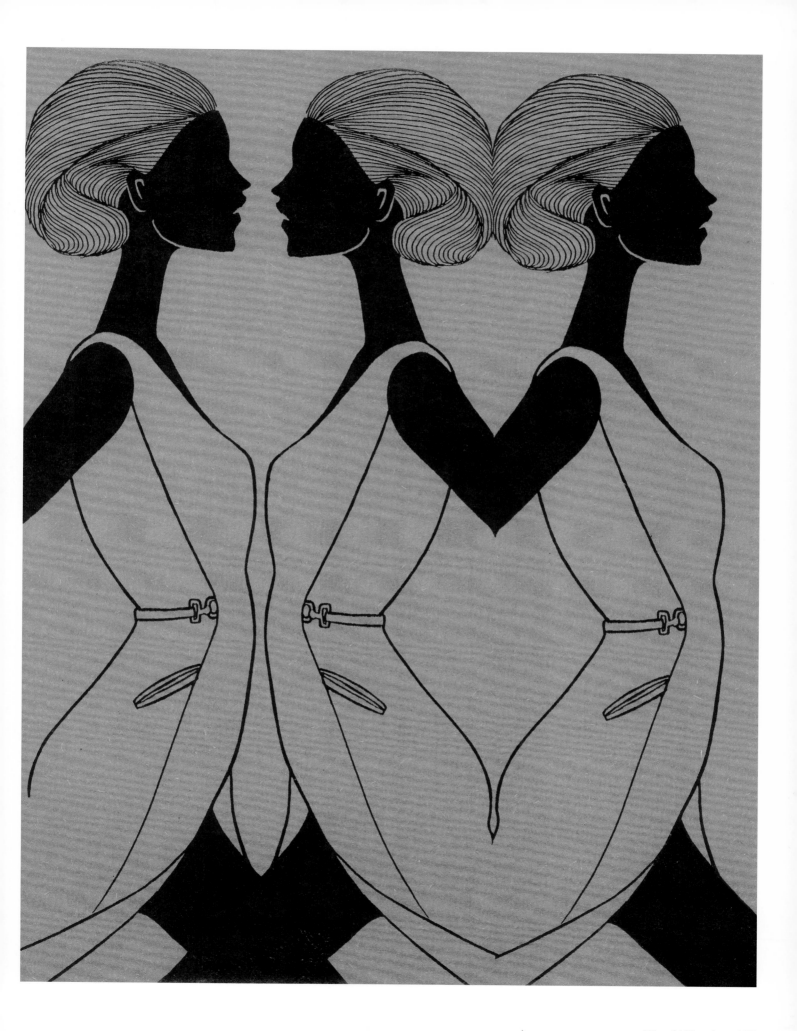

JULIE VERHOEVEN

It is perhaps her individualism and an approach that takes no prisoners that have made Julie Verhoeven an undoubted fashion illustration star, but she also embodies the commitment, dedication and the range of skills required to reach this level. Designing a catwalk collection, opening a boutique in Mayfair, creating erotic wallpaper, producing books of fashion illustrations and many more projects reflect the truth that simply being good at what you do is no longer enough. Verhoeven represents the pragmatic approach to fashion illustration also seen in the work of David Downton – they both understand that diversification and the ability to self-promote are what will take their work into another dimension.

Verhoeven's work is instantly recognizable, even though she has a range of techniques and styles, and this has created a school of Verhoeven wannabes who think that her curling irregular line and seemingly random page layout are simple to emulate. The truth is that her work is studied, professional and complex. Each piece offers a visual narrative and a balance of colour, which is the result of preparation, practice, skill, a finely tuned editorial eye and – most importantly – a gift for seeing things in a different way from other people. The observer is charmed, cajoled and seduced by her inventions, which offer a unique and almost eccentric view of fashion.

The invention of a specific type of Julie Verhoeven girl is a complex process and requires time and patience; such characters do not spring into the public consciousness overnight. Her sinuous line is reminiscent of the late Philippe Jullian's illustrations, with a slightly febrile quality. Her use of colour is extraordinary, as if she'd taken a box of paints and scattered its contents in seemingly random splashes across her figures, creating an almost firework-like explosion of effects. This is never used as a technique for its own sake, but is rather a carefully considered choice that is almost impossible to replicate. If at times there is a slight air of the seventies in the huge hair or layered patterns, as has been mentioned in press reviews, it is completely subsumed by the idiosyncratic way in which Verhoeven works her images. She is a total original – even down to the way she dresses herself.

Ho Ho Ho, Royal College of Arts Christmas card, 2008.

In the musical *Mame* the song goes 'The man in the moon is a lady'. It is unlikely that this was the inspiration behind this extraordinary visual conceit but it suits the image perfectly. There is a superb balance of excessive, almost crunchy, texture surrounding the face and the sad beauty of the portrait.

Below
The Pleasure is All Mine, The Sun,
2010.

The only word to describe this
image is 'dash': dashed off at
top speed no doubt, dash to see
it since it is a unique take on
fashion illustration and dash
it – how does she do it?

Facing page
Force a Smile, Flaunt, 2011.

The oblique glance of the subject
of this cover takes in the viewer
and manages to transform the hard
yellow with many other colours
to form a background colour that
supports rather than dominates.

*Where and when were you born
and where do you live now?*
Sevenoaks, Kent in 1969; now living
in London.

Any particular childhood influences?
Mum and Dad, *Misty* comics, *Bathers at
Asnières* by Seurat at the National Gallery,
open-topped London bus tour down the
Kings Road, *Top of the Pops* and *Hair,*
the musical.

What is your earliest drawing memory?
A magic garden drawing and a storyboard-
type set of drawings for 'She's Leaving
Home' by the Beatles.

What was your first professional work?
Artwork and in-house drawings for
John Galliano.

Do you have a preferred medium?
No preference. I love them all.

*Do you work in silence or with background
music/radio?*
Pounding, high-volume music/radio.

What would be your ideal commission?
No deadline, no roughs, no client and
a billion-pound fee.

*Are you a slow and careful or quick
and speedy draughtsman?*
Fast and reckless.

Do you keep a sketchbook?
Not anymore. I prefer carrier bags and
boxes full of loose pages of reference.

How would you describe your work?
Forever evolving and improving, I hope.

*Do you research your subjects? How do
you research?*
I always do an extensive amount of subject
research; an excessive amount of page
flicking and foraging in numerous libraries.

*How does your personal work relate
to your professional output?*
They both originate from the same source
matter/references/interests, but I am just
free to gallop off without a saddle, so to
speak, in my personal work.

Anything else you wish to tell the reader?
Drawing is King!

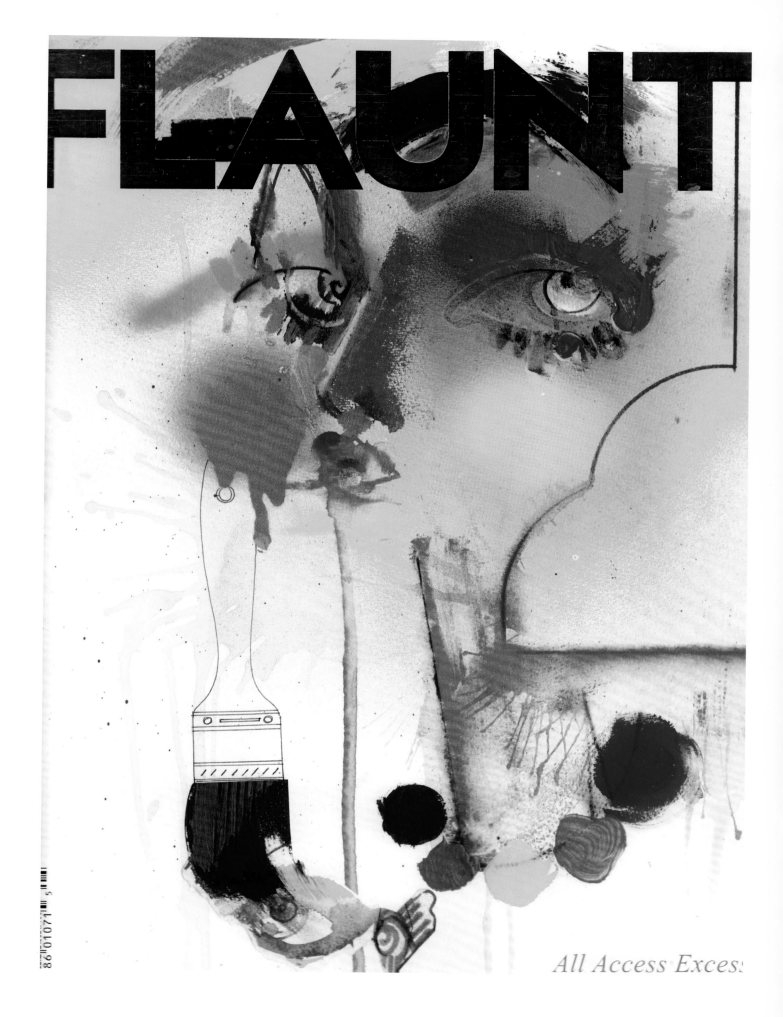

FLAUNT

All Access Excess

Above
Werk No.19 Club 21, CDC March, and *A Footprint of Manhood*, both 2012.

The abstraction of application in some areas of each of these images is balanced by the skill of the drawing in others. Balancing on a knife-edge between caricature and portrait they demonstrate Verhoeven's personal signature style perfectly.

Above and left
Hit Me With a Flower, on Marella
dress (detail) A/W 10, 2010 and
A Woman of a Certain Age, 2008.

The face and its specific character
and the glance of the subject are
at the heart of much of the work
of Verhoeven. Her subjects jump
off the page as they leap from
her skilled fingers in pastel, pen,
watercolour, crayon; every medium
combining in a textural and
arresting image.

Above
Cocky Bastard, 2010.

The Surrealist painter and
set and costume designer
Pavel Tchelitchew would
have recognized the layering
of storytelling in this piece.
The viewer is led through a
maze of images but left to
make their own interpretation.

Facing page
Fannying Around at Large, 2009.

This rhythmic creation seems
to need to move with a grinding
of wheels and a thrust to the
Jean Paul Gaultier-like bustier at
the centre. The use of the metallic
grey against the colour heightens
the mechanical, industrial feeling.

ANNABELLE VERHOYE

Combining impact with delicacy is a creative visual trick that not very many fashion illustrators can contrive; Annabelle Verhoye is one who can. Her multi-layered technique allied to complex illustrative constructions dazzles the eyes and leads the viewer down an enchanted pathway. The other special element of her work is her feeling for time, both in the sense of the hour of the day and the seasons of the year.

Gaze at one of Verhoye's creations and you'll know whether it's midday in a summer meadow, or midnight in a forest in winter. Her figures move through a haze of weather and flora, encapsulating a specific feeling yet without a hard edge or a literal element to them. This narrative quality is characteristic of many fashion illustrators' work, but what is different here is Verhoye's ability to suggest on the one hand and be specific on the other. Garments are hinted at rather than drawn in overworked detail, although there is a clear understanding implicit in the depiction of the clothing, be it a print all-in-one or ragged jeans.

As with many fashion illustrators whose work reflects contemporary image making there is a slight hint of the avatar about the weightlessness and fluidity of the characters – though they never approach cartoonishness. Although the figure is fully understood and conveyed, the ethereal effect of multi-layered techniques imparts a fantastical element to the implied story behind each visual.

CGI has broadened our visual horizons in many ways, and illustrators like Verhoye embrace the futuristic while maintaining a craft-based attitude.

For the contemporary romantic there is more than one style possibility – from sweet-pea soft to inventively bold. Her illustrations seduce in a manner that conveys the narrative of each rather than the skills that lie behind them.

Duftet wie gemalt, 2006.

Floating amidst the rosy and floral scene these fragrance bottles are being gazed upon by the model with elaborate hair and a richly printed asymmetric dress. Annabelle Verhoye combines the sharpness of line required for the containers with the softness of the flowers which form the liquids within them.

Kate, 2011.

This fashion portrait has a strongly cinematic feeling to its execution and cropping. Arrested motion, like a still from a movie or a screen grab, is shown in the expression and attitude of the model.

Where and when where you born, and where do you live now?
I was born in Wermelskirchen, Germany, grew up between France and Germany and finally moved to New York (Manhattan) in 1998 in order to do a Master of Fine Arts in Illustration at the School of Visual Arts.

Any particular childhood influences?
My father was a great gardener and had this almost unnatural love for beauty in nature.

What is your earliest drawing memory?
I used to draw a lot of princesses, with incredible eyelashes and high-heeled shoes who would be involved in a story that I cannot recall any more.

What was your first professional work?
My first professional work was an illustration on an Italian opera for *The New Yorker*.

Do you have a preferred medium?
Paintings behind glass:
My technique and conceptual framework is in many ways the polar opposite of many past and current approaches in two important ways. For example, I work in a reverse layering process on acrylic glass, sometimes obfuscating form with each application. The result is that my first layer of paint is often the first image the viewer sees, as opposed to the last brushstroke of an oil painting being the most forward facing. Just as a forest itself does not evolve as a predetermined collection of trees, my work begins and ends in a similarly natural way – uncalculated yet true to the spirit of my subject's sublime nature.

Illustrations in chine-collé:
Chine-collé combines delicate layers and precious webs of delightfully patterned Asian rice paper and textiles with a sophisticated line drawing. Each layer is scanned in individually into the computer and further amalgamated in Photoshop. The final output is digital.

Do you work in silence or with background music/radio?
I adore Frédéric Chopin and piano performances.

Are you a slow and careful or quick and speedy draughtsman?
I am slow and careful.

Do you keep a sketchbook?
I carry a little Moleskine book everywhere.

How would you describe your work?
My approach and technique are closer to
the realms of fine art, and therefore set my
work on a different level than most typical
illustrations. I try to produce the kind of
images that stop you in your tracks, hold
your attention and prevent you from turning
the page. My goal is to deliver a piece that
is beautiful and distinctive and which is so
congruent with the essence of the project that
it manifestly advances its cause. I am looking
for a deeper emotional response. I want
people not only to see but to feel.

*Do you research your subjects? How do
you research?*
I go to bookstores.

*How does your personal work relate
to your professional output?*
You can feel it.

Anything else you wish to tell the reader?
I consider myself blessed to have found
my inner voice and to follow my passion.

From a Mustard Seed, 2010.

Romantic mystery imbues this
image with a special quality since
the leaf-like shapes and branches
conform to no known foliage or
tree. The element of invention that
fashion illustration can impart is
admirably demonstrated here.

Above left

Pisces, *Joy* magazine, 2011.

Caught as she adjusts her huge sunglasses, our model is carrying two huge bags and is dressed in three floral prints. The busyness of the image is balanced by the harmony of blues and the repeated motif of the coral.

Above

Capricorn, *Joy* magazine, 2011.

The illustrator who dares to put horns on a model wearing giraffe print and accessorize it with a floral handbag is fearless and confident. The rich, dark background and the variety of illustration techniques used for horns, bag and dress are perfectly pitched to support this fantasy.

Right

Cancer, *Joy* magazine, 2011.

Silhouetted against pale and soft coloured texture, our fashionable surfers stand out in their rich crab and animal prints, their pale body tones and reptilian hair complementing the image balance.

Below

Virgin, chine-collé, *Joy* magazine, 2011.

Focusing directly on the viewer, this model sits amidst a bower of flowers – flowers that are not only on her clothing but also on her head since her wig is entirely composed of huge blossoms. The careful balance of colour between light and dark prevents the image from becoming muddled.

AUTUMN WHITEHURST

Autumn Whitehurst captures her subjects in a quirky way that offers surprises. She might show exquisite eyes and lips with the rest of the face almost lost; a girl takes a sip of a cooling drink through a straw, yet her body is pure line, eliminating the rest of the figure details. In this way Whitehurst removes the unnecessary from her images, edits them to make us focus on the element she wants us to see.

It is only possible to do this with supreme technical confidence. First, total knowledge of proportion structure and the mechanics of the body; if you are going to eliminate parts of it you need to know what, where and why. Second, the supporting lines must offer clues and indications even though the space between them is void. Finally, balance and harmony must be conveyed – if the eliminations are incorrect the observer will remain unconvinced. Whitehurst achieves all of these in her work.

The other key attraction of Whitehurst's fashion illustrations is a special view of colour and colour balance. There is a luminescence to her colours and a bloom around them, achieving an effect that is highly individual but not overpowering. Tints of autumn (perhaps unsurprisingly!) and spices pervade her colour palette. Warmth of tone adds to the embracing feeling of warmth in her handling of her subject, be it a pomegranate in the palm of a hand or a languid-eyed male model. In a sense her work is closer to the *Gazette du Bon Ton* artists and Georges Lepape or Eduardo Benito and their images for Paul Poiret or Charles Worth, than any of today's fashion illustrators.

In pure fashion terms Whitehurst is best known for her enchanting portrayals of eyes and eye make-up; it feels as though one could pick the iridescent shadows off the page. This feeling for cosmetic allure is continued in her wonderful renditions of nail varnish, notoriously difficult to portray with elegance. Whitehurst has the essential skill of balancing graphic minimalism against precise details according to the requirements of the image. This is the mark of the truly natural fashion illustrator.

Sugar and Skin, 2007.

The silky sheen on the pink bubble-gum complements the sheen on the model's skin perfectly, as the tight, low bun of her hair balances the bubble she has blown.

Right
Hyaluronic Acid, 2007.

More than a gaze and less than a stare, this model's fixed look invites speculation from the viewer. In her simple checked head square, tied peasant style at the nape of her neck, she is clean and neat in every way.

Below
Thom Yorke, 2008.

With his wonderfully spiked hair and artistic beard this man's portrait shows clearly the difference in the two sides of his face. The cascades of light place this realistic image in a mysterious milieu of creativity and fantasy.

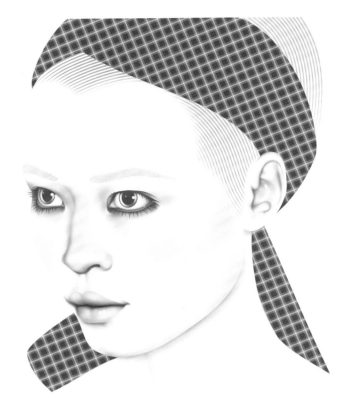

Where and when were you born and where do you live now?
I was born in Providence, Rhode Island, on 9 November 1973. I grew up in New Orleans, Louisiana, and now live in Brooklyn, New York.

Any particular childhood influences?
The environment I grew up in was very creatively charged. The shed my dad built behind our house looks like something from a Carl Larsson watercolour, and even now it houses a lot of strange old things, really mysterious objects that set my imagination off. There were lots of gallery openings and art festivals, parties and so on, not to mention Mardi Gras. Everyone would become engaged in the pleasure of preparing for carnival, which usually involved the endeavour of making things.

What is your earliest drawing memory?
I'm not sure how old I was but I very clearly remember drawing a she-mouse with my crayons. For whatever reason, instead of drawing the outlines of this she-mouse first, I scribbled her shape in with a fuzzy scribbling and then elaborated further by giving her a face and an apron.

What was your first professional work?
It was an illustration for the *City Paper* in Baltimore, Maryland. The article was titled *'Amour Fou'*; I don't remember what it was about but I do remember that it was slightly scandalous. Just slightly.

Do you have a preferred medium?
I have always worked digitally, from start to finish. It's inevitable though that I'll be introducing traditional media into my work at some point. I've been mulling over the possibilities for a while now...

Do you work in silence or with background music/radio?
It depends on where I am in the process and what time I'm working on it. When I'm trying to generate an idea or am actively thinking about my commission, I like absolute silence but if for example I'm engaged in rendering textures I definitely like a bit of music/radio to help me along. I prefer to hear my music on the radio, though. Sometimes I'm up really late and hearing the DJ's voice reminds me that I'm not the Omega Man.

What would be your ideal commission?
Any commission that provides me with the opportunity to connect and work with a truly inspired client is ideal. When a little inspiration rubs off on me from someone I really admire, I feel inexhaustable. If I were to meet any of my favourite designers and work with them in any capacity, that would be amazing.

Are you a slow and careful or quick and speedy draughtsman?
I'm so very slow and careful, it's as though I breathe between heartbeats sometimes. I haven't painted with an actual brush and paint in nearly a decade now but when I did I would cut a few bristles off my brush, just a little bit at a time here and there until I was left with one or two hairs and I'd really scratch out the finest line I could, as steadily as possible. I do intend to try to be the speedy draughtsman for just a part of my process... Just to put a right angle in my approach. I don't think it's healthy for me to go through familiar motions any longer than necessary.

Do you keep a sketchbook?
I was really diligent about keeping a sketchbook for many years and then stopped for a long time and only began again recently. My sketchbooks are not just sketches for my work, though... I keep to-do lists in them, recipes, jot down last night's dream, Scotch-tape chips of paint in them, will use a page for problem solving, etc.... They're for creative problem solving 24-7.

How would you describe your work?
I would describe my work as a contrast between textures... Simple. Beauty oriented, I guess...

Do you research your subjects? How do you research?
Researching my subjects is a pleasure. I've always loved researching as it would keep me in some dusty corner of the library for hours. Now, though, I do it on the internet... And when I'm not researching, if I should stumble across an image that makes me feel as though I have moths in my chest I pull the image for inspiration later.

How does your personal work relate to your professional output?
Honestly I've not had the opportunity to set aside time for my personal work in such a long while but I'm certain that there is a symbiotic relationship between the work that you do for the public and the work that you create for yourself. If you could ask me this question in another few years I could give you a better answer!

Above
Pomegranate, 2006.

A pomegranate in all its succulent splendour is held aloft, the seeds and juice running enticingly down the model's palm and wrist.

Right
Stress, 2006.

Almost albino in her whiteness of skin and hair, this model has an irritation in her eye, causing her to rub it. Her nail varnish and the eye and lip colours link together to form a visual focus for the image.

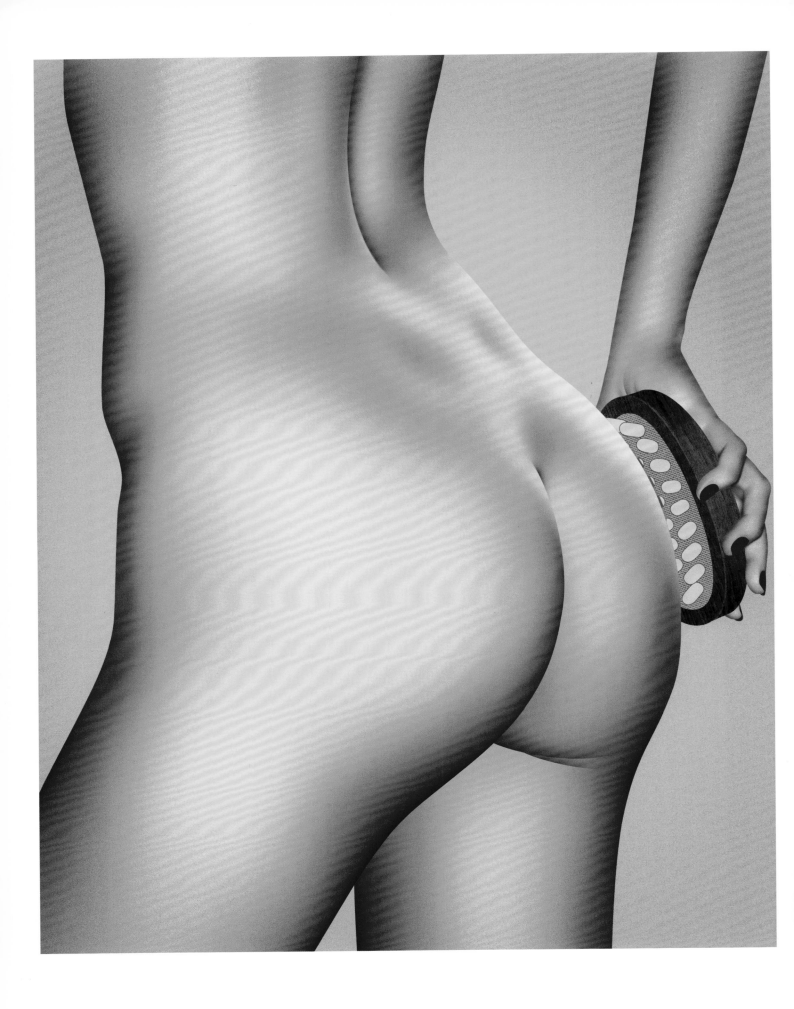

Facing page
Cellulite, 2007.

Health, beauty and skincare often require close-up treatment. Here, the bloom of the skin is exposed, offering the viewer an incentive to achieve a similar skin tone.

Below
Warm Up, 2007.

The juxtapostion of the smooth legs and scaley snakeskin shoes points up the exfoliating brush and its results. The cloudy background leaves the emphasis on the legs and the hand holding the brush.

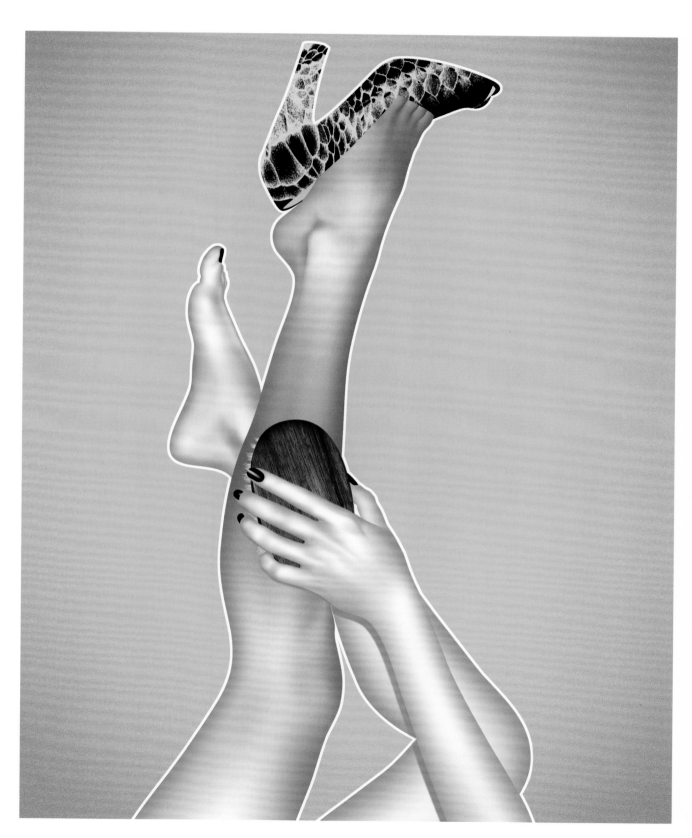

Autumn Whitehurst **195**

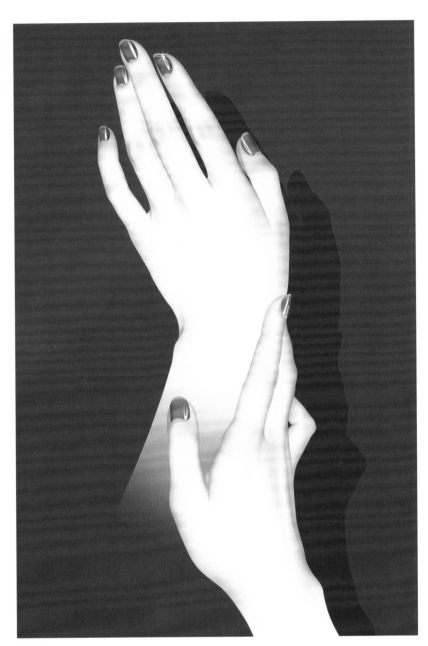

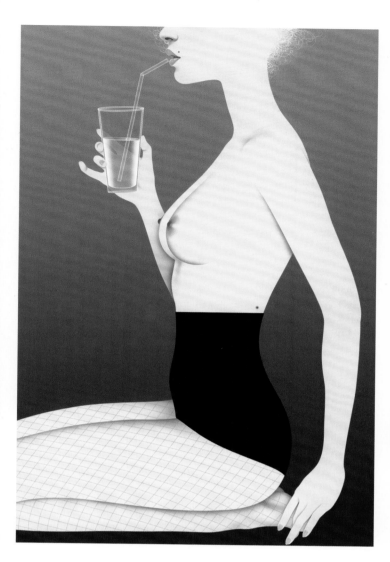

Above

In Shape, 2007.

Although this model is topless, the pose and the drink in its perfect glass renders the image cool rather than sexy; even the fishnet stockings are soft and subtle, as is the dark shaded background.

Above right

Psychodermatology, 2007.

Languor, tiredness and seduction, any of these could apply to this image as the model rests her hand so lightly against her forehead. Her eyelids shimmer and her mouth is heavily glossed, creating an image of mask-like perfection.

RICHARD PETER WINNETT

Attack in creation is often a splendid way to approach a subject, and Richard Peter Winnett certainly shows panache in his sexy and bold drawings. Yet there are other examples of Winnett's work that have a languor and gentleness, demonstrating that he is much more than a one-trick pony. What is especially potent within his work is a feeling for implied *mise-en-scène*. We know what is hinted at in the space within his drawings even when he eliminates most of it. His characters are never isolated from their environment; even his bold, linear silhouette drawings are strictly urban in their atmosphere.

Winnett has several styles. These include a fluid line, often on a black background, which is illustrative and loose, and a more worked realistic style, which seems to have a high-gloss relationship with international brands such as Gucci or Louis Vuitton. His portfolio demonstrates a mastery of drawing: a girl seated firmly, convincingly, on a chair, a hand holding a lipstick that actually seems to be gripping the case.

Winnett's work exudes the same understanding of fashion illustration as a communication tool dependent on solid drawing skills as, for example, Gerd Grimm's or Bernard Blossac's did in the twentieth century. To communicate fashion through illustration requires in-depth knowledge of the subject and an opinion about it – it is not sufficient to simply like clothes and mark making. The figures in Winnett's images bear witness to a real person wearing real fashion. Whether drawing lingerie, hairdressing, entire fashion collections or even mineral water, Winnett places his characters in an invented world for the pleasure of the viewer.

Although technically unlike Alberto Vargas's illustrations of pin-ups, Winnett's illustrations have a Vargas-like quality of sexiness without vulgarity, subtle exposure. His women in particular stretch and wind their way across the page as if held in some timeless boudoir of dreams. A love of women is a key characteristic of many fashion illustrators – there is nothing prurient in their gaze, simply a need to express admiration through the medium of illustration.

Dirty Blond Applying Red Lipstick, 2009.

Winnett captures the moment when a woman applies lipstick with all the focus on the profile of the face and torso. This timeless image links directly to the work of Eric and other fashion illustrators seemingly endlessly fascinated by the minutiae of women's fashionable behaviour.

Below
Cat Mask Coat, 2005.

Snuggled down in her frilled wrap, drinking seductively through a straw, it takes a second look to realize that the wrap is actually formed of cat masks.

Right
Blond in Fashion Print Chair, 2004.

A most unusual angle, and a heightened sense of using this viewpoint for the illustration, lends a staggering sexy confidence to this image, where the heels seem to raise the sitter back into the chair.

Below right
Tarot Card 'Flat' Girl, 2008.

Like a siren or even a sorceress this long-haired model crouches in front of a coruscating starburst of light, the fringe both hiding and at the same time accentuating her deeply made-up eyes.

Where and when were you born, and where do you live now?
I was born in Belleville, Ontario in Canada and currently live in Vancouver, BC. Our family moved from Canada down to the USA when I was young but I moved back for art school and have lived up here since. I've been on the west coast since graduating from NSCAD University on the east coast. I love Vancouver, with its beautiful scenery and laid-back lifestyle.

Any particular childhood influences?
I was definitely influenced by music videos, comic books, movies of all kinds, travelling throughout the USA, my older brother's artistic talent, flipping through glamour magazines in college through the present day, and artists like Patrick Nagel, Frank Miller, Picasso, designer David Carson, all things New York-style, plus Karl Lagerfeld's Chanel work.

What is your earliest drawing memory?
I remember practising drawing cartoon faces when I was about five years old, I think – trying to get the facial expression just right.

What was your first professional work?
The poster for a grand prix in Halifax, Nova Scotia, was my first commission. It was an oil painting of a F1 racecar.

Do you have a preferred medium?
I prefer mixed media – brush with ink, acrylic perhaps, then digital colour to finish.

Do you work in silence or with background music/radio?
Definitely music – alternative rock, trance or pop works great.

What would be your ideal commission?
A project with no artistic constraints and plenty of time and budget to produce the work is perfect. High expectations from everyone tend to produce the best results as well.

Are you a slow and careful or quick and speedy draughtsman?
The initial drawings tend to be quick and speedy to get the flow right, then the process slows down as more details and refinements are added.

Do you keep a sketchbook?
Yes – with lots of incoherent scribbles and repetitive contours.

How would you describe your work?
Lush color and sensual lines with a touch of chaos underneath the surface.

Do you research your subjects? How do you research?
Fashion mags and the internet mostly – often the client provides their own photography as well for reference.

How does your personal work relate to your professional output?
My personal work is more experimental and edgy. I can take more risks in the work.

Anything else you wish to tell the reader?
Always trust your instinct and remember to let go.

Red-haired Girl in Violet Lingerie, 2009.

This Marlene Dietrich-like image of lingerie and hosiery is timeless in its seductive glamour – the model gazes at the viewer through half-closed eyes in a way that is both calculating and mysterious.

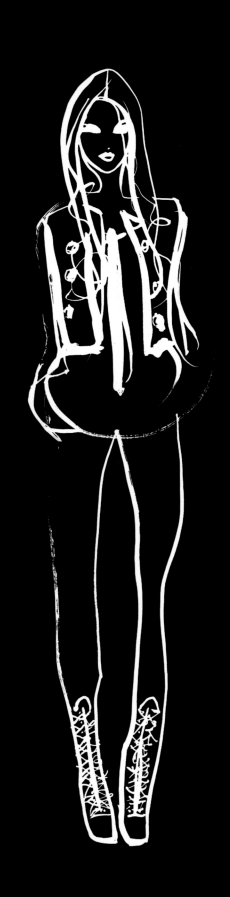

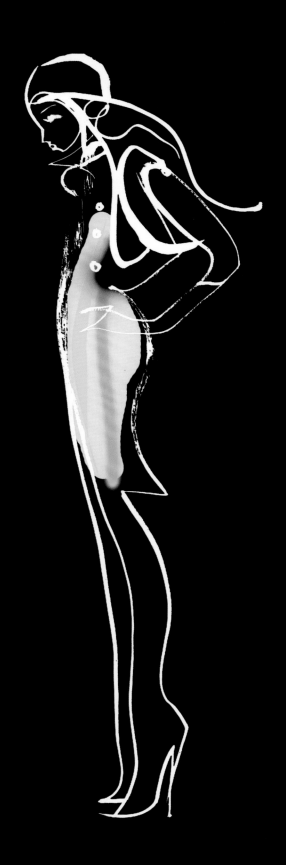

Above left
Polka-dot Dress, 2005.

Heightening a black and white
fashion illustration with colour
is a simple device but selecting
the accent colour requires an
expert eye. Here, Winnett opts
for an icy sea foam colour that
is totally unexpected.

Above
*Christian Dior Navy Blue Pinstripe
Suit and Tien Le Tux with Ring by
Paloma Picasso*, from 'In the Line
of Fashion', 2003.

Androgyny in illustration offers
opportunities to align the
similarities – here demonstrated
in the asymmetric fringes and
the striped suits.

Preceding pages
Faux Leather Biker Jacket and
Overdye Stretch Denim Jacket,
DKNY, 2008.

How many rejects were torn up
before the final effortless versions
appeared? Deceptively easy and
relaxed, this style of fashion
illustration is among the most
difficult to pull off successfully.

Adriana in Pink Lingerie, 2005.

Poised in front of a huge looking glass this model is ready and dressed for her portrait since she is wearing tiny black tulle mittens. The soft rose of the corset-stitched top perfectly complements her skin tones and accentuates the black bows and stockings.

IZAK ZENOU

To crowd the page with fashion girls jostling for centre stage and to gain our attention is a trick few can manage, but for Izak Zenou this is just one of the weapons he has at his disposal in an arsenal of talents. The observer sees a pure, line-perfect, sketch-like image of a languid floor-length evening dress; surely this must be his signature style? Yet another time, the image is a highly coloured and decorative view of a group of girls in the fashions of the moment, depicted down to the last eyelash and smudge of eyeshadow. Zenou renders the details of each fashion look – down to the bracelets, the heels and the flick of the fringe – with accuracy but without the slightest over-elaboration whatsoever.

This is the reason Zenou is so in demand for his work: the ability to seemingly dash off a sketch of a single perfect garment or to fill the page with animated figures worked through in explicit detail. His range encompasses single-colour work as well as the portrayal of the very specific colours of a season. However, there is one strong link between every image he creates: the women he conjures up in every single case have personality; they are bold enough to wear the latest fashions and carry them off with aplomb. In contrast to the hauteur usually seen on the catwalk, these women smile and chat, and shop, and live busy fashionable lives – they are not bloodless mannequins. Zenou's men are, if anything, even more eclectic and stylish – perfectly turned-out in fashion terms, they are modern dandies; the epitome of throwaway chic.

Although these men are superbly well dressed, they have a character and confidence to them rather than being effete, which means that they communicate to a broad range of consumers and not just the style elite. One of the interesting elements within Zenou's larger-scale works is his use of background; he often places figures against blurred imagery in a filmic manner. This allows him to suggest not only a mood and a setting for the fashions shown but a back story that draws the viewer in.

Untitled, John Lobb, for Hermès exhibition, 2006

This shaven-headed dandy is working it in this stylish menswear image from Zenou. The neutral palette selected for the image really makes the shirt and tie pop out, and the slim silhouette is offset by the vertical lines of the curtains.

Below
Personal, Prada, 2006.

Bottom
Fashion Now, india ink, 2011.

Sketch-style illustrations, which are used to communicate the essentials of a fashion of the moment, are a classic. As always the diagonal line of the arm and the sharp spaces support the image.

Right
Fake is Wild, 2010.

The caption points up the image perfectly. The fake fur bubble-shaped coat and animal-print legs are thrown into relief by the wild hair and the miniscule dog.

Where and when were you born and where do you live now?
I was born in Paris in 1964 and grew up there. My family is originally from Algeria. I have lived in New York City for the last 14 years.

Any particular childhood influences?
I grew up with five women in my household and that was surely a big influence. I drew my sister Isabel a lot. You could see her in much of my early work. I was also inspired by Audrey Hepburn and Inès de la Fressange, as well artists like Toulouse-Lautrec and René Gruau.

I attended evening classes at the Ecole des Arts Appliqués in Paris and while I was there I met people who inspired me to work in fashion. In particular there was one person who really encouraged me to go in this direction. I went to many fashion shows. I was drawn especially by the overall aesthetic of it rather than just the fashion itself. Later, I learned my craft by working in the fashion district where I trained the hard way, through experience.

My real breakthrough was with a magazine in Paris called *Depeche Mode*, which was a special fashion issue, and then some early projects with Chanel for the launch of the Allure fragrance.

What is your earliest drawing memory?
I have been drawing as long as I can remember. It was a gift I had early on. My earliest memory of drawing was clowns. I loved drawing horses and clowns. When I was about seven years old I drew my first clown. Everyone in my family was so excited about it. I was so self-critical that I tore it up.

What was your first professional work?
My first professional work as an illustrator was for an agency called Carlin International, which was a trend forecasting bureau. I was illustrating their books. I had a lot of breakthroughs with them because they also did advertising and I started doing storyboard drawings for them. They loved my work.

What was unique about my experience was that not only did I get to illustrate the images, but I also got to invent the clothes. I was part of the creative brainstorming when we were deciding what the upcoming trends were. I also collaborated with PromoStyl and Peclers, who are also trend forecasters.

Do you have a preferred medium?
My preferred medium is ink and watercolor.

Do you work in silence or with background music/radio?
I love to work with music, sometimes not. It depends on the intensity of the work. But music inspires me.

What would be your ideal commission?
I am grateful for everything I have done so far. One could say I have already had the greatest commissions. For me a great commission is what's coming next. I would enjoy creating a film and I would also enjoy doing collaborations with other artists.

How would you describe your work?
It's really hard for me to describe my own work, but for me my work is very spontaneous, and I believe it's honest. It is also very instinctual and intrinsically whimsical and is true to who I am and how I see the world.

Do you research your subjects? How do you research?
Most often I don't research and I draw more on things that I've seen and experienced for inspiration. I do research when I need to do something I'm less familiar with or something related to a specific brief. That research comes from magazines, from the web and I also take pictures. Mostly, I observe the world around me and get inspired by what I see.

I prefer when it comes from my head – then I don't feel closed in and restricted, and it's much more fluid and natural.

How does your personal work relate to your professional output?
I don't feel like I really have a professional agenda in my work, so it is more free. I go with the flow and where my inspiration takes me. Sometimes it's more dramatic than the commissions. I am always drawing for myself in between projects and this always keeps the creative juices flowing.

While creating a work, I need to be drawn in and seduced by the character that I'm drawing. When I am touched by the expression of an element of it, I know it's a successful piece; I know this when it comes alive and becomes real.

Anything else you wish to tell the reader?
I would like to say that for me what I realized in the last years was that I was moving women in a deep way and that is the most rewarding thing. If I make people feel good, then I have achieved my art.

Untitled, John Lobb for Hermès exhibition, 2006.

The raven may hint at the dandyism of Edgar Allan Poe but this dandy is resolutely bohemian and modern, from his carefully dishevelled hair down to his two-tone shoes.

The trick of communicating season and time with a fashion illustration is often hard to define. Here we can surmise it is late summer because of the breeze, the colour of the sea, the emptiness of the beach and the stiff breeze whipping her hair.

Above
Untitled, Frenchway Travel, 2009.

Possibly the most glamorous group ever spotted at an airport – one of the great advantages of fashion illustration. To find a crowd, however chic, which conformed to a colour palette without a stylist present, would indeed be extraordinary.

Right
Untitled, ArtAssure, 2011.

This art gallery scene is a slice of city living with a very stylish set caught by the illustrator. There is a special balance between the spectacle frames worn by the two men, respectively left and right of the image. Observe how the figure, who is possibly the artist, engages with the viewer.

Above
Untitled, Henri Bendel, 2011.

Henri Bendel bags are a sign to those in the know – since the sign for the store is half out of frame and the model being dragged along the pavement by her pack of dogs obscures a great deal of the shop window.

Above right
Untitled, Henri Bendel, 2011.

The poise of the dog and the femininity of the model are placed firmly in New York by the skyscraper image in a frame among those on the wall. The best picture within the picture, however, is the portrait of the dog holding a designer handbag in its mouth.

Above
Untitled, La Samaritaine, 2007.

By reducing the street scene in all
its complexity to a monochrome,
almost a black and white
photograph, the model in her
skinny-fitted red Chanel is
thrown into strong relief.

Right
Beach Girl, Henri Bendel, 2010.

Accessorizing a fashion illustration
is often part of the visual
storytelling. Here the striped beach
umbrellas and the multiple bangles
let the viewer know this is a chic
and fashionable resort.

BIBLIOGRAPHY

This listing does not include specialist portfolios or collaborations, or manuals on how to be a fashion illustrator.

Addade S-J. *Bernard Boutet de Monvel*, Les Editions de L'Amateur, Paris, 2001

Bachollet R., D. Bordet and A. Lelieur. *Paul Iribe*, Editions Denoel, Paris, 1982

Battersby M. *Art Deco Fashion: French Designers 1908–1925*, Academy Editions, London, 1974

Baudot F. *René Gruau*, Editions Assouline, Paris, 1998

Berning T. *100 Girls on Cheap Paper*, Chronicle Books, 2009

Blackman C. *100 Years of Fashion Illustration*, Laurence King, London, 2007

Bonnelle M. and M. Meneret. *SEM*, Pierre Fanlac, Perigueux, 1979

Borelli L. *Fashion Illustration Next*, Thames and Hudson, London, 2004

——. *Fashion Illustration Now*, Thames and Hudson, London, 2000

Bou L. *Trendy Fashion Illustrators*, Monsa, 2011

Cahriou J. *René Gruau*, Herscher, Paris, 1984

Caranicas P. *Antonio's People*, Thames and Hudson, London, 2004

Carco F. *Vertes*, Atheneum Publishing Co Inc, New York, 1946

Carlstedt C., V. Beckham and E. Von Unwerth. *That Extra Half Inch*, Harper Entertainment, 2007

Dawber M. *Big Book of Fashion Illustration: A World Sourcebook of Contemporary Illustration*, Batsford, London, 2007

——. *Great Big Book of Fashion Illustration*, Batsford 2e, London, 2011

——. *Imagemakers: Cutting Edge Fashion Illustration*, Mitchell Beazley, London 2004

Delhomme J.-P. *Art Contemporain*, Editions Denoël, Paris, 2001

——. *Design Addicts*, Thames and Hudson, London, 2007

——. *Les Choses Littéraires*, Editions Denoël, Paris, 2002

——. *Scènes de la Vie Parentale*, Editions Denoël, Paris, 2007

——. *The Cultivated Life: Artistic, Literary, and Decorating Drama*, Rizzoli International Publications, New York, 2009

Donovan B. *Advanced Fashion Drawing: Lifestyle Illustration*, Laurence King, London, 2010

Downton D. *Masters of Fashion Illustration*, Laurence King, London, 2010

Drake N. *Fashion Illustration To-day*, Thames and Hudson, London, 1987

Fogg M. *Fashion Illustration 1930–1970*, Harpers Bazaar, Batsford, London, 2010

Ginsberg M. *An Introduction to Fashion Illustration*, V and A/Compton/Pitman, London, 1980

Hemphill C. *Antonio's Girls*, Thames and Hudson, London, 1982

Kochno B. *Berard*, Thames and Hudson, London, 1988

Lepape C. and T. Defert. *Georges Lepape, ou l'élégance retrouvée*, Herscher, Paris, 1983

Ling T. and H. Murray. *What Lies Beneath: From Corset to Wonderbra*, Mercier Press, London, 2005

Lipmann A. *Divinely Elegant: The World of Ernst Dryden*, Pavilion Books Limited, London, 1989

Mauries P. *René Gruau*, Franco Maria Ricci, Milan, 1984

McDowell C., H. Brubach and J. Cahriou. *Drawing Fashion: A Century of Fashion Illustration*, Prestel, London, 2010

Mulcahy S. *Drawing Fashion: The Art of Kenneth Paul Block*, Pointed Leaf Press, New York, 2007

Nissen S. and V. Leret. *René Gruau: The First Century*, Thalia Publishing, Paris, 2010

Packer W. *Fashion Drawing in Vogue*, Coward McCann/Thames and Hudson, New York/London, 1983

——. *Fashion Drawings in Vogue: Carl Erickson*, Michael Joseph, London, 1989

——. *Fashion Drawings in Vogue: Rene Bouet-Willaumez*, Michael Joseph Limited, London, 1989

Paris P. and G. Koning. *Mode van A tot Z*, Lecturis Publishing, Netherlands, 2011

Paris P. *Fashion Illustration*, Waanders, Amsterdam, 2010

Ramos J. *Antonio 60.70.80: Three Decades of Fashion Illustration*, Thames and Hudson, London, 1995

René Gruau: Mode et Publicité, Palais Galliera, Paris, 1989

Ridley P. *Fashion Illustration*, Academy Editions, London, 1979

Roberts M. and G. Coddington. *Mr Snippy-The Snippy World of New Yorker Fashion Artist Michael Roberts*, Steidl, Germany, 2005

Roberts M. *Fashion Victims: the Catty Catalogue of Stylish Casualties*, Harper Collins, New York, 2008

Robinson J. *The Golden Age of Style*, Orbis Publishing Ltd, London, 1976

Romaine H. *La Couture Epinglée*, Editions Plume, Paris, 1990

———. *Revoir Paris Paris Paname*, Parigramme, Paris, 2001

Spencer C. *Erté*, Studio Vista, London, 1970

Tetart-Vittu F. *Le Dessin Sous Toutes Ses Coutures*, Paris Musées, Paris, 1995

Toledo R. and I. Toledo. *Roots of Style: Weaving Together Life, Love, and Fashion*, Celebra, New York, 2012

Toledo R. *The Style Dictionary*, Abbeville Press, New York, 1996

Verhoeven J. and A. Spaninks. *A Bit of Rough*, Stichting Germany, 2009

Verhoeven J. and B. Cole. *Fat Bottomed Girls*, London, 2003

Vertes M. and B. Holme. *Art and Fashion Studio Publications Incorporated*, New York and London, 1944

Vollbrach M. *Nothing Sacred*, Elliott Graphics Inc, New York, 1985, Paris, 1990

———. *Revoir Paris Paris Paname*, Parigramme, Paris, 2001

INDEX

CREDITS

5 © Bil Donovan/*Vanity Fair Italia*, photo editor: Chiara Zennaro

6 © Cédric Rivrain/Balenciaga

8 © Carlos Aponte

10 © Tanya Ling/image courtesy of tanyaling.com (represented by Fashion Illustration Gallery)

12 © David Downton

14–15 © Piet Paris, Amsterdam, Netherlands/Viktor & Rolf/photography: Peter Stigter, Netherlands

17 © Carlos Aponte/Gilbert & Lewis

18 left © Carlos Aponte/Gianfranco Ferré

18 right © Carlos Aponte/VISIONAIRE

19 top © Carlos Aponte/Christian Dior

19 bottom © Carlos Aponte

20 all © Carlos Aponte/Gilbert & Lewis

21 all © Carlos Aponte/Gilbert & Lewis

23 Tina Berning (represented by CWC International, Inc)/*A Guide to Looking and Feeling Fabulous Over Forty*. Penguin Books

25 Tina Berning (represented by CWC International, Inc)/*The New York Times*

25 top Tina Berning (represented by CWC International, Inc)/*Süddeutsche Zeitung Magazin*

25 bottom Tina Berning (represented by CWC International, Inc)/Fashiontrends, Branche und Business Fachverlag

26 top Tina Berning (represented by CWC International, Inc)/*Riot Magazine*

26 bottom Tina Berning (represented by CWC International, Inc)/Fashiontrends, Branche und Business Fachverlag

27 both Tina Berning (represented by CWC International, Inc)/Fashiontrends, Branche und Business Fachverlag

29 Jason Brooks/Personal Collection

30 top Jason Brooks/Private Collection

30 bottom Jason Brooks/for Fashion Illustration Gallery, London

31 Jason Brooks/Personal Collection

32 both Jason Brooks

33 Jason Brooks/personal collection

34 Jason Brooks/personal collection

35 Jason Brooks/personal collection

37 Cecilia Carlstedt

38 Cecilia Carlstedt/personal work

39 Cecilia Carlstedt/personal work

40 top Cecilia Carlstedt/client: H&M/art direction: Parasol

42 bottom Cecilia Carlstedt/client: Martini Gold (Russia)/art direction: James Eric Jones

41 both Cecilia Carlstedt/client: H&M/art direction: Stina Daag

43 © Jean-Philippe Delhomme

44 © Jean-Philippe Delhomme

45 © Jean-Philippe Delhomme

46 © Jean-Philippe Delhomme

47 both © Jean-Philippe Delhomme

48 both © Jean-Philippe Delhomme

49 © Jean-Philippe Delhomme

51 © Bil Donovan/Private Collection

52 © Bil Donovan/from *Birds of a Feather Shop Together*

53 left © Bil Donovan/promotion-writer/fashionista: Amy Fine Collins

53 right © Bil Donovan/Promotion

54 top © Bil Donovan

54 bottom © Bil Donovan/drawn from designer Ralph Rucci's couture collection

55 all © Bil Donovan

56 © Bil Donovan/Promotional Elle

57 © Bil Donovan/for Visual Poetry Show at Gallery Hanahou

59 © David Downton

60 both © David Downton

61 © David Downton/*Vogue* Australia September 2009 cover '50th Anniversary issue'.

62 © David Downton

63 both © David Downton

65 © Petra Dufkova

66 © Petra Dufkova

67 both © Petra Dufkova

68 both © Petra Dufkova

69 © Petra Dufkova/Stella McCartney

70 © Petra Dufkova

71 top left © Petra Dufkova/Iben Hoj

71 top right & bottom © Petra Dufkova

73 © Gary Fernández

74 both © Gary Fernández

75 both © Gary Fernández

76 both © Gary Fernández

77 both © Gary Fernández

79 © Jeffrey Fulvimari (represented by CWC International, Inc)

80 © Jeffrey Fulvimari (represented by CWC International, Inc)

81 © Jeffrey Fulvimari (represented by CWC International, Inc)

82 © Jeffrey Fulvimari (represented by CWC International, Inc)

83 © Jeffrey Fulvimari (represented by CWC International, Inc)

85 © Tobie Giddio

86 both © Tobie Giddio

87 © Tobie Giddio

88 © Tobie Giddio

89 top © Tobie Giddio/Alexander McQueen

89 bottom © Tobie Giddio/Chanel for Amica

91 © Richard Gray

92 both © Richard Gray

93 © Richard Gray/Miguel Adrover

94 © Richard Gray

95 top © Richard Gray

95 bottom © Richard Gray/*Flaunt* cover, issue 57, 2004

97 © Richard Haines

98 both © Richard Haines

99 © Richard Haines

100 © Richard Haines

101 © Richard Haines

102 © Richard Haines

103 all © Richard Haines

105 © KAREEM ILIYA

106 © KAREEM ILIYA

107 © KAREEM ILIYA

108 top © KAREEM ILIYA/*D Magazine*/*La Repubblica* for SODINI BIJOUX

108 bottom © KAREEM ILIYA/*D Magazine*/*La Repubblica* for MAX MARA OCCHIALI

109 © KAREEM ILIYA

111 © Jordi Labanda/Illustration Division

112 © Jordi Labanda/*La Vanguardia*, Barcelona

113 top left © Jordi Labanda

113 top right © Jordi Labanda/Frame for Grand Marnier TV Commercial

113 bottom © Jordi Labanda/Gucci *Il Corriere della Sera*

114 both © Jordi Labanda

115 both © Jordi Labanda

116 © Jordi Labanda

117 © Jordi Labanda

118 © Tanya Ling/NARS/image courtesy of tanyaling.com (represented by Fashion Illustration Gallery)

119 © Tanya Ling/Viktor & Rolf/image courtesy of tanyaling.com (represented by Fashion Illustration Gallery)

121 © Tanya Ling/image courtesy of tanyaling.com (represented by Fashion Illustration Gallery)

122 © Tanya Ling/Comme des Garcons/image courtesy of tanyaling.com (represented by Fashion Illustration Gallery)

123 © Tanya Ling/Christian Dior/image courtesy of tanyaling.com (represented by Fashion Illustration Gallery)

125 © Zoë More O'Ferrall

126 © © Zoë More O'Ferrall

127 © Zoë More O'Ferrall/for Top Shop

128 both © Zoë More O'Ferrall

129 all © Zoë More O'Ferrall

131 © Jenny Mörtsell

132 both © Jenny Mörtsell

133 both © Jenny Mörtsell

134 © Jenny Mörtsell

135 © Jenny Mörtsell

136 © Jenny Mörtsell

137 all © Jenny Mörtsell

139 © Piet Paris, Amsterdam, Netherlands

140 top © Piet Paris, Amsterdam, Netherlands

140 bottom © Piet Paris, Amsterdam, Netherlands/*Vogue* Japan 2003 © 2012 Condé Nast Publications Japan. All Rights Reserved

141 © Piet Paris, Amsterdam, Netherlands

142 © Piet Paris, Amsterdam, Netherlands

143 © Piet Paris, Amsterdam, Netherlands

144 © Piet Paris, Amsterdam, Netherlands

145 © Piet Paris, Amsterdam, Netherlands/Viktor & Rolf/ photography: Peter Stigter, Netherlands

147 © Stina Persson (represented by CWC International, Inc)

148 © Stina Persson (represented by CWC International, Inc)

149 © Stina Persson (represented by CWC International, Inc)

150 © Stina Persson (represented by CWC International, Inc)

151 © Stina Persson (represented by CWC International, Inc)

153 © Cédric Rivrain/Maison Martin Margiela

154 © Cédric Rivrain/Alexander McQueen

155 © Cédric Rivrain/Dolce & Gabbana

156 left © Cédric Rivrain/Balenciaga

156 right © Cédric Rivrain/Prada

157 © Cédric Rivrain/Lanvin

158 © Cédric Rivrain/Lanvin

159 top © Cédric Rivrain/Lanvin

159 bottom © Cédric Rivrain/Louis Vuitton

161 © Sara Singh

162 © Sara Singh

163 © Sara Singh

164 © Sara Singh

165 © Sara Singh

166 © Sara Singh

167 top © Sara Singh

167 bottom © Sara Singh/Estée Lauder

169 © Hiroshi Tanabe

170 both © Hiroshi Tanabe

171 all © Hiroshi Tanabe

172 all © Hiroshi Tanabe

173 both © Hiroshi Tanabe

174 © Hiroshi Tanabe

175 © Hiroshi Tanabe

177 © Julie Verhoeven/Royal College of Art

178 © Julie Verhoeven/*The Sun* newsaper

179 © Julie Verhoeven/*Flaunt* magazine, Spring 2011

180 © Julie Verhoeven/WERK No. 19 Club 21. CDG

181 top © Julie Verhoeven/Marella and Julie Verhoeven

181 bottom © Julie Verhoeven/courtesy of ZINGERpresents

182 © Julie Verhoeven/courtesy of ZINGERpresents

183 © Julie Verhoeven/MU, Eindhoven

THANK YOU

Firstly I would like to thank Helen Rochester, who commissioned the book, and Sophie Wise, my indefatigable editor. Sophie enabled me to write a better book than I thought I was capable of and I hope she is as happy with the result as I am.

Claire Gouldstone is a legend and I am certainly not the first to say this. As my picture researcher, she proved it time and again. In the simplest possible terms: thank you, Claire.

To the team at Praline who made the book, which contains so many images, look both cohesive and glamorous, while responding to all my 'suggestions': thank you very much.

To all the fashion illustrators contained in here: I would like to express my sincere gratitude for your time, support and, above all, your talent, which I hope you find appropriately celebrated within these pages. The joy of the book is the diversity of your approaches and the breadth of fashion styles and skills showcased. Perhaps it will encourage the next generation to continue the craft and art you all celebrate.

To Joelle Chariau at Galerie Bartsch-Chariau, Mark Kwakman at Piet Paris, Christine Cavallomagno at Jed Root, Laura Camerino at Jordi Labanda, Stephanie Pesakoff at Art Department, Erika at CWC International, Stacey Endress at Illustration Ltd, Michelle Edelman at Traffic NYC, and Willian Ling: I owe you all a truly huge amount of gratitude for your time and trouble in supporting the project and dealing with all the extra details that come from being included in the book.

Thank you also to Josie Wye, Paul Ziolkowski, Mark Andrew James and Lorna Selby for obvious reasons.

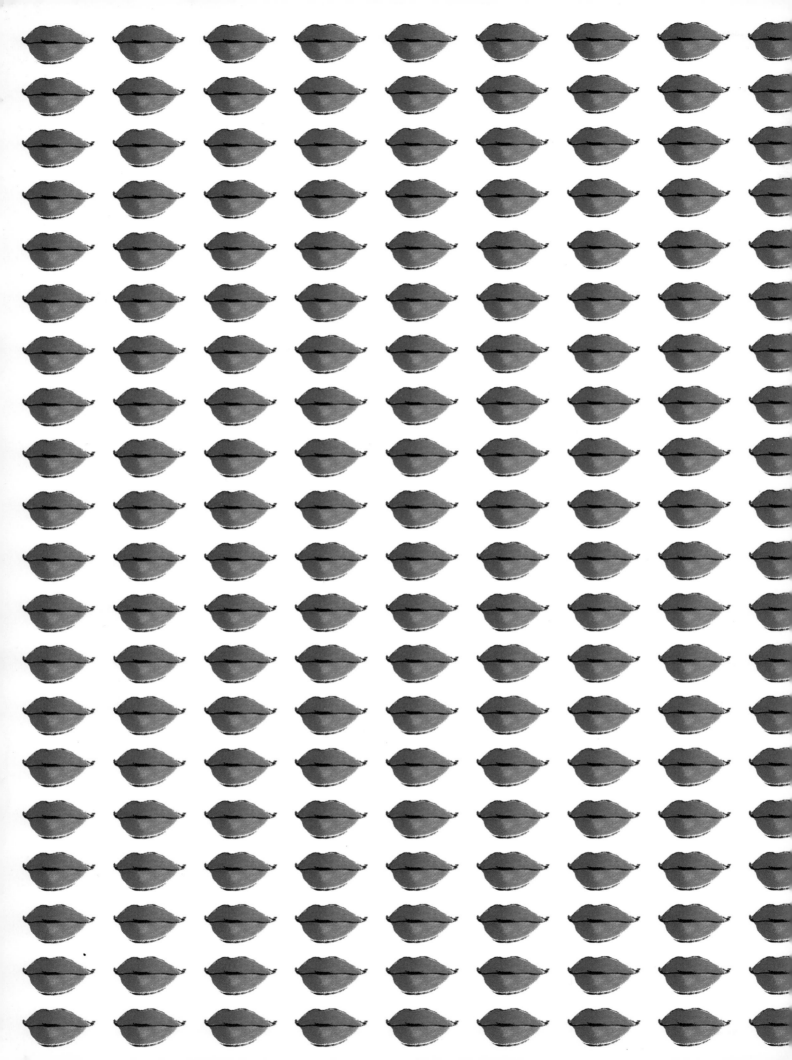

Rod,
Shadow
and
Glove

Pl. 1. BLACK THEATRE ROD PUPPETS: Angelo's Mother and Father, two endearing
characters from the play based on Quentin Blake's book *Angelo,* the story of a family of strolling players
in Italy. They are soft puppets with sewn and stuffed hands, foam plastic bodies and limbs, and polystyrene heads.

Rod,
Shadow
and
Glove

Puppets from the
Little Angel Theatre

John Wright

ROBERT HALE · LONDON

Robert Hale Limited
Clerkenwell House
Clerkenwell Green
London EC1R 0HT

Wright, John,
  Rod, shadow and glove puppets from the Little
Angel Theatre.
  1. Puppet making——Amateurs' manuals
I. Title
745.592'24   TT174.7

ISBN 0−7090−2628−5

Designed by Geoffrey Wadsley
Photoset in Sabon by
Kelly Typesetting Limited,
Bradford-on-Avon, Wiltshire
Printed in Great Britain by
BAS Printers Limited, Over Wallop, Hampshire
Bound by WBC Bookbinders Limited

Contents

List of Plates

All photographs by John Roberts except 13: Ulla
Finila and 2, 3, 20: Stefan Fichert.

List of Figures

Acknowledgements

Everything that has made this book possible can be traced back to the helpful support of others. You who I hope will benefit by its contents must be thankful to my wife Lyndie who with superb skill has designed and made many of the things described in these pages.

But the Little Angel Theatre which forms a setting for our creative activities would not exist without the devoted and tireless support of the members of Potheinos Council who are our theatre guardians, and the great generosity of Michael Marks who has done so much to keep the place going with both spiritual and financial backing. To these dear people I dedicate this humble work.

Members of the Potheinos Council are:

Noel Benjamin	Evelyn Crowne
Alan Judd	Ann Obermer
Fiona Phillips	Linda Sievi
George Speaight	David Stanfield

Preface

At some time in the course of your career as a puppeteer someone will ask you how you came to be interested in this crazy occupation with all its hazards, uncertainties and problems. Personally I have never been able to answer this question in a totally satisfactory way, but looking back to my days of innocence I can see now that some misguided motivation lead me to believe that, as a puppeteer, I could earn a living and still be free.

I believed that, if I could make puppets and write a play, I could be a company director as well and do everything necessary to launch entertainment of high aesthetic quality. I believed that I could do this and more without being under obligation to anyone and without being dependent on help from any quarter.

The truth of course dawned later, but by then I was so caught up in the fascinating problems of creation and management that it was impossible to do other than move further along the way I had unwittingly taken.

In writing this book I have a double purpose: on the one hand offering hope and encouragement and on the other giving constant warnings of difficulties to be overcome in order to arrive at the high standards of craftsmanship and theatrical expertise which alone will bring a satisfactory sense of achievement.

You may well be a genius but if you are not you may find that you will need help in many of the skills needed to make a good puppet company fully operative. Some people can draw, carve, paint and sew costumes; not many can do all these and be a carpenter, plan electrical wiring, drive a truck and speak the lines of a play as well. You may conclude that puppetry is best approached as a group activity and that it might be as well to review your resources in this light and plan your progress accordingly.

You may be discouraged at the outlay needed in terms of hard cash, but ingenuity will help. Bear in mind that, during the war years and after, materials of all kinds were hard to come by and yet much was achieved. My own first touring stage was built with

15

shelving from the cupboard of an old, disintegrating house, and the lighting was wired up with thick insulated copper wire found abandoned in an attic. Tin cans were spotlights, and the one and only dimmer, made from an old drainpipe, was of such a design as to be very nearly lethal on more than one occasion. Masking-curtains were of dyed hessian, backed and made lightproof with waterproof brown paper, hideously inflammable, which had lined the packing-cases of some consignment of goods from over the sea.

But with a dream in my mind I worked steadily on, knowing that it would all come right in the end. To begin with, I was totally involved in string-puppet production, and the perfection of this technique was my main interest for many years, but in 1950 Mr George Speaight arranged for a set of large glove puppets to be made for the Royal Shakespeare Company's production of *Bartholomew Fair* designed by the famous Motleys, and these were the first glove puppets to be made at my workbench. A smaller set of figures for a children's party show followed, but these somehow finished up in Ireland. A rod-puppet figure from a Russian company was lent to me for a time, and his beauty and great dignity made a deep impression, but it was not until 1964 that my wife Lyndie and I decided to take the glove puppet and the rod puppet seriously and go into production with this type of figure.

The decision was first inspired by an urge to increase the age range of our audiences with the production of a series of short plays which could be put together more quickly and effectively with glove puppets than with string puppets. We soon found that the variety of work in which we became involved was a valuable stimulant. We also found that a light glove- or a rod-puppet stage could be profitably operated in schools and small venues in which work with the heavier and more complex string-puppet set-up would have been impossible.

After the glove and rod productions were launched and the school touring unit was under way, we soon found ourselves venturing into other applications of the medium. A production of Noah was planned, and here we felt that rod puppets carved in a Romanesque style would be well suited to the boisterous medieval text we had in mind. This was followed by two large-scale productions, one of Stravinsky's *The Soldier's Tale* and the other of Menotti's *Amahl and the Night Visitors*, both made for the 1,100-seater Queen Elizabeth Hall where rod figures up to seven feet high and made of the lightest possible material were needed for obvious reasons.

Less important but still significant are the parts played by rod and glove puppets in two elaborate productions designed mainly for string puppets but using other techniques as well. In *Cupid and Psyche*, by Ann Obermer (based on the Robert Graves version of *The Golden Ass*, the gods are represented by rod puppets whose bulk and direct actions offset the light, uncertain movements of the string-puppet humans to good effect; then in Oscar Wilde's *The Fisherman and His Soul* the three journeys of the soul are acted out with rod puppets designed to give a dream-like quality to the scene.

16

Puppets from these productions and many more are shown in the illustrations which follow. Most of them were made by Lyndie, who is a designer and a superb and innovative craftswoman, able to work in many different types of material. This is really her book rather than mine.

The photographs, except where otherwise stated, were taken by John Roberts, another expert in many fields. He has included pictures of two of our leading puppet-operators, Christopher Leith and Ronnie LeDrew. Also included are pictures of puppets made by Stefan Fichert for two of the London Munich Puppet Players' productions. Stefan worked with us for about eight years, and we are proud to think that he owes something of his success as a maker of superb puppets to his association with the Little Angle Theatre.

I
Style
and
Technique

1
Style
and
Technique

1 Introduction

After half a century of near neglect the puppets are back with us again. It is difficult to say why ever they deserted us in the first place, and no one can really explain why they have come back, but the fact remains that, like so many other good things, they almost disappeared after World War I and they have only recently decided to return.

Who invented them in the first place remains a mystery. They filtered out of pre-history into the lives of the ancient Egyptians and the people of the Far Eastern early civilizations. They came in the form of crude models of men made of wood and terracotta and later they were shown as shadows cast by figures cut from animal hide. Some say they preceded actors, but who knows? Were the Greeks in their masks imitating the marionettes who had preceded them or was it the other way round?

They came in many forms in the past but never on such a prolific and varied scale as now. Today they appear in every shape and form from the purely traditional to the absolute *avant garde*, and they are made in many different ways—carved in wood, cast in rubber or plastic, scratched out of polystyrene, modelled in papier mâché, cut out of foam rubber, paper or leather or stitched out of cloth and stuffed with rags.

There are puppets to be found in almost every part of Europe, America, Canada and Australia, and when international gatherings take place, South America, India, China, Indonesia and Japan are often represented.

All manner of performance techniques, both ancient and modern, are to be found in use today, with perhaps the strongest accent on the various types of rod and glove puppets—the kind around which this book will be mainly centred.

The other most important types of puppet are of course the shadow puppets and the marionettes or string puppets. Of these two, perhaps the shadows are the ones to be gaining most rapidly in popularity. Though limited in appeal in some respects, their poetic value has a high potential which is rapidly being explored. The string puppet

21

on the other hand is sought after as the true traditional figure, the creature that is conjured up at the mention of the word.

But for puppeteers, the people who make and work with puppets, the glove (or hand) puppet and the rod puppet are the popular mediums of the day. The reasons for this are not far to seek. We live in an age which is out of breath and short of time. The string puppet, with its fifteen joints and sixteen or more parts, needs a high degree of knowledge and skill to design and construct, and the complex stringing and the patience and time required to master its effective manipulation make it an almost impossible

Pl. 2. THE TROJAN DONKEY is shown here with the Trojan horse ingeniously devised and made by Stefan Fichert. The story was dramatized by George Speaight and is spoken by him in narrative form out in front of the stage. A London Munich Puppet Players' production.

task for many. This applies especially to children, whose sense of time is foreshortened in keeping with their years. Glove puppets and rod puppets on the other hand are comparatively easy to make and work. Their mechanism is minimal or nil, and they

22

lend themselves to easy methods of structure and decoration which leave the imagination free to explore. The methods and materials used in making them are so varied that an aspiring craftsman can be almost certain to find a technique of construction to suit his particular creative urge, whether it be as a modeller or a woodcarver or one who can cut and stitch.

Glove and rod puppets have a more friendly feel about them too. They are there within reach to touch and fondle, unlike the marionette hanging aloof on his complex system of so easily tangled thread.

Audience reaction to the glove puppet is usually more spontaneous than to any other kind. Whether this is a hangover from our early days when Mr Punch and other lively figures came to our nurseries or whether it is something innate, confident and perhaps pleasantly aggressive about his nature that gives him this advantage is a moot point, but he definitely has the power to reach out and make contact with an audience, often under circumstances which would daunt his superior friend on strings.

The rod puppet comes somewhere in between the two, with a sure touch and a studied action; he has a stature of dignity and grace appealing to the intellect and quite foreign to the intimate knockabout world of the glove puppet. He has the same drawback as the glove puppet inasmuch as he is legless and must be presented against a playboard in an almost two-dimensional scheme. But although he appears on a stage which is similar in many ways to that of the glove puppet, he is a creature apart and must not be confused with any other in the application of his special talent.

There is a third type I must describe here. He is a cross between the rod and the glove puppet, having a head supported on a spinal rod as in the case of the true rod puppet and arms and hands on slightly tapering tubes worked by the thumb and fingers of the operator as in the glove puppet. He has qualities derived from both his parent figures, being easy to learn to operate and at the same time having the stance and dignity of the rod puppet together with the speed and certainty of touch of the true glove puppet. We call him the 'glove-rod' puppet.

In the course of this book other techniques and types of puppet are referred to and many ways of making them are described. The prosaic method of modelling and casting is given in some detail, with notes on the most-up-to-date materials available for use in this respect. There is a section on wood-carving, and this has been extended a little in accordance with my belief that there is a strong revival of interest in this craft. The uses of polystyrene with paper and glue are also carefully dealt with as a useful alternative. Costumes are referred to in some detail, and the making of animals, fishes, butterflies and birds.

It is hoped that by the time you have reached the end of Part II you will have sufficient knowledge and confidence to start on a programme of construction of whatever type of puppet creature, man, beast or insect, you need to populate your puppet world.

Part III will, I hope, serve to enlighten you on all important points relative to the staging and presentation of your puppets in the dramatic pieces you have selected for them.

I have assumed that the majority of puppeteers are compelled to use collapsible and easily movable stages, so I have concentrated on these rather than on any permanent structure, however humble. However, there are a couple of pages devoted to the permanent theatre, taking our Little Angel Theatre as a model and giving some notes on the building and the way in which it is being used.

There is a section on the making of small props and pieces of furniture, and in this I have simply taken examples that have come to hand in the form of props for the play *Wonder Island*. To do much more would be to venture out into a huge range of vastly differing items for which so many techniques and skills would be required as to make the subject unwieldy. It is hoped that the pieces described and illustrated will put you on the right track towards an inventive and resourceful solution of every problem and every project that looms on what might well turn out to be a very wide horizon.

2 Selection of Dramatic Material

Along with your research into the practical possibilities of puppet construction, you will doubtless be thinking in terms of the dramatic content of the performance towards which you are working.

You will be spending a great deal of time planning, designing and making puppets, props and settings for the piece you have in mind, so before it is too late you should consider seriously whether the material selected warrants the effort. Does the chosen theme spark off some response in

your personal attitudes or is it just a nice story with a pretty plot and no significant content? You may prefer it this way, but if so you may well feel, in the end, that you have wasted your time.

This point having been disposed of, the work should be analysed in other ways. Will it form an acceptable pattern of development, and is it a theme which will appeal to the type of audience you hope to attract? Are the characters strongly drawn and sufficiently varied? Have the main characters the personality needed to get through to an audience and lend power to the plot? And the plot—is it constructed as it should be? Look seriously at the play you propose to present and make sure that it is structured in a way that will grip your audience from first to last. Study the dialogue and make certain that it will be easy to speak and easy to understand, but by no means banal. Your characters will come to life, and their idiosyncracies will be emphasized by their speech as much as by their appearance. At the same time guard against over-writing: dialogue should be sparse and always to the point. Envisage your characters in detail at this point and work out in your mind's eye and with the aid of drawings how they are to be made and what their dimensions will be. Try to envisage their movements on stage and the kinds of furniture and setting each scene in the play will require.

There are more notes on planning and production in the chapter on rehearsal at the end of this book. Read them carefully and start off with a clear cut project in mind.

3 Wonder Island

In the course of this book I have chosen to refer to a play which was written and produced in our theatre and which used the glove-rod type of puppet very successfully.

It is not intended that you should copy or reproduce this play or any of the characters. The work is given purely to add colour and interest to that part of the text which deals with matters of design and construction, though of course many points of reference may come up in other areas. (Please note that the play is in copyright and may not be used for public performances without permission from the management of the Little Angel Theatre.)

The full text of the play is given on pp.

161–9. There are only a few characters in it. The first of these is Wizard Wonderful, a mad inventor who speaks with a strong foreign accent and who has produced a do-it-yourself flying-machine and wishes to try it out with the aid of a young and able person. This turns out to be Percy, a lively boy of undetermined age. Percy is out fishing in a small boat with his friend Mr Ninepence, a clown-like figure dressed in black torn coat and battered top-hat and with a cracked and crazy voice. Mr Ninepence shows reckless and indomitable courage in rescuing Percy from the clutches of the Wizard and his flying-machine. There are some fish, three butterflies and a charming cat which plays a small but important part.

The play, which runs only about twenty minutes, is a light-hearted piece intended for three puppeteers. It is in three scenes, the changes from one scene to the next being indicated by movements of scenery and changes of lighting without closing the proscenium curtain. Notes on the scene changes and in fact on all the action are given with the text of the play.

II
Puppet Construction

II
Puppet Construction

4 Heads

Rod and glove puppets are largely dependent on a form of mime as their means of expression, and it stands to reason that their heads and hands are their most important components.

The size and shape of a head, the proportion of the features and their arrangements and distortions will all give character and expression to a figure. The shape, size and coloration of the hands are of equal importance. Together these elements, when correctly used in certain relative positions and attitudes, will convey messages to members of an audience or will give rise to some dramatic impact upon them.

First to the matter of planning and design. It is always as well to try out ideas in the form of small, rough sketches before going too far. Once a clear idea of a character's appearance has been formed, a careful working drawing should be made. This drawing should be full scale—that is to say, it must be the exact size of the planned product, and it should show two matching aspects: full face and profile. The drawing must be accurate and clear so that it can be referred to without any doubt or variation when it comes to modelling or carving.

Some people prefer to model or carve directly without drawings but in my opinion, if you are a draughtsman with any ability at all, you should certainly make and use working drawings.

Figure 1 shows two aspects of a proposed head for a juvenile character. The head is wide with very simple, open features—a pert nose, smiling mouth and round button eyes—the epitome of fun and innocence and very easy to represent in the round.

Three different ways of making this head are given here. It would be as well to consider them carefully before you set to work. Modelling and casting might suit your particular style and ability better than wood-carving, or you may prefer to use polystyrene and paper—the simplest (but least effective) of all. Whichever you choose, bear in mind that it is as well to stick to one technique when making a set of puppets.

29

1 A working drawing for modelling or carving a
puppet's head

Modelling and casting a head

To model the head, start off by making a stand out of a length of broomstick about 12 inches (30cm) long plugged upright into a hole in the middle of a piece of one-inch or ¾ inch (2cm) plank or blockboard about 10 inches square (25cm).

The broomstick should be about the same diameter as the neck of the puppet is intended to be. If necessary it can be built up in thickness by winding a strip of paper round it where the neck is going to join into the head.

For a head of the size shown, plasticine will be the most convenient modelling-material to use. Modelling-clay is of course cheaper but it has certain disadvantages, being much more messy and more difficult to prepare. Plasticine is clean and needs no preparation other than perhaps a few drops of glycerine to soften it up. Clay on the other hand needs quite a lot of work to bring it to the right consistency and pliability, and it has to be handled out of doors or in some place where moisture and a few clay smears don't matter. Clay also has the disadvantage that it dries out and cracks if not kept constantly moist.

Whichever you use, clap a large handful of it onto the top of the broomstick you have mounted as a stand. Model it into a firm potato shape and then start to add contour and features by pressing small pellets of the modelling material onto it, slowly building up bulk and shape and referring constantly to your drawing. A pair of callipers will come in very useful here (see Plate 8). You can of course get the right shape by setting up a much larger initial mass and then cutting it away with a wire modelling-tool (Figure 2), a blunt table knife or an old teaspoon, but the process of building up the shape with small lumps of the modelling material is usually considered the most professional and satisfactory way of going to work (Plate 4). When the main shape of the head has been roughed out in this way, fill in and smooth over the surface of the head to a degree dictated by the design and the nature of the character, and then, with a modelling-tool, work on the detail of the eyes, mouth, nostrils and ears, bearing in mind of course that very fine detail will not be seen by a theatre audience and that broad effects are best.

At this stage, set the head up at eye-level and light it with a reading-lamp, looking at it and lighting it from different angles. This can be a valuable exercise as the sharp hard light will bring out various aspects of the modelling very strongly and also give some idea of how the head will look on stage.

When you are totally satisfied with the modelled head, you must switch from being a creative sculptor to being a craftsman, as the head is now to be cast in some material other than clay or plasticine.

The cast heads illustrated in this book are of rubber. They are light in weight and extremely strong. In spite of having been in use for nearly fifteen years, they show very little sign of wear and tear. If anything should happen to them, the negative moulds are still about somewhere, and duplicate heads could be cast at any time.

This is how a negative mould is made. It is an absorbing task and it requires skill and patience. First prepare some strips of card about 1½ inches (4cm) by 2 or 2½ (6cm) inches. Imagine a line dividing the head into two halves, back half and front half, and press the edges of the pieces of card into the clay or plasticine along this line until you have formed a wall of card from one side of

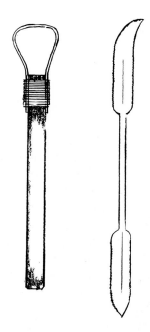

2 Modelling-tools

31

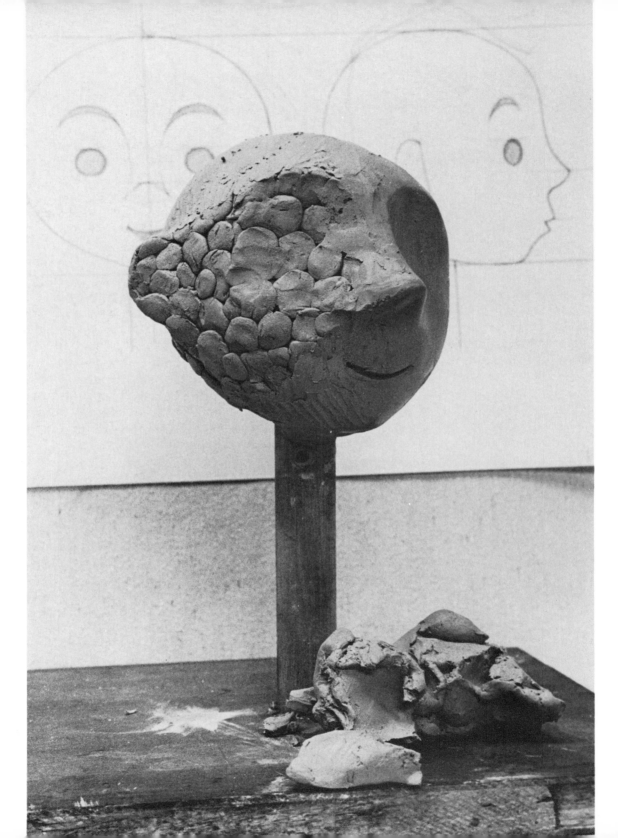

the wooden neck over the head to the other side (Plate 5). Place the head carefully face up, supporting the neck on a block of wood so that it is horizontal, and prepare the plaster of Paris from which the negative mould is to be made.

Plaster of Paris is best obtained from a chemist—they call it dental plaster but it is used mainly for plastering up broken limbs. A 5lb bag will be enough for your first experiments. Put about 1½ cups of the dry plaster in a heap in the middle of an old tin bowl and pour cold water round it until the plaster is nearly submerged but not quite (Figure 3). Stir the mixture up with your fingers, and as it begins to thicken to the consistency of cream, drip it onto the head, slowly at first and then faster as it begins to thicken and set (Plate 6). The thin, creamy plaster will fill all the detail recesses in the plasticine model. The thicker plaster will

3 Mixing plaster of Paris

cover it, and as the plaster approaches setting-point it can be slapped on and smeared into place to make a rough half round shape bordered by the card. It may take a little bit of practice to get it right but there is nothing difficult about it, and the process is totally fascinating. Clean superfluous plaster from the tin bowl immediately with cold water because once it sets hard it is very difficult to remove.

Give the mould half an hour to set finally and then turn the head over, keeping the neck horizontal on the block of wood as before. Carefully remove the cardboard strips. Using a sharp instrument of some sort, cut two shallow holes in the horizontal surface of the plaster so exposed. Rub a little light vaseline or grease of some sort onto this surface and into the two holes and patch up the slots left in the plaster by the removal of the cardboard strips. Mix plaster as before and apply it to the back of the head in exactly the same way as you did to the face, taking care not to finish up with an overlap of plaster which could, when it sets, make it impossible to get the two parts of the mould apart. If plaster runs from the back half of the mould down and round onto the face half, cut it away before it hardens. Go round the join with a blunt knife to make sure that no dribbles of plaster will link the two halves together.

Leave the plaster to harden for an hour or two and then carefully prise the two sections apart. The plasticine head within may well be partly destroyed in the course of this process as bits of it will stick to the inside of the mould, but this need not worry you. Examine the inside of the mould and carefully scoop away any fragments of plasticine

33

sticking in the hollows, taking care not to damage the plaster surface. Any air bubbles which have formed on the surface of the plasticine when the plaster was poured will now appear as small holes in the hardened plaster. These should be filled with plaster mixed with a little water and smoothed off. If this is not done, they will appear as warts on the final positive cast which is now to be made.

It is advisable to leave the mould to set and dry for a couple of days before making the first positive cast. There must be no moisture left in the plaster mould, and it should be at room temperature before the next process is undertaken. Carefully select the liquid rubber you are to use—it is sold in various consistencies. Buy the kind which is recommended for making hard rubber toys, and observe the instructions on the package. Fit together the two parts of the mould carefully and bind them round with string to hold them firm. Make a clay or plasticine base and stick the head mould into it upside down so that the neck hole is uppermost. See that it all stands firm in this position. Pour the liquid rubber into the hole, filling it to the top. Rock the mould about and tap it lightly to dislodge any bubbles of air which may be clinging to the inside of the mould. After about 10 minutes pour the rubber out again and back into the container. A film of liquid rubber will remain on the inner surface of the plaster negative mould. The process of pouring the rubber in and out of the mould may have to be repeated several times in order to get the right thickness of rubber. Follow the instructions given, and experiment until it all comes right.

The rubber will take about 10 to 12 hours to harden, and usually it is best to keep it in a warm atmosphere during this time. When it is ready, undo the string which is holding the two parts of the mould together and pull the halves apart gently. You should have a perfect hollow rubber head exactly like the plasticine model you started with and something about the weight and consistency of a tennis ball.

In the case of animals such as the seals from the mime *The Nine-Pointed Crown*, and the dogs in the play *Cupid and Psyche* (Plate 7) whose jaws are opened and closed by the hand of the operator (Figure 4), a much thinner or more pliant rubber will be required, but in every other respect the process of modelling and casting remains much the same except that it may be necessary to use some sort of a mock-up of the human hand as a basis for your modelling process. An old glove packed tight with scraps of cloth and mounted on a piece of wood cut from the crooked branch of a tree would be good, provided the whole thing is sufficiently firmly mounted not to sag with the weight of the clay or plasticine (Figure 5).

Right: Pl. 5. CASTING: A completed clay head lies face up ready to receive the plaster of Paris which will form the first half of the negative mould. The card surround which will separate the front half of the mould from the back half is shown embedded in the clay.

Below right: Pl. 6. CASTING: The plaster, first applied in the consistency of cream, begins to thicken and can be slapped on in large blobs. The whole face should be well covered by the time the plaster begins to set. The process, shown half finished here, takes only a few minutes.

When the plaster has fully set, the card will be removed. The surface so exposed will be carefully greased and the back of the head cast in the same way.

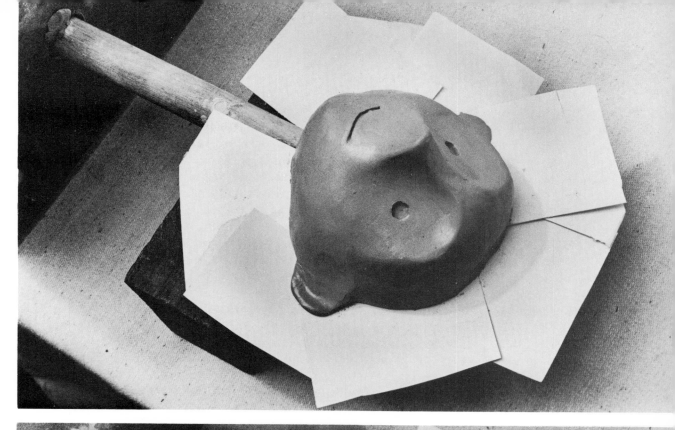

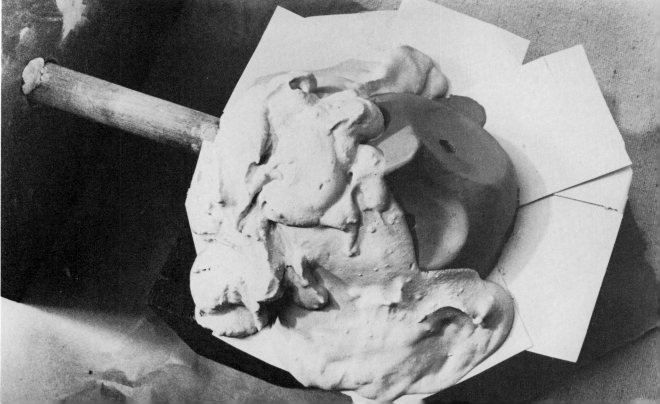

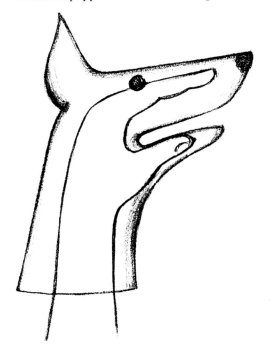

4 An animal puppet with a hand working its mouth

parts of the mould are used separately. Make sure that they are absolutely clean, and soak the inner surfaces with some thick oil or with soap. Press the plastic wood into the moulds a little at a time, making sure that it goes well into all the recesses. Stop when the layer of plastic wood is about ⅜ inch (1cm) thick. Carefully trim the edges level with the edges of the moulds so that there will be two flat surfaces to stick together when you extract the two halves of the head from the moulds. Make sure that the plastic wood is thoroughly dry before you try to get it out of the moulds. It dries rather quickly and shrinks a little in so doing. If it tends to dry too quickly while work is in progress, drying can be retarded by adding a few drops of castor oil.

When the rubber head has had a few days to dry out and set properly, it should be given an undercoat of a paint specially prepared for use with rubber. Ordinary emulsion and other watercolour-based paints will not stick properly to rubber, and oil paint is really not satisfactory.

Once the negative moulds are made, a head can be cast in a material other than rubber. You could try fibreglass but it is not recommended. It is extremely strong but so unpleasant to work with that it is really hardly worth it.

Plastic wood is often used. This moulds extremely well and is very durable. The two

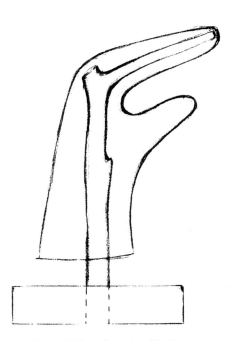

5 Core for modelling the animal in Figure 4

36

Heads made in this way are rather heavy, and of course the thicker the layer of plastic wood inside the mould, the heavier it will be. A balance must be found between the thin layer, which may be fragile, and the thick layer, which could be cumbersome.

Once the plastic wood has set and dried, it can be filled and sandpapered but it is very difficult to cut. It takes paint very well. It is usually supplied in tins, and most hardware and craft shops can supply it. Or you might try making it yourself by mixing fine

Pl. 7. A COMICAL SEAL and a not-so-funny three-headed dog-monster (Cerberus from the play *Cupid and Psyche*) are cast in thin, soft rubber and painted. The three dog heads are all from the same mould. All have mouths which can be operated by human hands. (See Figures 4 and 5.)

37

sawdust with nitro-cellulose varnish or polyester liquid resin.

A much lighter but less durable head can be made by pressing Celastic into the moulds. Celastic is a material used in shoe-manufacturing for strengthening and stiffening heels and toecaps. (For suppliers see Appendix 4.) It comes in large sheets and rolls, usually in three different thicknesses. For a 4 inch head the medium thickness would be best.

When it is soaked with acetone (nitro-cellulose thinner), it becomes soft and pliant and can be pressed into a mould so that it takes the shape of the head. Soap or vaseline can be used to prevent it sticking to the mould, or a layer of Clingfilm, but be careful in using the latter as, unless it is pressed into all the recesses very carefully, it may cause a loss of detail.

The nitro-cellulose thinner soon dries out of the Celastic, and another coat can be added for strength. Trim the edges of the Celastic very neatly to the edges of the mould. Stick the two parts of the head together with a little Bostik. Some care is needed here as the join must be invisible in the finished product.

Celastic is light and reasonably strong. It takes an undercoat of emulsion paint very well indeed. The thinners used for softening it are highly inflammable and should be used only in well-ventilated areas. It is advisable to use a mask to avoid breathing in the fumes, and wear rubber gloves when handling the thinner-soaked Celastic.

Carving a head in wood

Wood-carving is usually considered more difficult than modelling in clay or plasticine but it is a most satisfying pursuit, and the results are generally better than those produced in any other way.

In so far as materials are concerned, you will need some rather special wood but this will cost you less than plasticine, plaster of Paris and rubber. When it comes to tools, however, you can model with your bare hands and add detail with the aid of an old teaspoon or table knife, but wood-carving requires good chisels and gouges, and these are expensive and hard to come by.

The process of selecting, preparing and maintaining a set of chisels is such a special undertaking that I have decided to write a separate chapter about it and to put it in Appendix I, where it will not upset the balance of information on the three techniques under review in this chapter.

At this point, all I will suggest is that you purchase five good chisels : a shallow ½-inch (1.3cm) gouge and a deep ¼-inch (.6cm) gouge and three flats, one ⅝-inch (1.6cm), one 1 inch (2.5cm) wide and one fishtail ¼-inch (.6cm) flat. Secondhand ones are best: clean old tools free of rust and not less than 4 inches (10cm) long. The best makes are—or were—Addis, Herring Bros., Taylor and Tiranti. Of these I think Taylor's are the only ones being currently made, and in London Buck & Ryan, 101 Tottenham Court Road, W1, stock them. Once you have learned to handle your first five chisels, you will be able to enlarge your collection to suit your style of carving.

You will also need a good sharpening-stone (a hideously expensive item), a can of light machine oil and a vice. The vice should be fitted with wooden jaws, and these can be clad with cork for handling light, fragile work. Pieces of cork flooring-tile will do very well.

It will be necessary to fasten the vice to a strong table or a carpenter's bench, and the table or bench should be positioned in the workshop in such a way that it won't fall over when pressure or force is applied to it. Try putting it against a wall or in a corner. It may be necessary to fasten it down or brace it in some way against the impact of your onslaught with chisels. The notes on the selection and treatment of tools given in Appendix I should be studied and followed carefully. Chisels are usually sold unsharpened and some hours of hard work may be needed to bring them to a fit state for the tasks ahead.

As for wood, there are of course many different kinds available and suitable, but here at the Little Angel workshop we have narrowed our selection down to two varieties only. These are limewood and Jelutong. Lime trees grow in Britain and throughout Europe so there should never be a scarcity of this wood, which is strong, of medium weight and very pleasant indeed to carve. It is not a colourful or in any way decorative wood but this hardly matters as the puppets made from it will most likely be painted anyway. Timber merchants supplying the building trade do not usually stock limewood but there are many who specialize in wood for furniture-making or for musical instruments, and these are bound to carry supplies.

In purchasing wood, try to select a piece that looks clean and straight-grained. It will probably be rough sawn but this doesn't matter so long as it is straight and has the minimum of knots and faults. And of course it should be well cured and in dry condition. It is difficult for the beginner to tell whether a piece of wood is well seasoned or not but most timber merchants are fairly knowledgeable and will tell you whether that which they offer is ready for immediate use or whether it needs another year or two to mature properly.

The slab of wood you buy should be about 3 inches (8cm) thick. The heart (centre) of a tree trunk is the hardest, strongest part of the tree. The part nearest to the outer skin is the sweetest to carve and is quite strong enough for puppet-making provided it has no cracks or flaws. Ends of logs usually have splits and cracks, some of which go quite deep into the wood. So beware!

Jelutong, a rather unusual type of wood, is imported into Britain from Burma and Malaysia. It also grows in parts of Thailand. It is very light in weight and is easy to carve and shape. It is not very strong and therefore should not be used for puppet hands or parts requiring much detail. Simple heads can with advantage be carved in Jelutong but don't carve long noses or delicate ears out of it—they will probably suffer the first time they are dropped or bumped into anything. Jelutong comes in clean slabs, usually very straight and free of knots. Occasionally strange ducts run at odd angles through the wood but these are not indicative of any weakness in the material.

Jelutong can usually be found in fairly thick planks. Choose a bright piece with a yellowish tinge to it. Avoid bits with blue-grey stains. Examine the ends of logs for discoloration, which is a bad sign. Avoid pieces that are cracked or show any weaknesses. Jelutong is used for making the bulkier parts of puppets, so three- or four-inch (8 or 10cm) slabs are the most useful.

Learn to use your chisels before you start to carve anything. Follow the instructions for preparing and sharpening the new chisels given in Appendix I, then set up a scrap of waste wood in the vice, take your shallow half-inch (1.3cm) gouge and, holding the blade in your left hand and the handle firmly in your right hand (assuming that you are not left-handed of course), make some shallow cuts along the surface of the wood. Then change the angle of thrust and cut at an acute angle slightly down into the grain of the wood. Try the same with one of your deep gouges and note that with a deep gouge it is possible to cut easily across the grain as well as with it and into it. Always hold the chisel or gouge with both hands, and always work away from your body, never towards it. Keep your hands dry, and when you stop using a carving tool, wipe the blade with an oily rag. You may wish to use a mallet for clearing the wood more quickly, in which case you will hold the handle of your chisel in your left hand and the mallet in your right. Go carefully; too much violence will damage the fine cutting-edge of the steel blade.

Use a good-quality wooden mallet (Plate 8). Never hit the handle of a carving tool with a metal hammer or it will be damaged, and never hit it with the palm of your hand, or your hand will be damaged.

Spend as much time as you can spare cutting odd abstract shapes out of pieces of scrap wood, getting the feel of limewood

Pl. 8. *Right:* CARVING-TOOLS: A set of wood carving chisels and gouges with two types of callipers for comparative measuring, two mallets and stones for sharpening.

The chisels and gouges, which range in size from under $\frac{1}{8}$ in (3 mm) to 1 inch (2.5 cm), are part of a set which has been in use for over 45 years: the light-coloured mallet is new and made of elm, the dark one is a lignum vitae veteran. An Arkansas oilstone together with an old but still serviceable grindstone are also shown.

and Jelutong so that you can decide which you would prefer to use before you prepare to start on a head.

I assume that you will have a drawing prepared and that the head you propose to carve will be a fairly simple one about 4 or 4½ inches (11cm) high and 3 or 4 inches (8 or 10cm) across, without any difficult or fragile parts to it.

The head of a young girl as shown in Figure 6 would be a good example, and it might be as well to use Jelutong for this your first attempt.

Cut an oblong piece of 3 or 4 inch (8 or 10cm) thick Jelutong big enough to take the full-face drawing of the head to be carved with half an inch (1.3cm) or more to spare. Clean and sand the top surface of the block, and trace onto it the drawing of the head with the grain of the wood running from chin to crown. Take a piece of scrap pine-wood about 3 inches (7.5cm) across, 2 or 3 inches (5 or 8cm) thick and 4 or 5 inches (10 or 13cm) long and drill a ¼-inch (.6cm) hole through the centre of it. With a large wood-screw, fasten it to the back of the block of Jelutong you are about to carve. The screw should not penetrate the Jelutong more than about 1¼ inches (3cm). (See Figure 7.) The block of pine will form a base

for holding the Jelutong as carving proceeds. Fasten it firmly into the vice on your bench and draw some straight lines round the drawing of the head on the Jelutong. (These lines are shown as dotted lines in Figure 8.) On these lines make vertical saw cuts, cutting away as much as possible of the superfluous Jelutong. Follow this up by cutting vertically round the outline of the drawing with one of your flat chisels, taking care not to undercut the drawing (Figure 9). Think carefully before taking the next step, bearing in mind that whatever you carve away can never be replaced.

Start by rounding off the forehead and crown with a flat chisel, then turn the block round and carve the chin and cheeks, leaving the mouth and nose as protrusions to be tackled later. With a gouge, cut away shallow hollows beneath the lines of the

6 A drawing preparatory to carving or modelling a
  girl puppet's head

eyebrows and a deep channel down each
side of the nose. Look at the profile drawing
of the head and cut the profile of the nose.
This will then probably necessitate cutting
back the forehead, eyebrows and crown
again quite considerably. From this stage on

Pl. 9. *Right:* CARVING A HEAD, a process which
may take a day or two to complete, is shown here in its
early stages. The block of wood securely fastened to
its base (see Figure 7) has been cut down vertically
outside the outside line of the face traced onto it. The
nose has been roughly cut out and the forehead and
cheeks are being rounded off. Note the bulges left for
the eyes.

The working drawing is shown behind the carving
vice. The head should finish up looking something like
the one shown on page 44.

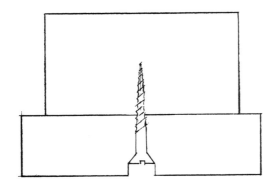

7 Base block with carving block attached

42

8 Preparing a block for carving

and nose of an average human head. The eyes look nearly straight forward. There are of course infinite and extreme variations but try to avoid making a face that is too flat. Not only are such faces ugly and unusual but they are difficult to light properly on a stage and difficult to see when used in profile to the audience.

Plate 9 shows work in progress on a head.

Avoid making undercuts during the first stages of the work, and go on cutting the face back until you are satisfied with the results. When you have reached a stage which you can regard as near perfect as your ability allows, turn the block over and release the carving from the base by undoing the screw which has been holding them

no hard and fast rules can be given but, if you examine the heads of the human beings about you, it will become apparent that the brows and forehead of a head are rounded, even dome-shaped, whereas the cheeks and jaws are much more pointed. Figure 10 shows diagrammatically what I am driving at. AA is the line of the forehead as seen from above, and BB is the line of the cheeks

Pl. 10. *Left:* PIERROT, a head carved in Jelutong as one of a set of eight glove puppets made for a television series called *The Puppet Man*. The head is painted with emulsion paint in two tones, (white and light brown); eyes and eyebrows are picked out in black Cryla. The skullcap is of black stockinette.

9 Vertical cut down the outline of the head

45

10 Contours of the head

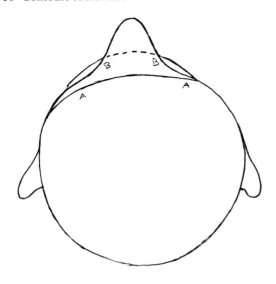

roughly and then unstick the two halves by dripping a little acetone onto the glued seam (thus softening the glue) and levering the two sections apart.

The back of the head can then be hollowed and the two parts stuck together again—this time more permanently. Use white PVA glue for this purpose, and keep the two parts together under pressure by binding them with string. When the glue has set, undo the string and drill a hole for the neck, enlarging it carefully to the right size with a gouge. The neck will go right up through the head to the top, and it can be fastened there immediately with a wood screw. (See Figure 12 for glove-puppet neck and Figure 13 for rod or rod/glove-puppet neck.) The head at this stage is ready for paint and a wig. For this turn to Section 5.

together. You now have the front half of the head complete except for the finishing touches.

Small heads (up to 2 inches [5cm]) need not be hollowed but large heads should be made light in weight, so fasten the half-head face down in the vice and, working very cautiously, cut out as much wood as you dare, using a ¼ or ½ inch (.65 or 1.3cm) gouge. Do not attempt to make the wood less than ⅜ inch (1cm) thick. Be very careful not to damage the face by cutting through the wood.

When the front half of the head has been hollowed out as far as you dare without risk of accident, stick it onto another block of Jelutong very lightly with a thin spread of Bostik or other nitro-cellulose based glue, and when the glue has set firmly, carve a back to the head. (Figure 11). Finish it off

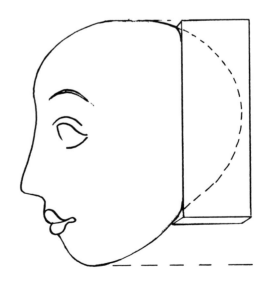

11 Carving a back to the head

46

12 A neck tube fastened into a head

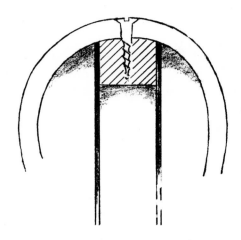

13 A rod fastened into a head

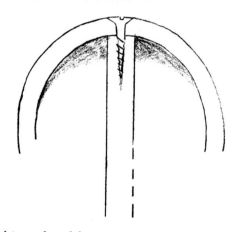

Making a head from polystyrene

The third suggestion for making a head is perhaps the easiest method, but it is one which produces results not quite so satisfactory as the other two.

Polystyrene is the basic material used and this, though it is very easily cut and shaped, does not lend itself to the formation of detailed or delicate shapes. To cut lips,

eyelids and ears in wood is a matter of skill and experience but to do the same in polystyrene is a near impossibility. The shapes designed for polystyrene therefore have to be absolutely as simple as possible.

The tools used for shaping polystyrene are easily obtained—a serrated breadknife for the initial cutting of the material, some files and rasps, a blunt penknife and an old teaspoon for scraping out hollows. These tools need not be sharp as polystyrene is soft and easy to work.

Acquisition of the material itself is a little more difficult. Even around the big centres such as London there are very few dealers in polystyrene, and those that do exist will supply only large slabs of the stuff. Your best bet is to find a firm which makes things out of polystyrene and who can supply you with off-cuts and the pieces they would otherwise throw away—the sort of places where they make displays for exhibitions and shop windows, for example. If possible, use flame-resistant or self-extinguishing polystyrene. Although your puppets are hardly likely to be submitted to fire risk, the material which you might keep in store and the sawdust and chips and scraps lying about in your workshop when you are at work could be a risk. Burning polystyrene gives off a most repulsive smell and heavy, dangerous fumes.

When you have worked the head into some sort of shape with the tools mentioned above, add the finishing touches with sandpaper, using two grades—coarse to begin with and then a medium fine.

Working with polystyrene is quite a knack, and some practice is required. Very often bits and pieces of the material will fall

47

away unexpectedly and you will have to start all over again. Fortunately the material is cheap and results can be obtained quickly, so not much time or money is wasted even if you have to make a head two or three times over to get it right.

The next stage is to cover the head with glue and paper or muslin. Prepare some pearl glue according to the notes given in Appendix 2, page 175, and cut some strong brown wrapping-paper into small pieces about 1½ (3.5cm) inches square.

At this stage you might like to try accentuating and strengthening the features by outlining them with string. Plate 16 shows a head very successfully treated in this way. Fairly thick white string is used, dipped in glue rather stronger than the glue you have used for papering the head. Eyebrows, eyelids, lips and even nostrils can be treated in this way, giving the head considerably more strength and carrying-power.

Mount the head on a spike of wood so that you have some way of holding it while you work on it, and paint the head with a thin, creamy coating of hot pearl glue. Soak the pieces of paper in a rather thinner solution of glue and apply them to the head, smoothing them over carefully and over-lapping each piece of paper with the next until the head is entirely covered. Continue with this activity until the head is covered with two or three layers of paper. Keep the glue hot and thin and smooth the paper out carefully as you go along. The neatness and efficiency of work at this stage will be reflected in the ultimate appearance of the head.

Some people prefer to use muslin rather

than brown paper for covering a poly-styrene head. You might like to experiment with other materials. For instance, in Plate 11 Blobbo's strawberry nose is surfaced with a piece of coarse sacking.

Set the head to dry in a warm place and consider the next step, which will be to apply a final finish to the surface. In Plates 1 and 34 two different methods are shown. *The Soldier's Tale* devils are simply painted with an undercoat of white emulsion and then a final cosmetic treatment with a polyurethane paint such as Cryla or Aquatex. For more crude effects poster paint or designer's watercolour can be used but these are not so lasting. In the case of the Angelo puppets shown in Plate 1 a very refined effect is obtained by coating the heads with a mixture of Alabastine and emulsion and rubbing it down with fine sandpaper until an almost porcelain finish is obtained. It may be necessary to repeat the process to obtain a perfect finish. This can then be painted with Cryla or Aquatex as desired.

Eyes should be added at this stage in the form of beads, cufflinks, buttons or small wooden balls sawn in half. Eyebrows, eyelids and mustachios can be accentuated with lines of string glued on as suggested earlier.

Wigs and other decorations and further ideas on painting heads are given in Section 5 which follows.

50

Pl. 12. *Left:* HAIRY RAUCHY, a strange fairy tale. The Giant and his wife are of foam plastic and Celastic with moving mouths. The others are simple rod puppets with heads, hands and bodies carved in Jelutong and limewood.

5 The Painting and Decorating of Heads

Heads cast in rubber require a special undercoat using a paint which will combine permanently with the surface of the rubber.

A second coating of Aquatex or Cryla flesh tint can be added and the final cosmetics worked on over that, using again the PVA-based paints Aquatex and Cryla.

A wooden head should first be given a light undercoat of thin, creamy emulsion paint using a flat brush with rather stiff bristles, leaving no brush marks and making sure that no superfluous paint remains in the hollows and recesses of the carving.

The moisture in the paint may possibly bring up or roughen the grain of the wood a little, in which case sandpaper it down gently after the paint has dried completely and give it another thin coat of the emulsion.

When you are sure that you have a smooth and even coat on the head, start the final work with your chosen paint, first flatting in the flesh tints with a soft brush and then getting down to the stronger details with the Cryla, Aquatex or what have you.

Oil paints must be used with discretion for painting puppets as they become shiny with age and with repainting. Even 'flat' oils seem to take on a shine when repainted and touched up as the years go by. Reflecting surfaces on a puppet should be avoided because they are difficult to light properly on stage and are detrimental to good visibility. For the same reason varnishes and polishes should never be used on the exposed surfaces of puppets unless some special effect is required.

Always use good-quality brushes, preferably sable—expensive, I know, but you will need only two or three, and they will last a lifetime if they are kept clean and are carefully looked after. Use a flat ¼ inch (.6cm) for laying on the foundation colour and two round ones—no.3 and no.5 will be about right for most other purposes. When a rough, unwashed character is being painted, use a fairly dark foundation colour and bring up the highlights as required. For a juvenile lead a light, slightly sunburnt foundation is best, and for young girls the pink-and-white or peaches-and-cream foundation could be appropriate. In middle and old age skins tend to turn greyish or slightly blue with some purple undertones and very little colour on the cheeks.

Lips are seldom bright red and, in fact, red is a colour which does not carry well. According to character, lips with a slightly brown, orange or purple tint look better on stage. Paint on lips can emphasize the shape and character of a mouth. Study pictures, portraits and human beings and learn all you can from source.

The colour on cheeks should be graded carefully and applied in such a way as to emphasize the shape of the face: a hollow face has a triangular shape to the cheek, a jolly face a round one and so on. The colour can be exaggerated a little as strong stage lighting tends to bleach colour out.

51

Eyes should be particularly strongly painted. Those that are realistically painted will give great emphasis to the character if the pupils are dark, either black or blue, the whites slightly bluish and the lines of the lids, upper and lower, rather over-emphasized. Experiment with eye-shadow over and above the eyes, using greys and greens and blues and watching your puppet in a mirror to see how these colours affect its appearance.

If you have not already used string to emphasize the features, you might like to try it at this stage for the eyebrows. Use thick, rough string for the bolder characters and thin parcel string for milder people and so on.

Eyebrows are most effective if painted black, and in fact they almost disappear from sight if they are not of some dark colour.

An old-fashioned idea is to put a small spot of red in the corners of the eyes. This in some strange way adds life to eyes on stage. It is worth trying.

In painting a paper-and-glue-clad polystyrene head, much the same procedure can be followed as for a wooden head.

The following notes apply to wigs and beards for all types of heads, the only difference being in the adhesive used.

Wigs and beards can be made of sisal string, cotton string, embroidery thread, wool of various textures, goathair, horsehair and the discarded feathers of birds.

Sisal is good for rough, tough characters, white cotton string for strong young men, embroidery thread for young girls and people with the well-groomed silky look.

Goathair and feathers are for witches and devils. (Plate 13 shows sisal used effectively on Noah and a thick, soft, white string wig on Noah's wife.)

Use rubber solution glue for sticking wigs onto rubber heads, and Bostick or other nitro-cellulose glue for the others. The latter type of glue can be dissolved away at will with the application of a little acetone, and this is a very useful characteristic when wigs have to be changed or renewed. Rubber glues can be dissolved with benzine or lighter fuel.

Here is a method of making a rather neat sort of string wig:

Take about 3 feet (1 metre) of thin white parcel string and tie a loop at its centre. Hook this loop round a nail in your bench or a piece of wood in the vice, knot the two pieces together a couple of inches (5cm) from the loop round the nail, and tie one of the free ends of string to your belt or to a cord round your waist.

Cut a number of lengths of the chosen material (string, sisal, embroidery thread) about 6 or 7 inches (17cm) long and arrange the pieces in groups of about three or four strands each on the bench. An easy way of cutting these lengths is to wind the thread round a 3 or 3½ inch (8cm) wide card or board and cut as shown in Figure 14. Next take one of the bunches of strands and lay it just next to the knot across the string which is stretched from your belt to the nail. Tie to this string by looping the loose string over it and fastening it with a single knot as shown in Figure 14. Pull tight the knot so formed and apply another bunch of three or four threads and knot them on likewise. Keeping all successive knots identical in direction

and degree of tension to the first one, continue to fasten bunches of thread on in this way until the wig is big enough for the head for which it is intended. It should cover the head from a point near the nape of the neck straight over the crown to a point on the brow which can be decided upon by trial and error. Dye the wig to the required shade with ordinary milliner's or household dye and stretch it out on a board to dry so that it will finish up straight and flat. The result will be a rather formal wig with a definite parting which can be stuck onto a head and then trimmed to requirements. The neat

Pl. 13. TWO CARVED HEADS in the style inspired by Romanesque sculpture in southern France and Spain. The heads are carved in limewood and painted. Noah's hair is of sisal fibre, and his wife's wig is of dyed, thick, soft, white string.

parting can be eliminated by pulling alternate strands of the material over and across to the other side.

If a rough, unkempt effect is needed, instead of using the method outlined above, try sticking bunches of strands onto the head at random. This is not as easy as it sounds but the chances are it will be

53

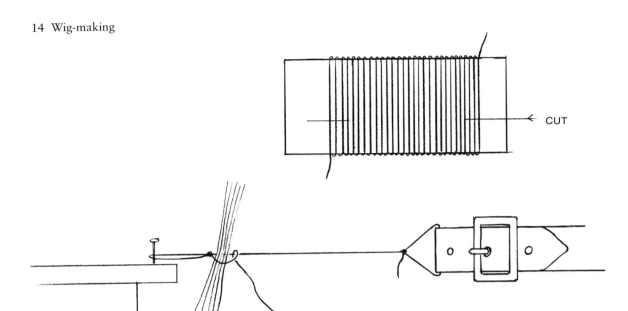

CUT

effective. Feathers and animal hair lend themselves to this treatment. Be careful always to use the absolute minimum of glue necessary.

In some cases it might be an advantage to make a base for the wig in the form of a skullcap of cloth or other material such as thin Celastic. If Celastic is used, cut it in a circle, soak it in acetone to soften it and press and mould it onto the head, having first covered the head with tin foil so that the Celastic can be removed when set and dry. Trim the edges as necessary.

6 Hands

Hands are almost as important as heads in establishing character. You should constantly observe the hands of those around you, noting their size and shape and the ways in which people use them to express themselves. Watch the shy and nervous way in which some people constantly cover up and conceal their hands—the flamboyant gestures of others and the display and posturing of yet others.

Carved wooden hands are by far the best. They need not be realistic but their design should be based on a study of human hands—the broad, strong hands of huntsmen, sailors and labourers, the long elegant hands of the idle, the short, active hands of artists, musicians and craftsmen, the distorted, claw-like hands of the greedy and dishonest and so on.

Witches and devils have very special hands, and they can be stylized and exaggerated in size just as their features usually are.

Make some careful drawings of hands, select the best pair for your purpose and draw them to scale, simplifying them as you go. As for size, you will notice that on average a hand is as long from the tips of the fingers to the wrist joint as the distance between the same character's chin and the middle of his brow. (See Figure 15.) Proportionally smaller hands however, are often used for glove puppets.

Look at Plate 14, which shows seven different pairs of hands carved in wood. This may give you some idea as to how carved hands can be effectively stylized. For hands, always use the best-quality limewood. Select a piece as wide and as deep

as necessary and at least two inches (5cm) longer than the finished hand will be. While the hand is being carved, this extra length will remain as a rectangular block attached to the wrist, and it will act as a base which can be firmly clamped in the vice as carving proceeds. (See Plate 15.)

In the case of glove and glove-rod puppets, this block will eventually form the wrist and will be rounded and tapered to take the tube which will form the arm of the puppet. Solid wrists are not advised for rod puppets, in which case the block will be sawn off as soon as the carving of the rest of the hand is complete.

Each hand should be traced onto such a block of wood, using tracing-paper and carbon paper. Having done this, fret out the hands with a bandsaw or machine fretsaw if available. If a machine saw is not available

15 Hand size in proportion to face

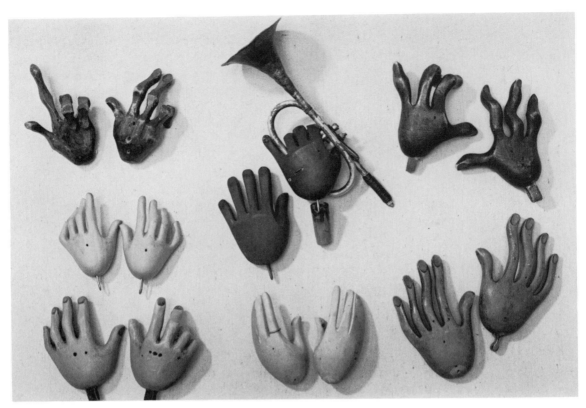

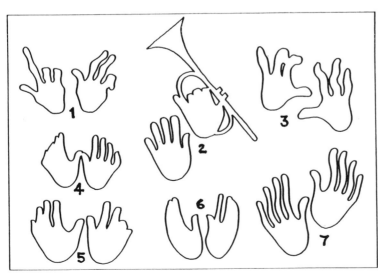

Pl. 14. *Above:* SEVEN PAIRS OF HANDS all carved in lime selected to show various character types. They are the hands of: 1. a witch; 2. a Negro jazz-player; 3. a devil; 4. a young maiden; 5. a young fisherman; 6. a fastidious character; 7. an elegant Anatolian dancer.

Pl. 15. *Right:* A HAND in the process of being carved. A part of the lime wood block from which the hand is being cut is retained as a base for holding the work in the carving-vice. If the hand is for a glove puppet, this block will be rounded off to form a wrist which will fit into the tapered tubular arm of the puppet. If it is for a rod puppet, the block will be cut off when carving is completed and a leather wrist joint will be fitted to the hand. (See Figure 26.)

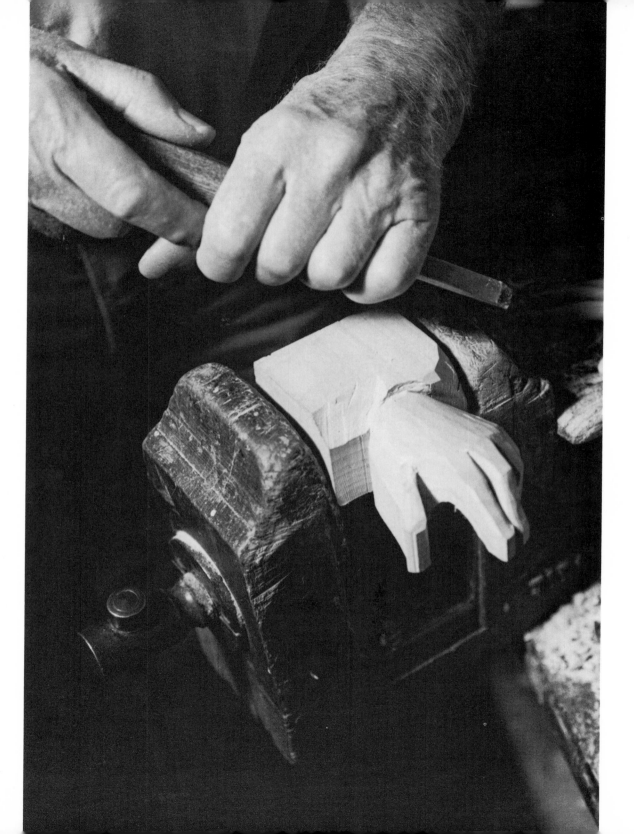

(as is more than likely), use a hand fretsaw, but be very careful to keep the cutting blade working vertically. This is most important. Also be sure to cut on the outside of the line you have traced onto the wood. If you cut on, or inside, the line, the cut-out hand will turn out to be smaller than indicated by the drawing (Figure 16).

Carve the back of the hand first and then turn it over and carve the palm of the hand and the underside of the fingers. Take your time about it, working carefully and studying the grain of the wood before each cut. A careless cut with a sharp chisel can lose half a wooden finger in half a second.

Look after your wood-carving tools. Delicate carving needs very sharp chisels.

It is easier by far to make hands out of cloth or felt but it is very difficult to make cloth hands look as though they belong to a carved or rubber-cast head. There are bound to be some people, however, who are unable to carve wooden hands for one reason or another, and for them cloth or felt sewn and stuffed would be the next best thing.

Avoid complex shapes—keep the cloth hands as simple as possible. It takes a little practice to get the size right as the cloth has to be cut big enough to allow for the material taken up by seams, thickness of the palm and the fingers. The wrist should finish off as a tube which will take the arm of the puppet. (See Figure 17.) When the sewing is done, turn the hand inside out and stuff it with scraps of material. Painting will have to be done with dyes rather than with paint as painted material tends to crack and disintegrate. Felt hands can be made in the same way.

7 Wrists

A hand for a rod puppet will be joined to the arm of the puppet by a leather loop whose ends are glued into a slot in the hand the loop being held in a square section slot in the arm by means of a wire pin (Figure 26). The action of this joint should be at right angles to the action of the elbow joint.

For a glove or glove-rod puppet, the wrist must be an integral part of the hand. It should be slightly tapered towards the hand and should be about 1 to 1¼ inches (2.5 to 3cm) long. The cardboard tube which accepts the thumb or finger of the operator will be glued on to it. (See Figure 18.) Tubes should be tried out at all stages for size. The thumbs and fingers of operators must be comfortable when at work.

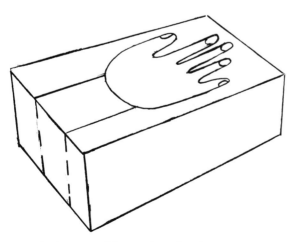

16 Block prepared for carving a hand

17 Arm and cloth hand for a glove or rod-glove puppet

18 Arm and wooden hand for a glove or rod-glove puppet

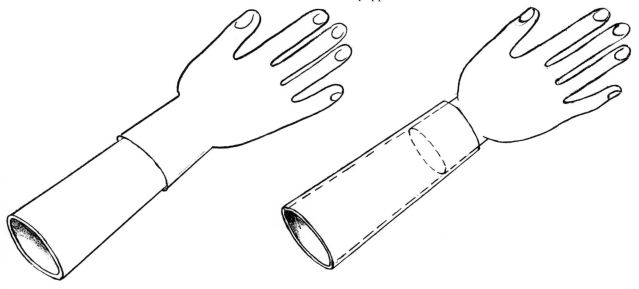

8 Completing the Glove Puppet

Other parts of the puppet can now be attended to. For a glove puppet you will need only arm tubes, a tube for the neck and the basic garment which will be joined on to these.

The neck tube should be not too long and should fit neatly into the hole at the base of the head. Some puppet operators support and control the head with the forefinger alone; others use two fingers, giving greater strength and variation to the movement. Design the neck tube according to your requirements, preferably allowing some space for a layer of foam plastic which will make the finger or fingers more comfortable.

The arm tubes are tapered and should, again with foam rubber as a lining, fit comfortably on to the thumb and either the second finger or the third and fourth fingers. Figure 19 shows and explains these variations. Tubes for arms and necks are best made of cartridge paper and pearl glue, the kind you have been using for sticking brown paper to polystyrene only thicker.

Take a length of dowel stick, mopstick or broomstick of the appropriate diameter and cover it with a layer of polythene (a piece cut from a shopping bag will do). Cut some strips of cartridge paper slightly wider than the length of the required tube. Wind the strips of cartridge paper round the polythene-covered broomstick, glueing it generously as you go. Four or five layers will

make a strong tube. The polythene, carefully used, will prevent the tube from sticking to the broomstick, and it should slip off easily when dry.

Tapered tubes for arms can be made in the same way except that the cartridge paper strips will have to be cut slightly curved instead of straight. They can be glued direct onto the tapered wrists of hands carved in wood, but in the case of felt or cloth hands without wooden wrists the tubes should be moulded on a specially prepared piece of dowel stick built up with

plasticine or clay, or a length of broomstick whittled down with a penknife. Some experiment is needed but it is worthwhile spending a little time on it as it is important to have arm tubes the right shape and size for the puppet-operator's thumbs and fingers. Always remember to allow some room for foam plastic lining as this adds greatly to the comfort and ultimate efficiency of the operators when performing.

The basic garment which holds the puppet together can best be made of strong calico or a light canvas. In designing it and sewing it up, great care should be taken to allow for space for the hand and arm of the operator and to avoid all corners and pockets which might prevent the smooth and easy entry of the operator's hand into the correct position inside the puppet.

The garment should be long enough to reach to the operator's elbow. Base your pattern on the shape shown in Figure 20 and continue to experiment until you are sure it is right. The garment will be glued at the appropriate places onto the neck tube and arm tubes, and when the glue is dry the puppet will be ready for the costumier.

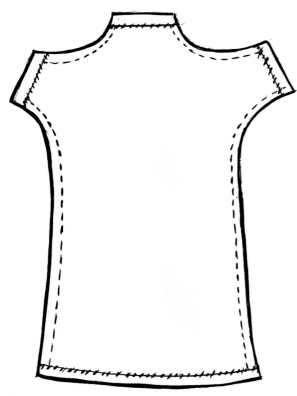

20 Pattern for a glove puppet's basic garment

9 Rod-puppet Variations

Rod puppets require a rather different treatment. The head, and in fact the whole puppet, is supported by a long ⅝ inch (1.6cm) thick dowel stick or broomhandle. (Figure 21). This should be at least 9 inches (23cm) longer than the total height of the puppet. The top end can be slightly rounded and fastened inside the top of a cast-rubber head or a hollow wooden head with a woodscrew as shown in Figure 13. Or in the cast of a solid wooden head or one made of polystyrene it can be glued into a hole drilled or cut to the right size. Six inches (15cm) of the lower end of the rod should be bound with thick white string fixed with a little Bostick or nitro-cellulose type glue to make a comfortable handle. But first mount the shoulder piece onto it. This can be a piece of Jelutong or other light wood as long as the width of the puppet's shoulders is to be and cut or carved to give the right slope to the shoulders according to the character. It should be of suitable thickness and depth to give some bulk to the figure. The spinal rod passes through a hole in the shoulder piece large enough for it to turn freely (Figure 22.) The shoulder piece is prevented from slipping down the spinal rod by a collar either made of wood drilled out to fit the rod and glued or fastened to it with a wood screw, or made of a small piece of rope (sash-cord thickness) glued to the rod and trimmed to form a neat circle.

A twist of the spinal rod will swing the head round to look right or left. If an up-and-down tilt is required for the head, a special method of mounting it must be undertaken.

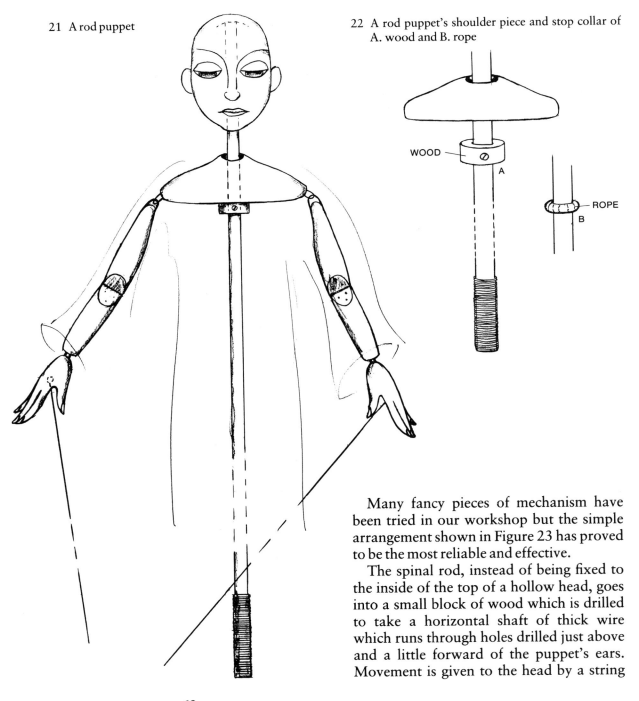

21 A rod puppet

22 A rod puppet's shoulder piece and stop collar of A. wood and B. rope

WOOD

A

ROPE

B

Many fancy pieces of mechanism have been tried in our workshop but the simple arrangement shown in Figure 23 has proved to be the most reliable and effective.

The spinal rod, instead of being fixed to the inside of the top of a hollow head, goes into a small block of wood which is drilled to take a horizontal shaft of thick wire which runs through holes drilled just above and a little forward of the puppet's ears. Movement is given to the head by a string

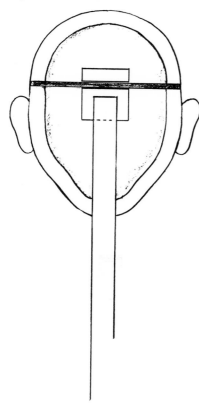

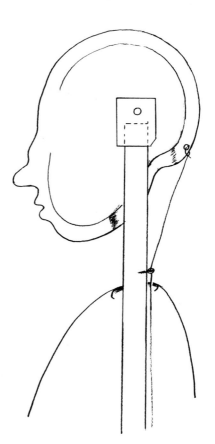

(thick nylon is good) which runs from a hole at the base of the back of the skull through screw-eyes in the spinal rod to a curtain ring which is pulled by the operator's thumb or forefinger. When he pulls the curtain ring down, the head looks up.

Rod-puppet arms are best made partly of wood and partly of leather. Figure 24 shows an arm made in this way. The forearm is made of wood squared off at the elbow. The upper arm is a double strip of leather fastened by glueing it and binding it with thread to the squared-off part of the forearm. The loop formed at the shoulder

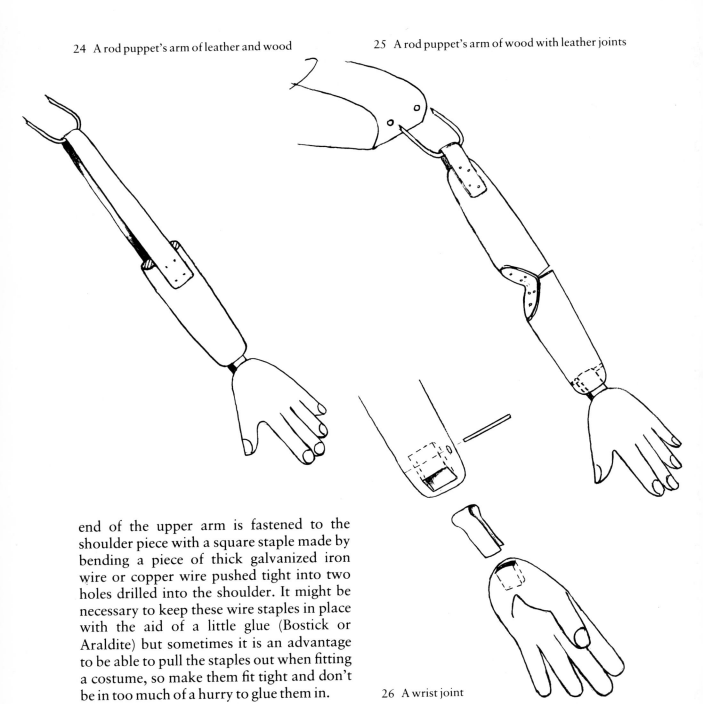

24 A rod puppet's arm of leather and wood

25 A rod puppet's arm of wood with leather joints

end of the upper arm is fastened to the shoulder piece with a square staple made by bending a piece of thick galvanized iron wire or copper wire pushed tight into two holes drilled into the shoulder. It might be necessary to keep these wire staples in place with the aid of a little glue (Bostick or Araldite) but sometimes it is an advantage to be able to pull the staples out when fitting a costume, so make them fit tight and don't be in too much of a hurry to glue them in.

26 A wrist joint

Another and perhaps more efficient type of arm can be made as shown in Figure 25. Here both parts of the arm are made of wood. The upper part is attached to the shoulder by a glued-on leather strip forming a loop which goes through a wire staple as in Figure 24. The two parts of the arm are joined by an elbow joint made by cutting away the wooden ends at an angle of 45 degrees and glueing on an oval strip of soft leather to form a hinge. The action of this joint should be at right angles to the action of the wrist joint. The shoulder joint should have enough leather to enable the upper arm to swing round at any angle to the shoulder.

The best way to fasten the hands onto the lower arms is again with leather. A couple of adjacent holes are drilled into the wrist end of the hand and, with the aid of a narrow chisel, these are joined up and squared off to form a slot in the wood. The two ends of a loop of leather are glued into this slot. A much larger hole is drilled into the wrist end of the forearm and squared off, and the leather loop is held in this by a pin made of soft galvanized iron wire. The drawing in Figure 26 should be referred to if the procedure is not clear. The hands are operated by thin rods made of stiff steel wire. Each rod has a dowel stick handle at one end and at the other a loop of thin soft wire glued on with Araldite. These loops are threaded to the palms of the puppet's hands with strong thread.

Your figure is now ready for the basic garment, which in this case is probably a straight tubular affair glued to the shoulder piece and in length somewhat longer than the final costume will be. Tubular cloth arms can be added if a little more substance is necessary, and the costume can be padded with shaped foam plastic to give form to the body of the figure. This is of course essential for female figures such as those shown in Plate 16 or stout figures of either sex. For glue use Copydex or Bostick or a rubber glue.

In making a rod puppet, take into consideration the weight factor, and do not design a costume that is going to impose a strain on operators. The matter of weight should in fact be considered right from the start. It would be a mistake, for instance, to plan a large rod figure with a wooden head and bulky shoulders and arms. For puppets over 2½ feet (75cm) in height, polystyrene should be used wherever possible and the clothing should be of the lightest possible material. The strain of supporting a heavy rod figure can be back-breaking.

10 Rod-glove Puppets

Here in our theatre we have a troupe of rod-glove puppets, the type mentioned briefly on page 23. Two of the characters, known as Percy and Martha, are shown in Plate 20. They are typical members of this most useful, tough and durable troupe. Their heads are cast in rubber, and their hands are carved out of wood. There is no reason why their heads should not instead be of wood or even polystyrene, though the latter might prove rather too fragile for such a hard-working, vigorous family. The wigs which adorn their heads are of wool, and their eyes are coloured buttons.

They are called rod-glove puppets because they are made partly as rod puppets, partly as glove puppets. As can be

65

seen in Figure 27 their hands are fastened to tapering cardboard tubes, and their heads are supported on spinal rods as with true rod puppets.

They have distinct possibilities inasmuch as they are easy to operate and have the quick direct action of the glove puppet together with some of the stance, dignity and proportions of the rod puppet. They are best made to an overall size of not more than 24 inches (60cm) which of course is

Pl. 16. *Above:* ROD PUPPETS IN ACTION: Juno stands by as Venus strikes a pose in the able hands of Ronnie LeDrew, a talented and versatile puppet operator. Venus is a leading character in the play *Cupid and Psyche* by Ann Obermer, based on a story in the Robert Graves version of *The Golden Ass.*

Pl. 17. *Right:* CHRISTOPHER LEITH speaks the part of Noah as he operates the main character in this play, one of the earliest to be included in the repertoire of the Little Angel Theatre. Note the positions of puppet and operator in relation to the playboard which divides the auditorium from the acting area.

66

27 Holding a rod-glove puppet

pieces are circular knobs of limewood drilled out to take the spinal rods in an easy fit. To make them, drill the holes first in a piece of sound limewood about ¾ to 1 inch (2 to 2.5 cm) thick, then draw a circle round each hole about 1¾ inches (4.5 cm) diameter and saw the pieces out with a fretsaw (Figure 28). If you saw the pieces first and then try to drill them, they will most likely split in the drilling process. Each puppet should have two such pieces. One acts as the shoulder piece and has the puppet's basic garment glued to it; the other is fixed to the spinal rod by means of a small wood screw in such a position as to hold the

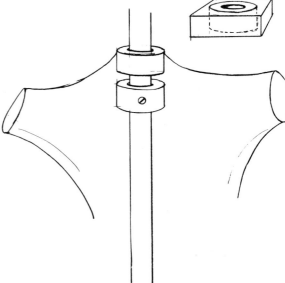

28 The shoulder and spinal rod of a rod-glove puppet

bigger than a normal glove puppet but not as tall as a rod puppet can be.

If you have followed the notes on making glove and rod puppets in Sections 4 to 9, you will need no further instructions except where the shoulder piece is concerned. Because the glove-rod puppet has a limited arm span, the shoulder piece is much smaller than with the usual rod puppet. In the case of the puppets shown, the shoulder

68

shoulder piece and prevent it from slipping down the spinal rod. The shoulder piece should turn freely on the rod, and friction between moving parts should be eased with a little talcum powder or French chalk. By and large the construction of the average glove-rod character should be no more difficult than that of an ordinary glove puppet, and you will find it easier to learn to use him than either the glove puppet or the rod puppet.

To get the best out of him, he should be operated with two hands, one hand holding the spinal rod loosely and supplying movement to the arms, and the other hand holding the lower end of the rod and using it to twist the head in different directions. If no head action is required, the figure can of course be operated by one hand only, leaving the other hand free for other work.

11 Costumes

Costumes can now be considered more fully. The scope of costume design is as unlimited for the puppet stage as it is for the human theatrical scene.

A few rules can be observed (and broken if you wish). Fine detail, for instance, is not usually effective because of the small proportions of the figures. Embroidery and appliqué are inclined to stiffen a costume out of all proportion, and in the same way very thick or very new material will be disproportionately stiff for small figures. Use soft, flowing materials where possible. Old, much-laundered, good-quality linens and cottons are invaluable, and silks where appropriate are ideal. Serge tweeds and stiff denims have limited uses. The costume should not restrict the movement of a puppet in any way. The fact that male rod and glove puppets have no legs and consequently no trousers should be countered by making the lower skirtlike part of the costume dark and insignificant in colour and accentuating the upper part with masculine-style strong tones. In Plate 20, you will notice, Percy has a well-cut swagger to his coat with strong lapels and some brass buttons, whereas Martha has pale, soft, vertical lines and a small lacy collar.

Study old paintings for ideas on costume and decoration and style, and refer when in doubt to the many very sound books on period costume available to all.

Plate 35 shows a Clown and a Wizard. The Wizard is perhaps rather too heavily ridiculed in a yellow and black cloak, sharp pointed hat and all those stars. But he is after all a somewhat comical figure, and being the bad man of the piece he must not invoke too much admiration or sympathy. The Clown on the other hand is a lovable and slightly pathetic figure. The battered top hat and bedraggled coat and bow tie, typical essentials to the clown figure, are invaluable in establishing his character.

A costume, especially for a rod puppet, should flow properly and if possible add something extra to the shape of the supposed body beneath. Plate 18 shows three very special rod puppets beautifully costumed for Oscar Wilde's *The Fisherman and his Soul*. The material used is pure silk carefully dyed. The colours in no way clash with the face make-up of the characters and at the same time match up well with the décor—another important point to watch.

69

Pl. 18. *Left:* THREE ROD PUPPETS from Oscar Wilde's *The Fisherman and his Soul.* On a lonely sea shore at night the Soul tells the Fisherman of his three journeys. As he speaks, the action is played out by stylized characters such as these shown behind a gauze and lit in such a way as to give a dream-like quality to the scene.

Pl. 19. *Above: THE REEVE'S TALE*
(Chaucer): Robust, uninhibited design and strongly carved figures go to make this set of puppets by Stefan Fichert a joy to behold. They take part in a programme entitled 'Shakespeare and Co' consisting of short pieces from different periods of English Literature.

12 Animals in General

In all forms of puppetry, figures representing animals need to be treated quite differently from those designed as human beings. The string puppet animal has a horizontal control instead of an upright one—but where glove puppets are concerned the problem of control is not so easily solved. The upright human character conceals the upright hand and arm of the operator. The horizontal dog conceals the hand and wrist of the operator but not the forearm, which looks unsightly protruding from the back end of the dog.

The solution is either to design the animal as a rod puppet or to have it as a glove puppet but only three-quarters visible. This latter is the better solution of the two as dogs, rabbits squirrels and many other animals spend much of their time squatting with their bodies at an angle of 45 degrees anyway, and in this position the operator's arm is concealed. (See Figures 29A and B.)

How the legs should be made to work is the next problem. The back legs, if they are to be seen at all, must be shaped and positioned so that they dangle down,

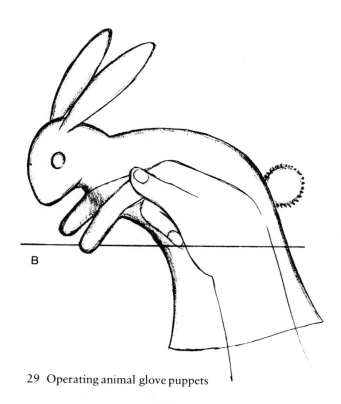

29 Operating animal glove puppets

73

catching a little movement by contact with the playboard. The front legs can be similar or they can be operated by light rods both held in the hand which is not supporting the body of the puppet. An alternative method would be to design the figure so that the fingers of the hand supporting the puppet fit into the front legs from within. This gives a rather creepy-crawly movement to the animal, good for rodent types and pussy-cats but not for horses and the more noble animals. Rather than use the fingers of the operating hand as front legs, you may wish to apply them to the mouth of the animal, giving the beast a distinctive Muppet characteristic and lending to the head the possibility of excruciating and sometimes humorous distortion.

It is assumed, of course, that these animals will be made largely out of soft materials such as foam plastic preferably covered with stockinette material so that it will be protected without losing its elasticity. Some examples are illustrated in Plate 21, which shows three animals including a large frog made out of two pieces of foam plastic each about 12 x 8 x 3 inches (30 x 20 x 8cm) thick.

One piece suitably shaped and hollowed out forms the top half of the entire frog, and the other piece the lower half. The operator's hand works the mouth. The legs, carefully shaped and stiffened in such a way as not to distort, are animated simply by the movement of the puppet. They are of Celastic, each leg being in one piece and joined to the body with a strip of leather glued into a deep slit in the body. The eyes are ping-pong balls. The entire figure is covered in the sort of stretch material that underpants are made of. He is painted with dyes (strong green). His lips are of Celastic shaped to accept the operator's fingers and thumb. The inside of the mouth is painted red. The forearm of the operator is clad in part of a black sock so that it is somewhat disguised if and when the frog jumps up from the playboard.

Dogs, wolves and animals that need big, expressive mouths can all be made in this way, choosing of course suitable materials for fur or hide. Horses and bovine animals on the other hand are probably best made as rod puppets even when they are used in conjunction with glove or glove-rod figures. Here polystyrene comes into its own again as it is easy to shape into the elegant lines needed to suggest a horse or deer, and it is light enough not to cause distress when used for the bulkier body of a bull or a cow.

Again the legs are in one piece and made of Celastic and suspended on thick cord from slots cut into the under part of the body (Figure 30). The neck can be sections of polystyrene carefully shaped and threaded together on two lengths of cord whose ends are carefully glued into the head and shoulders of the animal. The animal is supported by a rod glued into a hole in its middle, and its head is supported and controlled by a second, lighter rod hinged into a slot cut below and behind the lower jaw.

Polystyrene is liable to crumble and weaken at the point where a rod or cord is glued into it. To prevent this hazard, a plug of wood prepared with the necessary hole or slot to take the cord or rod can be glued into the polystyrene and covered in with glued cloth or brown paper (Figure 31).

Pl. 21. ANIMAL HAND PUPPETS made for a film called *Hollow Tree Home* and subsequently absorbed into various items in the Little Angel Theatre repertoire. The Green Frog is the most popular of the three. He is made out of foam plastic and has a big mouth and rolling ping-pong ball eyes. See Section 10. The Squirrel is less active; she has paws worked by rods, and a tail which twitches. Nicholas Allsorts also has paws worked on rods but his ears are his main attraction. Worked by the first and second fingers of the operator's hand, they can move through a vast range of expressive action. His facial distortions are fascinating.

75

30 A rod-puppet cow

polystyrene. The supporting rods are fastened into these two end pieces of wood, and the head, which can be of wood or polystyrene covered with paper and glue or of wood, is on a piece of dowel rod fastened at an angle into the front end wooden block (Figure 32). A fine degree of acrobatic distortion can be evolved with an animal made in this way.

Comical animals and skinny animals can be made by threading chunks of polystyrene onto two pieces of cord and using that as a spine over which a hide of rough, frayed woollen blanket is hung. For strength and durability it might be as well to have the two end pieces made of wood rather than

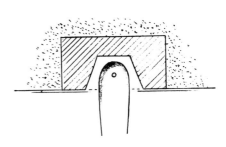

32 A comical horse

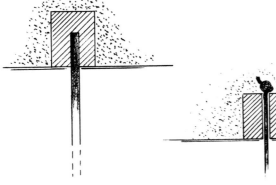

31 Fastening a rod, rope or limb to a polystyrene body

76

13 A Special Kind of Cat

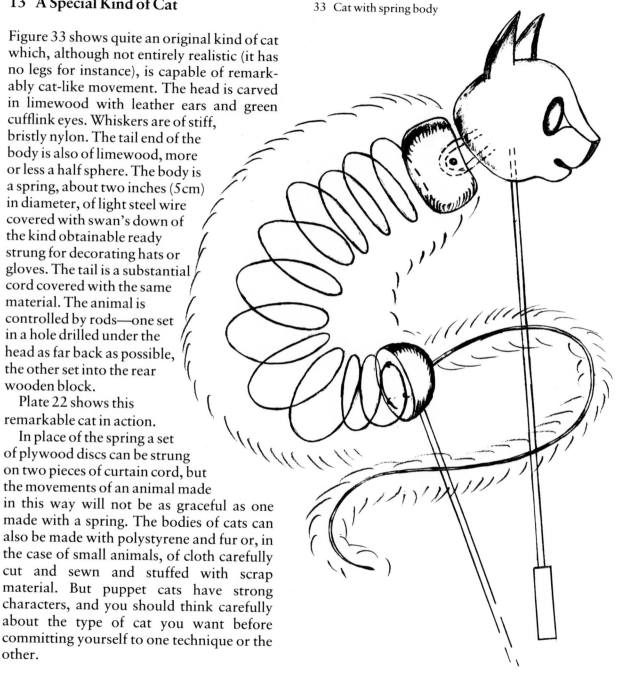

Figure 33 shows quite an original kind of cat which, although not entirely realistic (it has no legs for instance), is capable of remarkably cat-like movement. The head is carved in limewood with leather ears and green cufflink eyes. Whiskers are of stiff, bristly nylon. The tail end of the body is also of limewood, more or less a half sphere. The body is a spring, about two inches (5 cm) in diameter, of light steel wire covered with swan's down of the kind obtainable ready strung for decorating hats or gloves. The tail is a substantial cord covered with the same material. The animal is controlled by rods—one set in a hole drilled under the head as far back as possible, the other set into the rear wooden block.

Plate 22 shows this remarkable cat in action.

In place of the spring a set of plywood discs can be strung on two pieces of curtain cord, but the movements of an animal made in this way will not be as graceful as one made with a spring. The bodies of cats can also be made with polystyrene and fur or, in the case of small animals, of cloth carefully cut and sewn and stuffed with scrap material. But puppet cats have strong characters, and you should think carefully about the type of cat you want before committing yourself to one technique or the other.

77

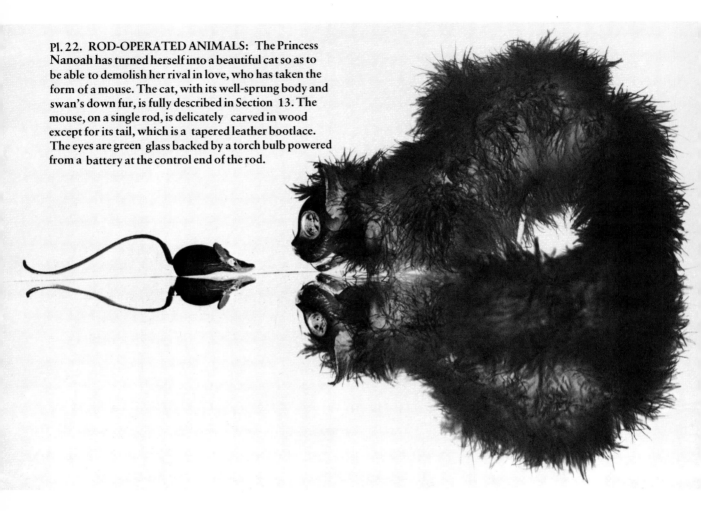

14 Fish

In *Wonder Island* the Wizard Wonderful catches a very large fish, much to his satisfaction. To make this fish a piece of light three-ply was cut to the shape of the fish but without its tail. This plywood piece was used as a stiffener for the body, which was made out of thick upholstering material in the form of a bag which was then padded out on either side of the plywood until it was of the right bulk. Before the fish was finally sewn up, a wooden socket 5 inches (12cm) long and 1 inch (2.5cm) square was drilled out to take a ½ inch (1.3cm) dowel rod and glued and pinned to the middle underside of the plywood as shown in Figure 34. The ½ inch (1.3cm) dowel is used for controlling the fish when it is swimming horizontally and just showing above the playboard.

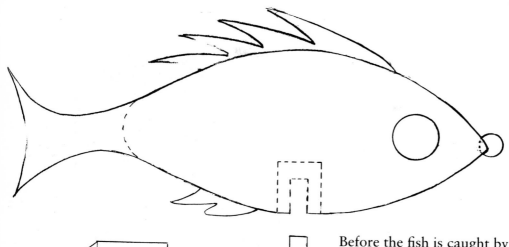

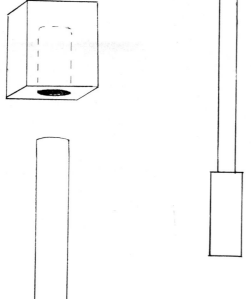

34 Fish with detachable control rod

Before the fish is caught by the Wizard and hauled up above the playboard into full view, the control rod is pulled out of the socket.

A ½ ·inch (1.3cm) curtain ring is sewn strongly to the fish's nose so that the Wizard can hook it out of the sea with his line and wire fish-hook.

Note that it is easier to select material of the right colour for the fish than to have to paint it. The fish eyes are large buttons of some sort, preferably shiny or of mother of pearl with a circle of dark shiny paper or a black sequin stuck on for a pupil. The tail should be only loosely stuffed so that it has some movement.

The small fishes caught by Percy and Mr Ninepence off Wonder Island are made purely out of material or coloured felt sewn up and stuffed with cloth. They are about 4 inches (10cm) long and need no stiffening of any sort. Small wire rings are sewn to their noses, and they are coloured according to the text of the play—a blue one, a yellow one, a pink one and a black-and-white striped one, 'a very interesting specimen', as Mr Ninepence says.

15 Butterflies and Birds

These should be made of very light, flimsy material and mounted each on a single stiff steel wire for control.

We have made butterflies out of thin white, good-quality typing paper cut to the right shape, slightly folded down the spine and then painted with watercolour. They are fastened to their steel wires with Bostick and a few stitches or with small pieces of masking tape. The important thing is not to interfere with the elasticity of the paper or the flapping action of the wings will be reduced. You might like to bend at a slight angle that section of the wire to which a butterfly is fastened. To do this, heat the wire at the point where it is to be bent in a gas jet and bend it while it is red hot. The other end of the wire can be drilled into a length of dowel stick to form a handle. You might have a little difficulty in finding the right sort of wire for this job as stiff steel wire is not usually carried by the average ironmonger. We have found that model-aeroplane shops are usually the most consistent suppliers. The wire comes in various thicknesses; a little experimentation is needed to select the thickness best suited to your purpose. Puppet butterflies, by the way, are usually made very large in proportion to the human figures associated with them.

Birds can be treated in much the same way except that their bodies and heads need to be three dimensional and should therefore be either of material stuffed or better still of carved wood or moulded Celastic. If the bird is fairly small and for casual use

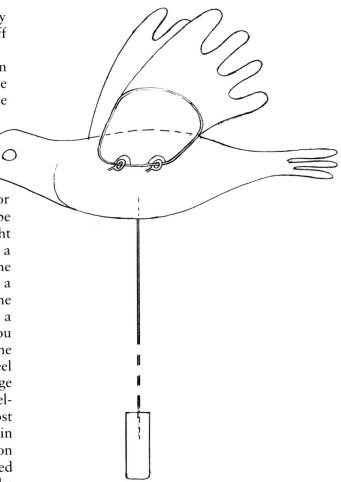

only, hinged paper wings will probably be good enough, but if the bird is an important character the wings must be capable of a more convincing action. You might like to try a small wire frame hinged onto a wooden body with a couple of small screw-eyes as shown in Figure 35. The wire should

80

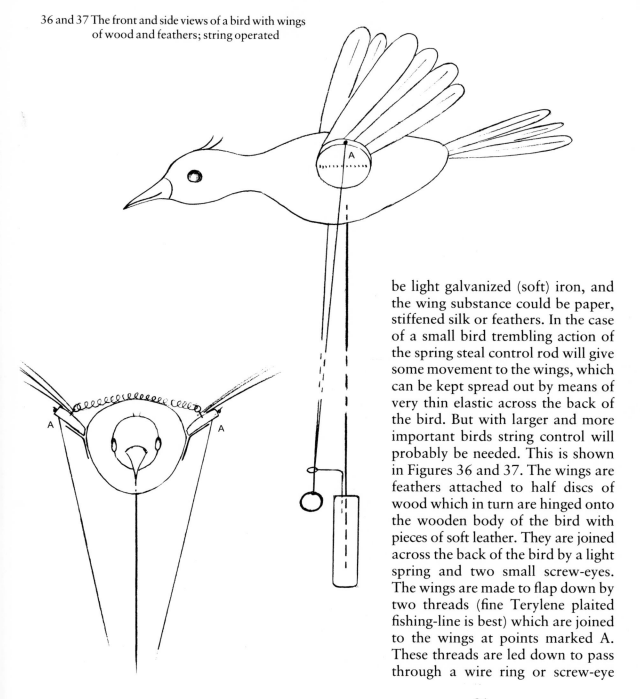

36 and 37 The front and side views of a bird with wings
of wood and feathers; string operated

be light galvanized (soft) iron, and the wing substance could be paper, stiffened silk or feathers. In the case of a small bird trembling action of the spring steal control rod will give some movement to the wings, which can be kept spread out by means of very thin elastic across the back of the bird. But with larger and more important birds string control will probably be needed. This is shown in Figures 36 and 37. The wings are feathers attached to half discs of wood which in turn are hinged onto the wooden body of the bird with pieces of soft leather. They are joined across the back of the bird by a light spring and two small screw-eyes. The wings are made to flap down by two threads (fine Terylene plaited fishing-line is best) which are joined to the wings at points marked A. These threads are led down to pass through a wire ring or screw-eye

81

attached to the wooden handle at the end of the wire rod which supports and controls the bird. The threads are joined to a large curtain ring which the operator pulls down and releases with the forefinger of the hand which holds the control. A second string could be attached to a hinged lower beak if required, giving the bird even greater possibilities. If this is done, a piece of elastic should be used to draw the beak shut against the pull of the string.

III

The Theatre, the Stage, the Props and Sets

The Theatre, the Stage, the Props and Sets

16 A Theatre for your Puppets

The construction of a theatre for staging your glove or rod puppets will need much thought and careful planning. You may be amongst the lucky ones who have the facilities available for setting up a permanent stage—that is to say, an available building or part of a building which can be converted to a small theatre. A barn, a disused warehouse, a billiards room or a room in a college or recreation centre might be available and might or might not be suitable.

The first absolute essentials are space and accessibility. To work under cramped conditions can be a misery. For an audience to have to struggle to get in and out of a building is dangerous.

To seat 100 people, about 700 square feet (65 square metres) will be needed. Roughly half of this will be taken up by seating, and the rest will go to aisles and entrance ways and the area between the front row of seats and the stage. At least two exits will be needed; preferably one of these should lead directly out of the building onto a street or unrestricted open space. Exit doors should open outwards and should have special crush-bar fittings if they are to be fastened during performances. It should be possible to rake the auditorium—in other words, to have the seats arranged on a sloping floor with a rise of about 3 feet (90cm) in 30 feet (9m) or more. Windows should be capable of being blacked out solidly and sound-proofed into the bargain.

A good-size permanent stage area would be 10 feet (3m) deep by 20 feet (6m) across, although only a small part of this, say 8 feet (2.4m) deep by 12 feet (3.6m) across, would be used as stage space; the rest would be for holding puppets and scenery ready for a call on stage.

Some sort of foyer space is a great advantage, and of course there must be toilets and backstage storage and a place for the coats and belongings of the puppeteers.

If there is to be a fly system for backdrops, quite a considerable ceiling height will be needed. If this is not available, then of course a system of rollers can be used instead. But in any case an absolute minimum ceiling height for the stage areas should be 11 feet (3.3m). With a ceiling as low as this, at least three narrow borders will be needed for effective masking. A system of masking for wings on either side will be necessary as well. Figure 38 gives an idea of how masking arrangements would be worked out for premises with the front row of seats 10 feet (3m) from the proscenium and a stage space of 10 feet (3m) by 20 feet (6m) with a ceiling 12 feet (3.6m) above. Two borders about 2 feet (61cm) deep would be required at the points marked B and two wings each side (marked W).

Matters concerning lighting-equipment and procedure are dealt with in a later section, where descriptions of various lamps are given together with ideas for fixing them to a touring-stage framework. In a permanent theatre the same lights can be used, though one would be inclined to use more of the spotlights and perhaps larger mushroom-type lamps than with a touring stage. This will be made feasible by the availability of more rigid support for the heavier lamps.

It should be borne in mind that with a permanent set-up more stage space might be available, in which case a greater pro-portion of lighting power will be needed. I suggest that vertical beams of 2 x 4 inch (5 x 10cm) timber be bolted to the walls on either side of the stage from floor to ceiling at intervals of 3 feet (1 metre) or less. Horizontal battens can be fastened to these at any point, and lamps or lamp brackets bolted to them wherever required. This will give a great deal of flexibility when it comes

to positioning lights. The same timbers, fitted with suitable brackets, can be used for supporting beams across the ceiling for borders, wings and backcloths or backcloth rollers. That is, of course, if direct support from roof beams or ceiling structure is not possible.

Some method should be evolved for supporting spotlights and houselights above the auditorium. Unless there are very solid beams from which spotlights can be hung, it is better to use metal brackets bolted to the walls. These brackets should be very rigid so that positions of lamps fastened to them do not vary from day to day. All spotlamps in the auditorium should have safety chains arranged so that, if they work loose for any reason, they cannot fall on the heads of members of the audience. Houselights will need dual control so that they can be dimmed out slowly from backstage or switched on and off from some point front of house for cleaners and maintenance purposes.

The proscenium opening is shown in Figure 38 as being 7 x 4 feet (2.1 x 1.2m) quite satisfactory for glove and glove-rod puppets but a little low for rod puppets.

Obviously an oblong building is much more adaptable than a square one. The panel which contains the proscenium arch between the stage area

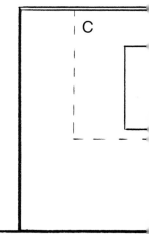

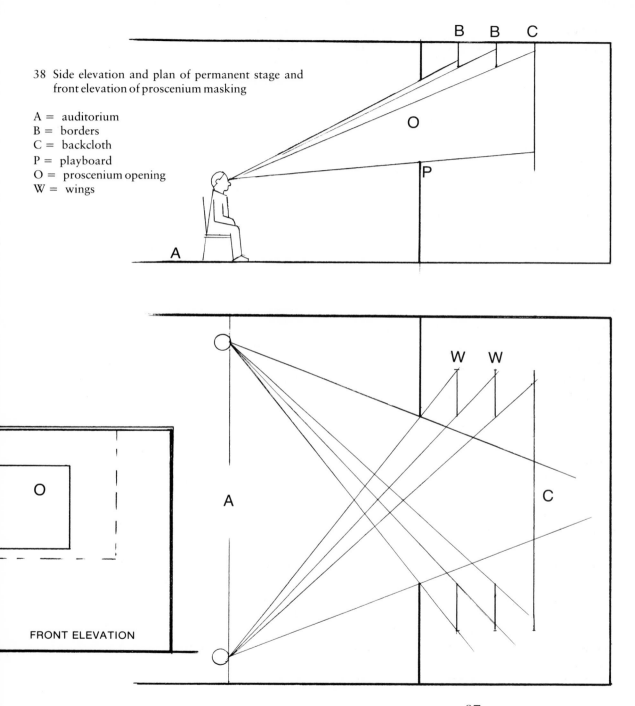

38 Side elevation and plan of permanent stage and
   front elevation of proscenium masking

A = auditorium
B = borders
C = backcloth
P = playboard
O = proscenium opening
W = wings

FRONT ELEVATION

87

and the auditorium should be of non-inflammable material. This poses a problem now that asbestos is forbidden. Perhaps a framework of heavy timber 2 x 3 inches (5 x 7.5cm) faced back and front with some sort of plasterboard would be the answer. Thick timber is considered safe because it takes some time to catch fire and remains rigid until it burns right through. Metal of equal strength (but thinner of course) distorts under heat and collapses much more quickly. Ask your local fire superintendent for advice before you launch out on any venture which might concern him.

Again get expert advice if you propose to cut through a brick wall to make a proscenium opening. Most borough councils have building superintendents who are ready to help. If an opening through a brick wall is necessary, it should be made as large as possible and then be masked in to the required size. Too much brickwork round a proscenium will give puppet-operators a very cut-off feeling.

Other points to consider are easy access from backstage to foyer areas and hence to the auditorium. This is essential, and office, storage and kitchen space must also be carefully planned.

You may pick up some other ideas as to how a permanent theatre could be installed from the following description of the Little Angel Theatre premises. The building in its original form consisted of a Victorian hall with pitched roof of slate supported by heavy timber trusses on very thick brick walls with arched windows in the south wall adjoining the grounds of St Mary's Church, Islington. It is often thought to have been an old church hall but actually it was owned and used by two Temperance societies until it suffered bomb damage in 1940, after which it was abandoned and suffered serious decay for twenty years. On the north side of the building was a reception area under a lean-to roof. Trees were growing here when we first moved in. The Western end of the site had originally contained a stage area, a small yard, two lavatories and a kitchen. Within this area all but the kitchen had been totally wrecked.

The reception area down the north side of the hall now contains the foyer, a small kitchen and a coffee-bar counter, one end of which is used as a box office. At the far end from the main entrance there are swing doors leading to an area containing three toilets, one of which is arranged for wheelchair accommodation.

The auditorium is 40 feet (12m) long and 20 feet (6m) wide. Our architect decided to rake the floor by excavation rather than by building up. This proved to be an expensive and troublesome operation and many tons of soil had to be removed and the walls had to be underpinned with concrete.

As can be seen from Figure 39, we have built-up seats on a level area at the rear of the hall. The main blocks of seats are on a central sloping area which drops to 3 feet (90cm) below normal floor-level. There is another flat area between the front row of seats and the proscenium. On this we have built a very useful apron stage 3 feet (90cm) high and 3 feet (90cm) deep. On the slanting area there is a 4 foot (1.2m) central aisle between two rows of benches. The benches are of very solid Pyrana pine, each holding five adults or six children. The benches are screwed to the floor and padded with foam

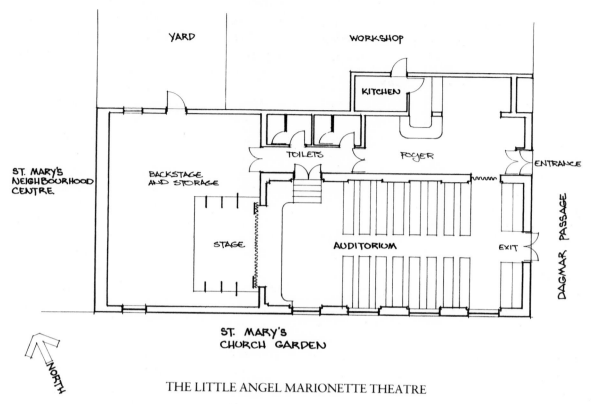

YARD

WORKSHOP

KITCHEN

TOILETS

FOYER

ENTRANCE

ST. MARY'S
NEIGHBOURHOOD
CENTRE

BACKSTAGE
AND STORAGE

DAGMAR PASSAGE

STAGE

AUDITORIUM

EXIT

NORTH

ST. MARY'S
CHURCH GARDEN

THE LITTLE ANGEL MARIONETTE THEATRE

39 Plan of a permanent puppet theatre

rubber covered with furnishing material in four colours. The front row of seats is ten feet (3m) from the proscenium opening, and to the right of this area there are wooden steps up to a door which leads to the lavatories and to another door which opens onto the side of the stage.

The central aisle leads up and back across a flat area straight to a 4 foot (1.2m) emergency exit door which opens outward directly on to the pavement and forecourt of the theatre. On the left it turns to a curtained doorway through to the foyer and main entrance.

The proscenium opening in the heavy brick end wall of the auditorium is 12 feet (3.6m) wide and 7 feet (2.1m) high from the 3 foot (90cm) apron stage (Plate 23). This opening is usally masked down to 9 feet (2.7m) by 4½ feet (1.3m) with variable blockboard borders and side pieces (known as 'tormentors'). The stage area is housed by a modern structure of brick erected in 1967. It has an asphalted concrete roof which is almost soundproof, and heavy shutters on the windows. It is roughly 30 feet (9m) square and 23 feet (7m) high. This height enables us to fly backcloths. Below there is a

89

Pl. 23. *Left:* THE PROSCENIUM ARCH of the Little Angel Theatre as seen from the middle of the auditorium. It has a carved frame surround and is 12 x 7 feet (3.66 x 2.13m) over a 3 foot (90 cm) high apron stage. Behind the purple front curtain the proscenium is masked down with adjustable blockboard panels to 9 feet (2.75 m) wide and 4¼ feet (1.30 m) high. Above the proscenium arch is another 3 foot (90 cm) opening through which figures or effects can be operated from a high gallery.

storage basement which also contains the central-heating boiler. There is a high gallery at the rear which supports two small offices and a puppet storeroom.

The actual stage area is 16 x 8 feet (4.8 x 2.4m) and is in the form of a pit with floor-level the same as the floor-level of the front row of seats in the auditorium. There is wing space at normal floor-level (3 feet [90cm] above pit floor-level) at sides and back. (Plate 24).

The playboard (which in a puppet theatre represents the stage floor) is variable in height and is set back about 2 feet (60cm) from the proscenium. This allows spotlamps behind the proscenium to be used effectively on the playboard area. Other lamps can be set up at almost any point in the wings or from the gallery above.

There are two such galleries as the theatre is used also for string puppets. These galleries are not, of course, necessary for the presentation of rod or glove puppets but a narrow one over the proscenium can be very useful nevertheless.

Backcloths and centre-drops are suspended by woven nylon cord running through a system of large screw-eyes and down to a set of cleats on a heavy horizontal batten bolted to the uprights which in turn

are bolted to the walls as described earlier. The sets of screw eyes are arranged at 4 inch (10cm) intervals and about twenty-five sets of lines are available.

The switchboard and dimmer-control system is of very mixed genre, some of it old but still effective and giving a total of forty-five stage circuits plus working lights and power points and houselights. For sound-equipment there is a substantial deck supported on heavy brackets to a side wall so that it will not be affected by vibration from the floor. In the auditorium sound insulation is adequate though not complete. Black-out is absolute except when exit lights are on.

The floor is of cork tiles on hardboard over concrete, giving a comfortable, silent yet hardwearing surface.

The theatre was opened in 1961 under very primitive conditions. At first only the barest essentials were available. Improvements and developments, based on knowledge gained by experience, have been made at intervals over the years.

So much for the permanent stage and all that it implies. But it is more than likely that you will be planning a fully mobile stage rather than one with a fixed address, so before going on with the all-important matters of scene-painting and stage lighting it might be advisable to deal with the possibilities and problems to be met with in designing and making a touring stage.

17 A Touring Stage

Some considerable skill in the art of carpentry and construction will be required for

Pl. 24. THE COMPANY at work in *Noah* as seen from back stage left looking diagonally across to stage right front. Noah's wife, with her back to the audience, is arguing with her husband, who shouts down at her from his newly constructed ark (not yet afloat) while two of his sons look on. The ark has no back to it. It is supported on a pyramid like structure which acts as a fulcrum for the seesaw action of the craft when the storm is raging at sea. The animals (flat cut-outs) can be seen stacked on the shelf far right.
1. Ark, 2. Stand for Ark, 3. Playboard, 4. Proscenium opening, 5. Wings, 6. Shelf, 7. Animals

the building of a stage that fits together easily, withstands the rough and tumble of a life on tour and at the same time looks good to the audience on every occasion. Many different requirements will come under survey in deciding the size and type of structure to be embarked upon. You will have to take into consideration how and where your stage will be used, transported and stored, the number of operators to be involved and the complexity of the shows envisaged.

If you propose to work alone, a sort of enlarged Punch and Judy booth from 4 to 6 feet (1.2 to 1.8m) wide and about 8½ feet (2.5m) high will probably suffice, but for such productions as *Wonder Island*, using three operators, a minimum size would be about 10½ feet (3.2m) across with a proscenium opening of about 4½ feet (1.4m). My suggestions for such a stage are put forward in the drawing shown in Figure 40. Dimensions can, of course, be varied to suit your own ideas and requirements. The width of the proscenium opening for instance could be increased to 6 feet (1.8m) simply by making the central horizontal flat E 1½ feet (45cm) longer. Obviously the height of the playboard must be such as to conceal the heads of operators, and the size of the proscenium must be in keeping with the size of puppets made. Other dimensions are purely optional.

A stage structure of the type under discussion is usually referred to as a 'fit-up'. For easy transport and storage the component parts of your fit-up could best be in the form of frames made of wood and covered with canvas or cloth. In theatrical language these are called 'flats', and it is convenient to refer to them as such. Sometimes two flats are hinged permanently together, in which case they are called 'book-flats', and sometimes they are joined together with detachable hinges called 'pin-hinges'. A pin-hinge is made by knocking out the normal straight pin which keeps the two parts of the hinge together and substituting a looped piece of wire of slightly smaller diameter than the original. (See Figure 41.)

18 Making and Covering Flats

Flats of the required size are best made of pine about 2 by 1 inches (5 by 2.5cm) planed. The pieces are joined with carefully cut triangles of pine 1 inch (2.5cm) thick glued and pinned with long panel pins. (See Figure 42.) Mortice joints can be used instead, and they would be preferable, but special skill is required for morticing, and I find the triangular block method perfectly adequate.

Figure 43 shows timber cut and laid out ready to be joined up to form a flat 8½ feet (2.6m) high and 3 feet (90cm) wide. Two cross-pieces are shown. These will give strength to the structure and, as you will see later, will be useful for supporting shelves for props and puppets. An extra cross-piece is shown in dotted line and marked K in the drawing. This extra piece will be included only in flats D and F where its function will be to support lighting-brackets each side of the proscenium opening. (When you come to canvassing the flats, note that the canvas should not be glued onto these cross-pieces.)

93

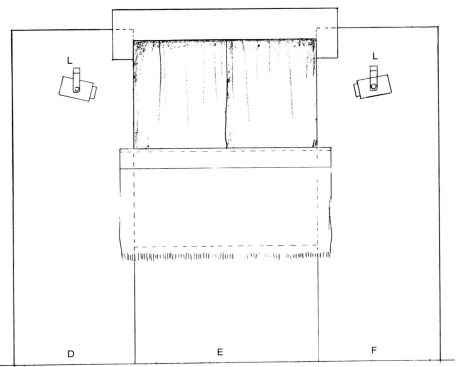

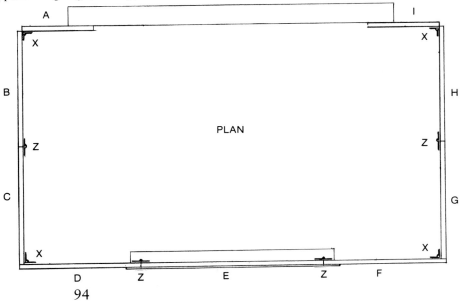

FRONT ELEVATION

40 Front view and plan of a portable glove– or
rod-puppet touring stage (or fit-up)

94

41 Detachable pin-hinge

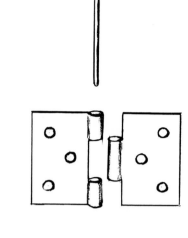

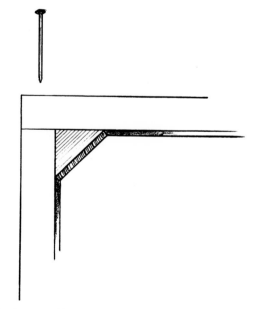

42 Corner of frame for a flat

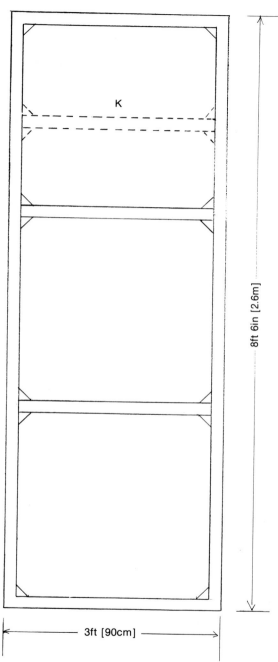

K

8ft 6in [2.6m]

3ft [90cm]

43 Layout of timber for a flat for a touring fit-up

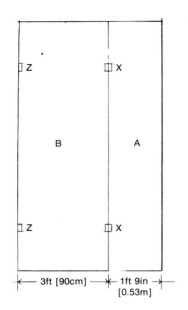

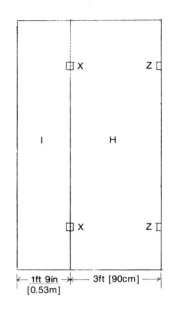

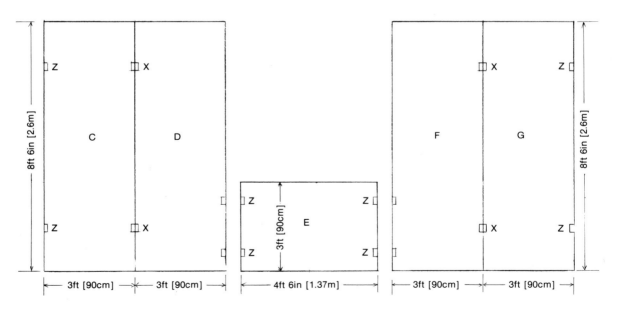

44 Diagram of flats required for a touring fit-up
X = permanent hinge   Z = pin-hinge

96

Make sure that all right angles are perfect. If you feel that extra strength is required at the corners, drill holes and drive 3 or 4 inch (7.5 or 10cm) nails in as shown in Figure 42.

The fit-up will consist of four hinged book-flats and one plain flat, a playboard, a proscenium pelmet and a structure for holding painted sets or curtains.

The book-flats and plain flats when folded and packed together will form a pack about 8½ x 3 feet and 10 inches thick (2.6m x 90cm x 25cm). The proscenium and playboard together will form a bundle about 8 feet long and 1 foot square (2.4m x 30cm). For transportation a box will have to be provided for lighting and props and another for the puppets probably about 6 or 7 cubic feet (0.2 cubic metres) in all.

The timber selected for the construction of your fit-up should be straight lightweight pine as free from knots as possible. Old, well-seasoned or secondhand wood is less likely to distort than any other. Seek a timber merchant of good repute and select your wood personally or see that it is well selected for you. Time spent with the timber merchant is always worthwhile. Figure 44 shows the flats laid out diagrammatically so that the task of measuring and cutting the timber can be set about systematically. The flats are marked alphabetically A to I. Flats will be hinged together at points marked X and pin-hinged at points marked Z. Flats A and B, H and I are hinged in the ordinary way. Flats C and D, F and G are joined with the hinges set in an inch (2.5cm) or so in order to conceal the edges of flat C and G from the audience. (See Figure 45.)

But before you hinge the flats together, attend to the matter of covering them. Two

45 'Set-back' hinge for book-flats C,D and F,G (See Figure 40)

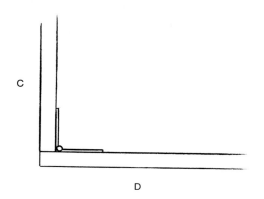

alternatives present themselves the flats can be draped with hanging curtain material or canvas, or they can be covered with canvas or thick calico, glued all round and painted.

If the first method is used, select strong poppers and fasten them at regular intervals along the top battens of the frames and onto the canvas at corresponding points. Fasten one or more poppers onto each upright as well, about a foot (30cm) from the base, to keep the canvas or curtaining from being disturbed by wind or movement of puppeteers when the fit-up is in use. Velcro tape can be used instead of poppers; it gives very satisfactory results.

The frames and covers should be code-marked to make sure that each cover is attached to its proper frame. It would make a nice finish if the coverings on D and F could be made large enough to lap around the corner edge on to C and G. Whatever material is used for covering, it should be thoughtfully selected as it will make an important visual impact on an audience assembling for a show. The material should be attractive to look at but not too colourful or garish. Bright colours and stripes might have a dazzling effect which your puppets will have to live up to or overcome when the show begins.

I have neglected to mention the matter of fireproofing, which is all-important. If you select a woollen material or a material known as noyle silk, you need have no fear as these are flame-resistant. Likewise canvas and even calico can be obtained ready fireproofed from theatrical suppliers. Otherwise you should take steps to fireproof the material yourself. This can be done by simply purchasing a can of fireproofing solution and spraying it onto the material according to the instructions of the manufacturers. You can make your own fireproofing mixture (see note in Appendix 3, Page 180 for recipe) but the ready-made mixtures are superior.

For covering the frames according to the second suggestion mentioned above, cut the canvas or calico you have selected about 4 inches (10cm) bigger all round than the frame you are about to cover. Put the frame down on the floor or other large enough work surface and fasten the calico to it at each corner with a tack or staple from a staple-gun. See that the material is stretched very slightly and be sure at the same time that it does not distort the rectangle of the frame. Tack or staple the material to the frame right round, starting at the centre of each side and working towards the corners and placing your row of tacks or staples half an inch (1.3cm) from the *inner* edge of the timber of the frame. Again be careful not to distort the frame by stretching the material too hard or in the wrong direction.

Now take a pot of carpenter's glue prepared from pearl glue as described in Appendix 2. See that the glue is hot and of thin, creamy consistency and, lifting up the material by its outer 4 inch (10cm) fringe, coat the timber underneath it from the line of tacks or staples to its outer edge and press the material down onto it, pulling it slightly outwards to keep it smooth and rubbing it hard with a rag pad soaked in water as hot as you can handle. It is an advantage to have two people working simultaneously on all this so that the glueing and pressing down can continue without a break. The hot, damp pad should have the effect of flattening the material and bringing some of the glue up through it to the surface, making sure of a bond which will defy destruction for years to come. When you are satisfied that a neat job has been done, take a very sharp knife and trim the superfluous canvas or calico off straight along the edge of the wood, making sure that nothing is left to curl round the edges. For painting these flats see the notes on scene-painting in Section 22.

N.B.: Flats covered with calico or canvas need special handling and packing. Handle them by their wooden frames only. Never touch the canvas, and do not let anything press or rub against it.

19 The Playboard

At this stage it would be advisable to assemble the hinged-up flats into their proper positions before going on to make the proscenium pelmet and the playboard. You will have a 10½ x 6 foot (3.2 x

1.8metre) space enclosed except for an opening at the back.

The proscenium opening will be 4½ x 5 feet (1.4 x 1.5m), and the next task will be to make a playboard of variable height to set onto the lower edge of this opening.

A good width for a playboard is about 4 inches (10cm), and the thickness should not be less than ¾ inch (1.9cm); ⅞ inch (2.2cm) would be better. So select a good piece of 4 x ¾ or ⅞ inch (10 × 1.9 or 2cm) pine 5 feet

(1.5m) long, bearing in mind that this is the stage on which furniture and props will be placed and above which your puppets are to play in every performance. The plank should be smoothed and sandpapered to a fine degree, with the edge away from the audience slightly rounded for the comfort of the puppet-operators and to reduce wear and tear on puppets and their costumes.

Along the forward edge of the playboard a 6 inch (15cm) strip of ½ inch (1.3cm)

46 One end of playboard detail and supporting member of flat F

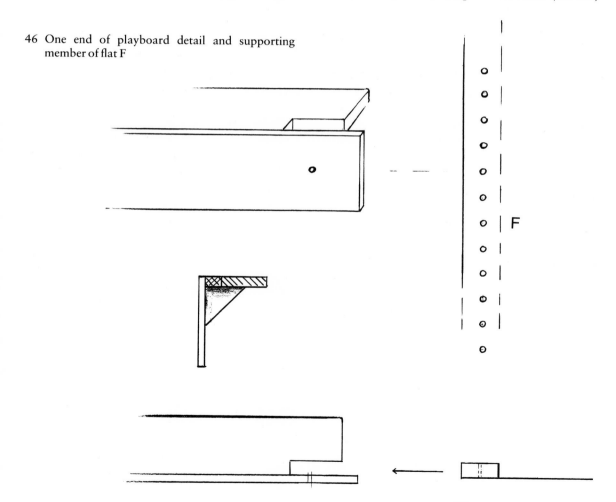

99

blockboard or ¼ inch (.6cm) plywood should be carefully fastened with wood screws. This strip should be capable of taking a good finish and should be a little longer than the playboard at each end. (Total 5 feet 3 inches [1.6m]).

The playboard is held in position by two ¼ inch (.6cm) carriage bolts fastened through two of a series of holes drilled at 1 inch (2.5cm) intervals up the sides of the flats which border the proscenium opening. These holes should be so planned and drilled as to give a maximum height to the playboard of 6 feet (1.8m) from ground-level and a minimum of 4 feet (1.2m). (See Figure 46.) To complete the arrangement a fringe is required. This should be deep enough to cover the opening between flats D and F whatever the height of the playboard. It can be Velcrotaped under the front flange of the playboard so that it can be removed during transportation or changed to suit the mood of the play. The fringe should be scalloped or cut to some pattern and decorated with braid or ball-fringe according to your fancy.

20 The Proscenium Pelmet

The proscenium pelmet must now be tackled. This can be basically a frame made of 2 x 1 inch (5 x 2.5cm) pine in the form of an oblong 5½ feet (1.7m) long and 9 inches (23cm) deep with ends extended down by about 6 inches (15cm) faced and backed with 4mm plywood. The frame is so constructed that the lower corners can be slipped over the top inner corners of the flats D and F. The plywood covering these corners is extended down to give added security. Figure 47 gives an overall idea of the framework, and Figure 48 shows the detail of the extended lower corners. To save plywood, the backing on the frame can be restricted to an oblong piece 6 x 15 inches (15 x 38cm) at each end.

The curtain rail could be fixed permanently to the back of the proscenium pelmet, but for easy dismantling and transportation it is really better to have it on a separate batten of wood. If the curtain is of a heavy material, this batten should be a little stronger than the 2 x 1 inch (5 x 2.5cm)

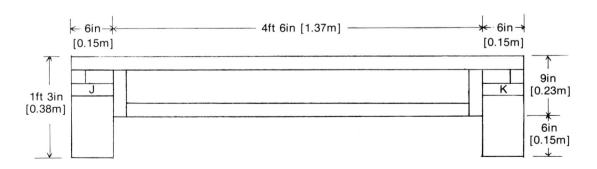

47 Front elevation of pelmet over proscenium arch

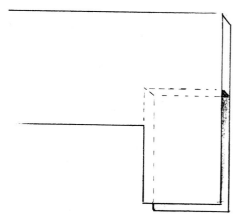

48 Clip-on end of proscenium pelmet and corner of flat F

Two lengths of plastic curtain rail should be fastened to the underside of the batten with a 3 inch (7.5cm) overlap so that the two sections of the curtain when closed will not show a gap. The outer ends of the

Flat F

curtain rail should go right out to the end of the batten so that the curtains can be pulled out of sight when opened. Figure 50 shows how to join up the curtain cord. A is a fixed pulley, B a fixed double pulley and C a swinging pulley with a weight attached, or pulled down with a light spring. Curtain

you have used up until now. I suggest a 2½ x 1 inch (6.3 x 2.5cm) or even 3 x 1 inch (7.5 x 2.5cm). It should run about a foot (30cm) longer at each end than the width of the prosecenium, making it 6½ feet (2m) for a 4½ feet (1.4m) proscenium.

At a point near to each end there should be a lug of wood 4 inches (10cm) long by 2 x 1 inches (5x2.5cm) socketed in as shown in Figure 49 and fitted with a stout round-headed screw which can be hooked into a keyhole slot cut in the back plate at each end of the proscenium pelmet.

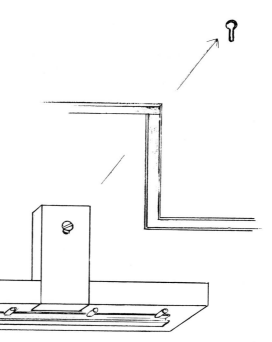

49 Front curtain-rail support. (Keyhole is *behind* pelmet)

101

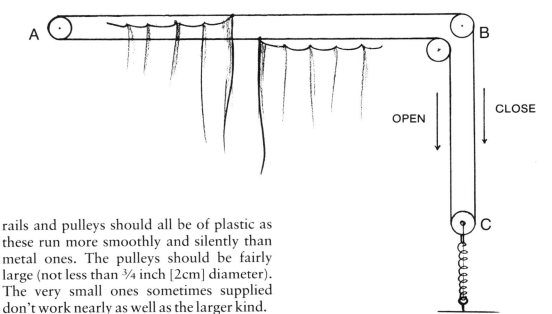

OPEN

CLOSE

rails and pulleys should all be of plastic as these run more smoothly and silently than metal ones. The pulleys should be fairly large (not less than ¾ inch [2cm] diameter). The very small ones sometimes supplied don't work nearly as well as the larger kind.

The curtain material is, of course, a matter of your choice. Again I would stress that it should be modest in design and colouring and, of course, it should match up with the general scheme. It must be light-proof, and a lining may be needed in order to make it so.

21   A Support for Curtains and/or Backdrops

We now come to the all-important matter of backing to the stage area. Curtains can be useful but rather mundane, and I think you will agree that a set of painted backdrops would add a great deal more to a production in every way.

As we are still involved with the structural side of our staging, we will review the possibilities of setting up a frame to support a series of backdrops before dealing with the matter of designing and painting the cloths themselves.

It is obvious that something like the pelmet structure is best dropped into place or clipped on rather than being held by bolts. Figures 51 and 52 show how the same principle can be applied to the backdrop support. Actually two bolts can be used to keep the arrangement totally rigid, but these may not be necessary; if they are, being at a low level they should be easy enough to apply. The drawings show in front and side elevation a box panel which supports and conceals three aluminium rollers each with a backdrop attached. The panel is a strip of 4 mm (5/32″) plywood 8 feet x 11 inches (2.5m x 28cm). The upper edge is glued and

102

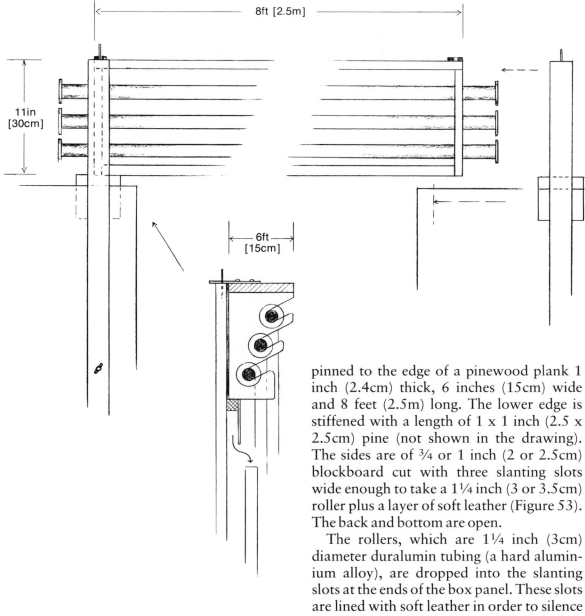

8ft [2.5m]

11in [30cm]

6ft [15cm]

52 Side elevation of three-roller unit showing clip-on to flat A or F

pinned to the edge of a pinewood plank 1 inch (2.4cm) thick, 6 inches (15cm) wide and 8 feet (2.5m) long. The lower edge is stiffened with a length of 1 x 1 inch (2.5 x 2.5cm) pine (not shown in the drawing). The sides are of ¾ or 1 inch (2 or 2.5cm) blockboard cut with three slanting slots wide enough to take a 1¼ inch (3 or 3.5cm) roller plus a layer of soft leather (Figure 53). The back and bottom are open.

The rollers, which are 1¼ inch (3cm) diameter duralumin tubing (a hard aluminium alloy), are dropped into the slanting slots at the ends of the box panel. These slots are lined with soft leather in order to silence the rollers and enable them to run smoothly. The top edge of each painted backdrop is

53 Side view of three-roller container showing metal
    plate used in raising and lowering it

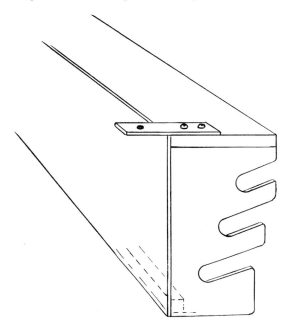

The battens themselves are held upright in position by clipping them onto the tops of flats A and I. The clips used are made of blocks of 4 x 1 x 1 inch (10 x 2.5 x 2.5cm) wood and strong 4 mm (5/32") plywood as shown in detail Figure 54 (Thin plywood is always referred to in millimetres when bought and sold). In this way your three backdrops can be assembled and heaved up into position above without anyone having to climb onto chairs or ladders.

glued to its roller (with Copydex glue) very carefully so that it will roll perfectly straight without running off at the ends. The rollers are longer than the width of the backdrops so that a cord can be wound round each end—one to roll the cloth up and one to pull it down. Each cord has a small weight and a loop at the end.

The box panel with its rollers is supported at each end by a 2 inch (5cm) vertical batten 1 inch (2.5cm) thick and 8 feet (2.5m) long. At the end of each of these is a metal spike made by hammering a 4 inch (10cm) nail into a hole drilled exactly into the top of the batten and then cutting the head off (Figure 54). The spikes at the ends of the batten fit through holes in metal plates attached at the ends of the box panel. (See detail Figure 53.)

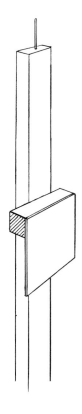

54 Batten with clip and spike for raising and
    supporting three-roller unit

Added refinement could be in the form of strips of plywood pinned to the upright battens so as to mask the ends of the backdrop rollers. The cords which roll the rollers when raising or lowering a backdrop will be concealed by the edges of flats A and I. Each cord by the way is fastened to its roller by threading the end through a hole drilled in the metal and then tying a large knot inside the tube. Cords fastened at the right-hand ends of the rollers should be for unwinding them and so lowering the backdrop and those fastened at the left end for raising them. (See Figure 55.) Some experiment will be required to get the length of the cords right.

The height at which the backdrop rollers should be held is a matter for discrimination. It may be useful to have the clips on the uprights adjustable as the height of the backcloth will depend upon the sightlines, and the sightlines will vary from one venue to the next. But for a start you can estimate the sightlines, taking a fairly average sort of set-up and drawing it up diagrammatically. Figure 56 is a diagram of the stage set-up at one end of a small hall or a classroom with no platform, a flat floor and the audience seated on benches with the front row about 10 feet (3m) from the stage. AB represents

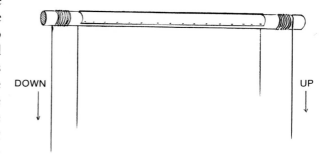

55 Method of stringing for rolling and unrolling backcloths

DOWN   UP

the lines of vision from the front row, and CD the lines of vision from the back row 25 feet (7.5m) back. Your backdrop therefore should be visible at points A and D. This means that the effective part of your painted drop should be not less than 6 feet (1.8m), and to this you should add about a foot (30cm) for the roller and another 6 inches (15cm) for wastage in pinning it to the floor or to a paint frame. (See Section 22 painting backdrops.)

As to the width, this will be determined by your stage. Make it 8 feet (2.5m) across and trim it down to size later.

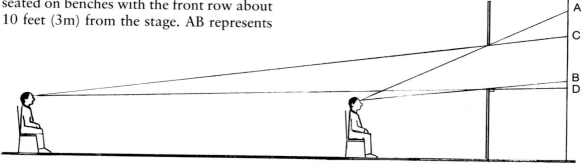

56 Sightlines as from front and back seats of auditorium

105

22 Painting Backdrops, Set Pieces and Props

The above paragraphs lead us to the preparation of the backdrops required. These are best made of unbleached calico of good quality. Scene-painting canvas can be used, but for backdrops of the size needed for puppets the canvas would be unnecessarily heavy—and of course it is more expensive. Fireproofed calico can be obtained but if it is not easily available ordinary calico can be used and a fireproofing applied.

Most scene-painters believe that their work can be done only with the use of a paint frame but, although a paint frame gives added joy to the work, it is not really necessary provided you have sufficient floor space to spread the cloth out horizontally. A clear, clean wooden floor is best to work on.

Assuming that you have a suitable floor, cover it with two layers of newspaper, measure the cloth out, making it about six inches larger each way than its final size is to be, and tack or staple it down, starting at the four corners and stretching it very slightly. Take extreme care to see that it remains exactly rectangular. Fill in along the edges, straightening them out as you go with tacks or staples about 5 or 6 inches (13 or 15cm) apart.

The next step is to treat the cloth with a very thin mixture of glue-size made by dissolving two dessertspoonfuls of pearl glue in a quart of hot water (just below boiling point). If the pearl glue can be soaked in a little cold water for a few hours first, it will dissolve very readily in the hot water. Using a flat brush, paint the cloth evenly with this mixture and leave it to dry. This process is called 'sizing' the cloth, and the effect is to make it non-absorbent so that clean edges can be made with brush strokes using dyes and very fluid paints.

Only very thin paint should be used for painting cloths that are to be rolled up as these will be. Dyes are excellent if you can handle them. Cryla and similar paints are excellent but expensive. Oil paints are out because of their inflammable nature. The concentrates used for tinting emulsion paints are worth experimenting with but the cheapest and most effective paints are the dry colours used by theatre scene-painters. To handle them effectively, some experience is necessary. The colours are obtained in powder form and mixed in with glue-size made in the same way as the mixture described earlier to be used for 'sizing' the cloth except that the glue-size used for mixing paint should have a higher glue content. Try four dessertspoons of pearl glue per quart (litre) of boiling water—but experiment may be necessary. If the paint you have mixed rubs off when dry, more glue is needed. If the cloth goes hard like cardboard, too much glue has been used. Most scene-painters when they are laying out a cloth for painting will nail a spare piece of the same cloth to a board, size it and use it for experimentation. This is particularly necessary when using scene paint as some of it dries unexpectedly much lighter in tone than anticipated.

When the cloth is painted to your satisfaction and is totally dry, cut it to the right size with a sharp blade and lift it off the floor. Some newspaper may have stuck to the back of it (this is a sign that the initial coating of glue size was mixed too strong).

A steam iron will help to get the paper loose if it doesn't peel off easily. The cloth is then ready to be stuck to the duralumin roller. Do not attempt to paint or in any way moisten the cloth when it is no longer stretched on the floor. If you do, it will buckle and distort irredeemably.

Painting on a scene frame is the same in general practice. The frame can be made quite simply out of 2 x 1 inch (5 x 2.5cm) pine with a strong plywood triangle at the back of each corner, preferably held on with screws rather than nails or glue so that it can be altered or dismantled at will. If the frame is 6 feet (1.8m) or more, it should be braced with a cross-member fastened with screws to the back of it at centre to prevent the upper and lower battens being drawn together when the cloth shrinks under the treatment of glue-size. The frame should be bigger in size than the finished trimmed cloth is to be. About 6 inches (15cm) each way should be sufficient. Tack or staple the cloth to the frame, stretching it very slightly just as you would if you were working on a floor. There are certain advantages in working on a paint frame. One is that the frame can be held upright or sloping slightly, and under these circumstances the glue-size and the paint to be applied later will dry much more quickly than if the work was being done on the floor. Another and even more important advantage is that the painter can view and assess the progress of his work from a comparative distance.

Returning to the matter of sightlines, it must be obvious that the most important elements of your design must be kept well away from the outer fringes of the back-drop. Members of the audience sitting on the extreme right or left of the auditorium will find that their view of the set is partly masked by one side or the other of the proscenium, while those sitting very far forward or to the back of the auditorium will miss the lower edge or the top section of the scene respectively. Your drop scenes should be planned and painted accordingly.

The painting of set pieces (three-ply buildings, polystyrene rocks etc) can be carried out in the same way but it might be an advantage to use a more solid kind of paint. As your set piece will probably not be of flexible material, glue-size will not be necessary and a substantial coat of emulsion paint can be applied instead. A set of rocks, for instance, made of polystyrene and covered with paper and glue for strength (using 2 inch [5cm] scraps of paper), can be given a ground coat of white emulsion and painted with dye or treated with Cryla, giving some beautiful effects. Once you have gained a little experience, never be afraid to experiment.

The painting of props will, of course, depend on the materials from which they have been made. As the objects are mostly small, care should be taken not to clog them with thick paint. Metal things can cause problems and you might have to use a special undercoat known as metal-primer before you can get a paint to stick. Firms selling car accessories can usually supply small quantities of primer. The other spray paints they stock can also be useful. Metallic paints are no problem—spray cans of gold and silver, for instance, are easily obtainable from most hardware shops and from branches of Woolworths.

Here are one or two final notes for the scene- or prop-painter.

1. Always clean and dry brushes immediately after use. This applies especially to brushes used for emulsion paint, which, if it hardens (as it does very quickly), cannot be dislodged without damage to the brush.

2. Glue-size should be used when still slightly warm. It tends to thicken as it gets cold, and when really cold it will jellify.

3. Glue-size and paint mixed with glue-size putrefy after a few days. If you wish to prevent this, mix a few drops of disinfectant with the paint or size (Jeyes Fluid, Dettol or Pine Tar disinfectant, for example). Otherwise throw the paint out and rinse all containers with water. The smell of bad glue-size is very disagreeable.

4. It is best always to paint in daylight. Plain electric light distorts colour, especially blues and blacks. When the work is finished, it can be tested out under coloured light, and this can be very useful.

23 Design and Construction of Sets and Furniture

Glove and rod puppets are operated from below and have virtually no stage floor. Settings and furniture and props to be used in presenting them must obviously be designed accordingly. They must appear to be at the correct level when seen in conjunction with a puppet. Some of the movable ones, such as the boat (to be described later), a cut-out resembling the sun or the moon or some clouds are best supported by rods held by puppet-operators, but the fixed ones—tables, chairs etc—must be supported by

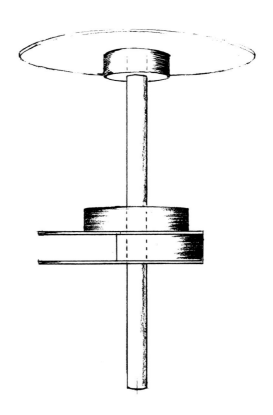

57 A round table with clip for attaching to playboard

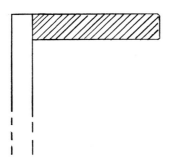

108

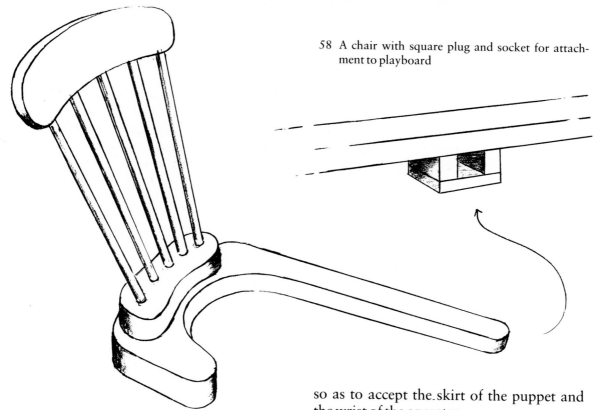

something solid and immovable such as the playboard or the framework of the stage. A round table, for example, can be made as shown in Figure 57. The single supporting leg has two three-ply discs at its base. These are separated by a piece of wood exactly the same thickness as the playboard. This forms a fairly flexible clip which enables an operator to fix the table firmly at any point on the playboard.

Another method is to use a box socket made of wood and fastened under the playboard as shown in Figure 58. The article of furniture, in this case a chair, has a neatly fitting length of wood which can be plugged into the socket when required. The chair, you will note, has a part of the seat cut away so as to accept the skirt of the puppet and the wrist of the operator.

In the play *Wonder Island*, the cage in which Percy is held prisoner by the Wizard is supported by a three-ply clip as in the case of the table. The cage is made of two rings fretted out of block board (¾ inch—2cm) forming top and bottom of a framework of bars made of ½ inch (1.3cm) dowel stick and painted with black emulsion. The plywood clip which holds it to the playboard is shaped and fastened to the underside of the lower blockboard ring with two wood screws. There is no door to the cage as Percy appears within the cage at the opening of the scene, and he is removed, cage and all, by the Wizard at the end of the scene.

The island which gives the play its name is a simple half-round structure of wire and

109

sacking on a wooden frame; its base has a vertical square section plug about six inches long which sockets into the top of an upright pole which in turn is fastened to the centre of a small wooden platform about 18 inches (46cm) square. This platform is fitted with casters of the type usually associated with beds, sofas and large armchairs. The upright pole supports the island at the height of the playboard.

The boat used in the same scene has sides made of bent plywood. (See Plate 25.) It is supported by a square section wooden handle about 8 inches (20cm) long fastened to the outside of the side of the boat away from the audience. The boat has no floor and no seats. An operator can hold the boat with one hand and with the other hand operate a puppet through the bottomless boat. A second operator works another puppet in the boat. They hook a large fish. The fish drags the boat across the sea at great speed. Clouds, cut out and painted three-ply on dowel rods, flash overhead, accentuating the sense of speed. Suddenly the island is wheeled in and the boat collides with it.

The island has a secret door which is the entrance to a cave. The door is a plywood panel sliding vertically up in wooden grooves and activated by a string through a screw eye above. Puppets entering the cave go through this door and disappear behind the island. In the next scene the island is turned about-face so that its black, hollow, reverse side forms the interior of the cave.

The do-it-yourself flying-machine which the Wizard has made is a primitive affair. It has a flat body a little bigger than Percy's torso and two flat wings fastened to it at the shoulder points by loops of string. The whole structure is hung onto Percy's shoulders by a pair of wire hooks and Percy's arms are spread out on the wings and fastened with either bands of elastic or tape and Velcro. The machine with Percy fastened to it is held aloft by means of a heavy dowel with a handle bound with string. The wings, decorated with pieces of silk and feathers, are worked by strings which run from below up through two looped antennae which are fastened to a block of wood on the back of the structure. (See Figure 59.) A soft white rope is looped around Percy's waist, and the Wizard holds the end of this and controls Percy and the machine rather as if he were flying a kite.

24 A Support for Props and Set Pieces

When we first produced *Noah*, the figure of God had to appear very suddenly and quietly out of the darkness backstage. We decided to wheel Him on in a black-out, and a platform on silent casters was built and fitted with a pivoting extendable frame. At the highest point of the frame we set up God in the form of a large set piece with movable mouth. The apparatus on which He was

Pl. 25. *Right:* GLOVE-ROD PUPPETS IN ACTION: In the play *Wonder Island* Percy and Mr Ninepence are seen, as from back stage, fishing from their boat. The boat has two sides but is bottomless. The fish (a blue one and a black-and-white striped one) are of coloured felt sewn and stuffed with cloth and fitted with small rings on their noses for the fishermens' wire fish-hooks. Knots on the fishing-lines, in keeping with Mr Ninepence's untidy nature, give added visibility to the lines.

59 Wizard Wonderful's do-it-yourself flying-machine. Note terry-clip T for Percy's neck and Velcro patches VV for holding his arms to the wings

conveyed became known as 'God's trolley'. We now have several versions of God's trolley, and we find them extremely useful for supporting sets, props or even a second playboard in the middle of the stage.

The most favoured one has a base of ¾ inch (2cm) blockboard 2½ feet x 2 feet [75cm x 60cm] (See Figure 60.) This size is optional, but be careful: if it is too large, it will obstruct the feet of operators; if it is too small, the structure will tend to topple over. It should be fitted with modern swivel-type casters at one end and a strip of wood at the other end to keep it level. This strip of wood keeps the trolley steady when it is in a set position; it has, of course, to be lifted slightly off the floor when the trolley is moved. The framework supported by the trolley is made of 2 x 1 inch (5 x 2.5cm) pine screwed and bracketed firmly onto the base. If it is to be a fixed height, it should be as high as your playboard but it is best to make it variable, in which case two frames are made, one being 2 x 4 feet (60cm x 1.2 metres) high; the other, 2 x 3 feet (60 x 90cm), is bolted to it with ¼ inch (.6cm) carriage bolts with wing-nuts and large washers. The bolt holes are slotted so that the frame can extend to a total height of 6 feet 6 inches (2 metres) with a 6 inch (15cm) overlap and down to 4 feet 2 inches (1.2m) with the maximum overlap.

The sliding parts can be rubbed with candle wax or polished and treated with French chalk or talcum powder (not rice powder).

As you can see if you refer again to Figure 60, the upper frame of the trolley is finished off with a horizontal plank of 4 x 1 inches (10 x 2.5cm) and 2¼ feet (70cm) long. This

60 A 'God's trolley' with extending frame

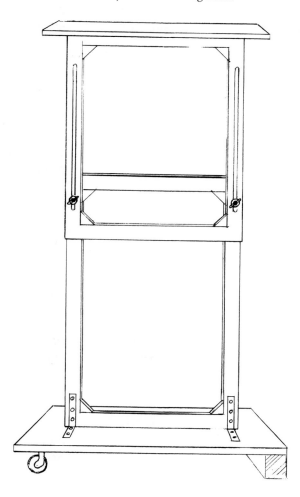

acts as a platform onto which props and settings can be clipped, bolted or clamped. If, as is very likely, the whole structure plus a piece of scenery looks a bit top-heavy, the base should be weighted to prevent a disaster. If you have nothing suitable to use as weights, they can be made by cutting up strips of lead sheeting 12 x 2 inches (30 x

5cm) and laying them one on top of the other until you have a slab about 1½ to 2 (4 to 5cm) inches thick. (Builders' merchants usually stock lead sheeting.) The layers of lead can be hammered together and then bound up with thin wire or drilled and nailed to a piece of wood of equal size.

Another very satisfactory way of making weights is to make a mould out of pieces of scrap plank and fill it with molten scrap lead piping. Scrap-iron merchants usually carry disused lead piping or can tell you where it can be obtained. The lead can be melted down in an old, unwanted iron or aluminium pot over a gas-burner. Handle molten lead very carefully: it can cause nasty burns. Work down at floor-level as much as possible and see that there are no children about.

Set pieces supported by this trolley structure can be painted cut-out plywood bracketed onto a ¾ inch (2cm) wooden base or they can be partly in the round, with side walls and roofs of buildings foreshortened and slanting away. Rocks and pieces of rugged scenery can be made of polystyrene, preferably on a wooden base and covered with layers of paper and glue or skrim or hessian depending on the quality of surface required. But bear in mind that the structure should not be required to hold anything too bulky or heavy.

It may be necessary to have a second playboard in a production, and the trolley can be used to support this. The length of the second playboard will have to be carefully considered as puppeteers will have to be able to pass round it at both ends; in other respects (thickness of timber and so on), it should be as similar as possible to the main playboard so that props and furniture can be swapped from one to the other.

The second playboard can be faced with a strip of ½ inch (1.3cm) blockboard 6 inches (15cm) wide, depending on sightline requirements, and this can be added to by a fringe of glued and painted canvas.

25 Props and Prop-making

Making props for a puppet production can be a fascinating occupation. The objects required can be of such infinite variety that it is difficult to give any specific instructions. Here is a description of how props for *Wonder Island* and certain other productions were made. By studying these, together with some notes on useful materials and tools, it is hoped that you will get an idea of how to set about making whatever is required.

Fishing rods as used in the opening of the play. Half inch (1.3cm) dowel sticks are cut to about 1½ to 2 feet (45 to 60cm) and equipped with small screw eyes about an inch (2.5cm) from each end. A length of thin string known as 'brickys' (bricklayers') line is threaded through the screw eyes. To one end a curtain ring is tied and to the other a hook made from a piece of soft galvanized iron wire is fastened. When a fish is caught, the wire hook is passed through a wire loop sewn to the nose of the fish. The fish is hauled up into view by the operator pulling the curtain ring down with his free hand.

Telescope as used by the Wizard Wonderful. Three pieces of dowel stick of

114

different diameters are drilled and fastened into each other. A stiff vertical wire drilled into the middle at the point of balance supports the telescope which is finished in black and gold paint. The supporting wire can be fitted with a 4 inch (10cm) dowel stick handle which will make it easier to use with accuracy.

The barrel of gunpowder is an old miniature sherry barrel, but that is difficult to find nowadays so it might be best to make a polystyrene barrel and glue some strips of thick cardboard onto it using carpenter's glue or the special glue used for polystyrene mentioned in Appendix 2. The cardboard strips will have to be tapered at each end and some trial-and-error tactics used to get the degree of taper correct. The bands representing the barrel hoops would best be made of strips of canvas folded to give thickness and glued on carefully. A flat, vertical wooden handle is glued into a hole in the bottom of the barrel about an inch (2.5cm) from the edge furthest away from the side presented to the audience. This handle enables an operator to set the barrel on the playboard in view of the audience without showing a hand. The barrel is not hollow but the polystyrene can be scooped out at the top just enough for Mr Ninepence to stick his rather large nose into it when he smells gunpowder.

Kitchen utensils and crockery can be made of cardboard but a better material is Celastic. It is strong and can be moulded into a fixed shape when softened with acetone. Acetone should only be used out of doors or in a well-ventilated room as the fumes can be damaging if inhaled. The fumes are highly inflammable. Celastic can be obtained in rolls or large sheets and in several different thicknesses. It is an idea to have a few pieces handy when making props. It can be pressed into moulds or over plasticine or clay shapes which can then be scooped out as soon as the acetone has evaporated. Celatic is a material used in the shoe-making industry for strengthening toe caps and heels. It is rather difficult to come by. See Appendix 4 for known suppliers in Britain.

A shelf for holding small props can be made by bracketing two planks together at right angles and fitting them with square strip aluminium hooks like the ones shown in Figure 64 made for supporting lamp-holders. They can be hooked onto the cross battens shown in Figure 43 at any convenient point. They should also be fitted with pairs of padded dowel stick pegs for hanging puppets, the pegs being placed just wide enough apart to accept the necks of the puppets which then hang by their heads. (See Figure 61.)

26 Stage Lighting and Lighting-Equipment

Lighting for the puppet theatre can be a most absorbing subject. A show can always be enhanced by good lighting, and it can certainly be ruined by bad lighting or by total neglect of lighting. Diaghilev, the famous Russian Ballet impresario, is said to have used light like paint. He was a great artist and, together with a group of dedi-

115

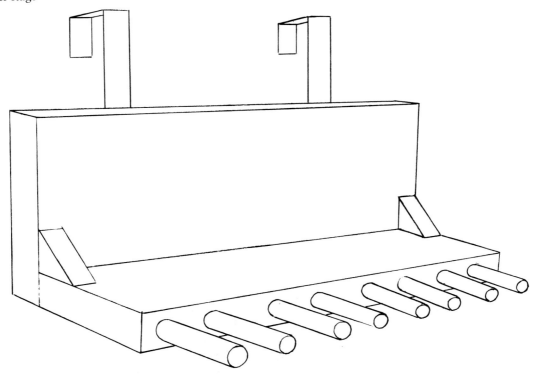

cated people, he produced some amazing results. That was a long time ago. Nowadays we have available very much more sophisticated and efficient equipment than Diaghilev had, and there is absolutely no excuse for not lighting our puppets and their stage scenery to very good effect indeed.

There are various ways of producing light for theatre, and various standard types of lamp have been evolved over the years. For the uninitiated here is a brief descriptive list. (And see Plate 26.)

Floods are lamps so arranged as to throw light evenly over a wide area. The larger ones (up to 1,000 watts) can be very cumbersome and of not much use to a puppeteer. The smallest can be any size you like—a 100 watt household-type lamp set in a tin can makes an excellent flood. If a mushroom-shaped mirror light is used, so much the better. A type of light known as PAR (Parabolic Aluminised Reflector) is common and is made in various colours, usually pretty basic but very useful.

Spots will throw a hard-edged circular patch of light. Lenses are used for this purpose, and it will depend on these and their focusing potential to give a large or small patch of light at a given distance. A spot giving a narrow beam of light is said to

116

THEATRE LIGHTING-EQUIPMENT
as described in Section 26 on stage
lighting. The reference diagram shows:

1. Pattern 23 Stand Electric spot-light.
2. Long-focus lens attachment for
   Pattern 23.
3. A very useful mushroom-shaped,
   100-watt silver reflector lamp with
   adjustable lamp-holder.
4. Strip-light with holder and reflector.
5. Minuette spotlight, Fresnel type
   (soft focus) made by CCT.
6. Known as a Par 38 light. Very tough,
   made in four different colours and clear.
7. A big mushroom-shaped light (150
   watts with reflector) is mounted in a
   large beer can held on a wooden
   adjustable stand.
8. A selection of colour slides.

Also shown: Two metal slide-holders
and a safety chain.

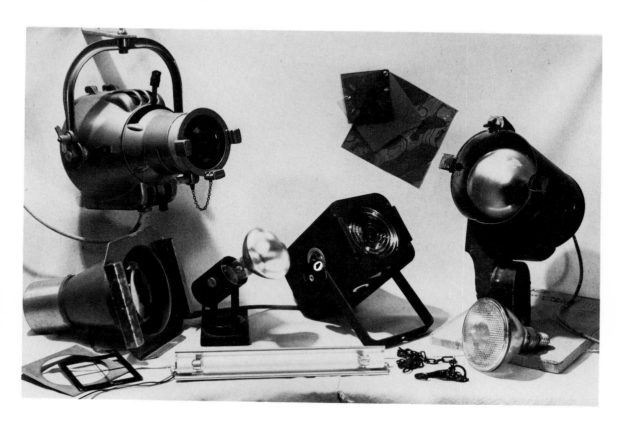

have a long focus, and one which has a wider beam is called a short focus lamp. An enormous number of spotlights of different kinds have been made recently but the Strand Electric 'Pattern 23', available with long or short focus, held the market for a number of years. Rather a large lamp for puppeteers.

A profile spot has a very sharp focus, enabling one to throw a beam of any shape with the aid of various masking devices.

A Fresnel spot is a type of lamp which gives a soft pool of light instead of a hard circle. It is very much in favour with puppeteers, usually giving a light of better quality than the profile spot. It can be focused—in other words, the pool of light can be made larger or smaller, but there is always a good deal of spill. (This means that a certain amount of light is discernible outside the main pool of light.) Fresnel spots are sometimes made quite small in size. A very good medium size is the CCT Minuette, using between 250 and 500 watts and giving a clean light with good colour value (see p.117).

A Tungsten-filament light is the normal household lamp in which the light is given by the resistance of the filament wire which causes it to turn white hot (or nearly so) without melting. It does not burn up as it is suspended in a vacuum. The light given is actually not a clean white, and the slightly brown or yellow tint can give disappointing results when thrown on blues or blacks. This can be counter-acted by throwing the light through a pale blue slide but this causes some loss of power.

The Quartz Halogen light has come into favour recently as it gives a clean white effect which mixes well with colour. A number of very good Quartz Halogen spots have come on the market recently, and a special fitting can be used for converting old Pattern 23 lamps to Quartz Halogen. The lamps are expensive but you get more light for the power used than with the common tungsten filament. It is possible to get Quartz Halogen lamps which work at a very low voltage. A 12-volt lamp has such a small element that it can be used to throw clearly defined shadows without the aid of lenses. Power from the 240-volt mains can be transformed down to 12 volts by using a small transformer. Special connecting plugs should be used on the 12-volt circuit so as to avoid accidentally plugging a 12-volt lamp into a 240-volt circuit, which would blow it instantly.

A strip light is a filament light in tubular form, useful for giving a weak spread of light from a trough or from behind or under a ledge.

Fluorescent light is not often used for stage lighting as it is difficult to control and flickers when first switched on. It has two good characteristics—it is inexpensive to run and it gives off no heat.

Ultra-violet light produces ultra-violet rays only. These react on certain substances and not others. (Uses in the theatre to be described later see page 158.)

27 Using the Equipment

Rod and glove puppets have a great advantage over string puppets inasmuch as they can be lit from above, but at the same time they are inclined to perform very far

118

forward, almost under the arch of the proscenium in fact, and this poses a problem because a light falling too vertically can have an ugly effect on a face.

So light the rod or glove puppets on the playboard by means of two or more spots (or other lights) directed from either side out front in and down at an angle of 45 degrees to the vertical, crossing the beams of light so that the stage-left area is lit from the right and the stage-right area from the left.

How you position and support these lamps is a matter of choice. Lamps free standing on tripods or other forms of lampstand are ideal from a lighting point of view but they do constitute a danger to the audience, especially where children are concerned. If lampstands have to be used, they should have extremely wide, heavy bases or the bases should be fastened to the floor in some way. It is difficult to envisage a way in which lampstands could be made totally accident-proof but, if they are to be used, this must be done.

Ideally some other means of supporting these exterior lights should be worked out. If your stage is a permanent fixture in a building, lights can be slung from a beam above or mounted on brackets fastened to walls, but a touring stage should be self-contained and capable of supporting all the equipment used.

Brackets slung out from the flats on either side of the proscenium would seem to be the answer, and these can be devised in various ways. I suggest neatly made wooden brackets, carefully designed to be bolted onto the flats marked D and F in Figure 40 and protruding horizontally from the points marked L. Figure 62 shows side and front view of one such bracket. It is made of two pieces 2 x 1 inch (5 x 2.5cm) nicely finished pine held at right angles to each other by a triangular piece fastened in with glue and wood screws. The horizontal piece is finished off with a piece of stout iron strip drilled to take a bolt which in turn holds the lamp. The upright part of the device is bolted through the covering of the flat to two horizontal battens; the lower one is part of the normal structure of the flat, the upper one is placed specially in position to take the bolt which supports the upper end of the bracket but it will be used also for lights which will be mounted inside the framework of the stage and which are to be discussed later.

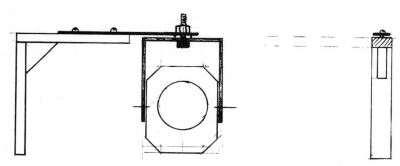

62 Bracket for out-front spotlight

The lamps used outside the proscenium should be either spotlights or lights so devised that they do not spill too widely. It would be a good idea to visit a firm dealing in the sort of fittings designed for lighting shop windows and exhibitions. You might find some useful patterns which will cost a great deal less than the average stage spotlight. If you do decide to buy stage spotlights, consider the Minuette, a 250-500 watt Fresnel lamp made by a firm called CCT. This lamp, which was mentioned on p.118, is light in weight and moderate in size, but even so it could look large and clumsy outside your proscenium. It is, of course, ideal for a permanent theatre.

Lights of the type shown in Figure 63 might suit you better and will certainly be much cheaper to instal. The lamp shown is a simple shop-window or exhibition type of fitting with a screw cap reflector-type mushroom-shaped bulb obtainable in 100 or 150 watt size. The 100 watt size gives a very clean light and, suitably masked, would look good, two each on either side of your proscenium opening. This means less light than if you had, say, two 250 watt spots but the quality of light would be satisfactory and a greater variation of colour would be available. The 150 watt could be considered but these are much more bulky and more difficult to mask down.

Within the proscenium more lights of the same type can be added to give direct effect from either side onto the playboard area. I suggest two more of the 100 watt mushroom type for this purpose and another two to be directed onto the central stage area.

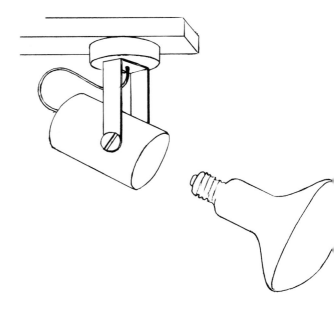

63 Adjustable lamp-holder mounted on batten

The holders of these lamps can be mounted onto strips of 3 x 1 inch (7.5 x 2.5cm) pine each fitted with a hook made of 1 inch (2.5cm) aluminium strip which will enable it to be attached to the special batten K (Figure 43). They should be mounted singly or in pairs as in Figure 64. They should be beamed down at an angle, and in positioning them care must be taken to make sure that they will not interfere with the curtain which will be drawn out to either side when opened, or with the puppets which will make entrances and exits from the playboard. The backdrop will also need to be effectively lit, but this is no very great problem. Again mushroom lamps in holders mounted on boards with aluminium hooks can be used very effectively, this time hung on side flats about half-way back.

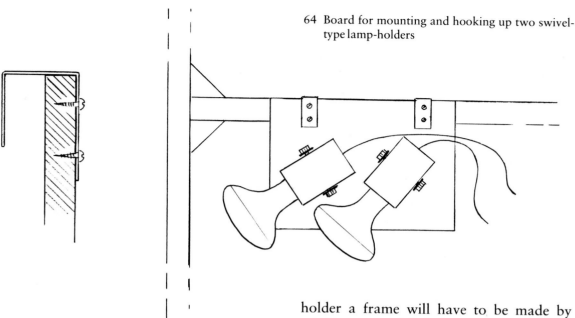

64 Board for mounting and hooking up two swivel-type lamp-holders

The above-mentioned lights are reasonable in price and effective in many ways but they have no facility for throwing coloured light, so some sort of attachment will have to be devised for this purpose. Sheets of coloured gelatine were used for half a century for giving colour to stage lighting, and the pieces so used became known as 'gels'. Gelatine has recently been supplanted by other, more durable materials. Two of the popular trade-names of these are Cinemoid and Roscaline, and there must be many more—but whatever they are, backstage we still call them 'gels'.

So a frame of some sort is needed for supporting gels in front of each of the lights you use. Theatrical spotlights are supplied complete with gel-holders but for the mushroom bulb in its exhibition light-holder a frame will have to be made by cutting a round hole in a square piece of light aluminium or tin sheet and then bending the edges round on three sides, leaving the fourth side open so that the gel can be slipped into place. (See Figure 65.) This can be kept in place in front of the light by means of a stiff piece of soft iron wire fastened to the wooden base of the lamp assembly by two round-headed screws. If

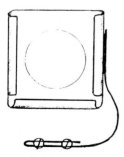

65 Sheet metal holder for colour slides

121

tin is used for the gel-holder, it can be soldered onto the wire—if aluminium, the wire will have to be attached by bending it through two holes drilled down one side of the sheet or by simply sticking it on with Araldite.

At maximum your proscenium and playboard area will be lit by eight lamps, four outside and four inside; the backdrop may need another four lamps, and you will need another lamp or two to light the central playing area back from the playboard. This gives a total of fourteen lamps. If more powerful lamps are used, of course, fewer will be needed but I think you will get more subtle results by using fourteen 100-watt lamps than with, say, ten of 100 watt and two 250-watt spotlights.

Whatever the answer, a switchboard and some system of variable control will be needed before you can try it all out, so read on through the next section and plan the rest of your lighting set-up according to whatever is available.

28 Lighting Control

The apparatus used for the control of an electric lighting circuit is commonly known as a 'dimmer'. There are three main types of dimmer in common use: resistance, induction and thyrister.

Resistance dimmers are now somewhat out of favour, their size and weight being the chief factors against them. Certainly they are cumbersome—a 500-watt Strand Electric resistance dimmer measures 20 x 6 x 5 inches (50 x 15 x 12.5 cm) and weighs about 10lbs. Control is effected by running a carbon contact slide up and down a double spiral core of resistance wire, so effecting a greater or lesser resistance to the current passing through. These dimmers are easy to work with accuracy and are very tough and durable, but as well as being bulky have a disadvantage in that they can only handle in a satisfactory way the precise power load for which they were designed. If, for instance, a 500-watt dimmer is in circuit with a 500-watt lamp, it will give an even control of light from zero to full power. But if a 250-watt lamp is put in the circuit, the light will come up abruptly after the scale mark leaves zero and be almost at full power soon after the mark leaves half-way. This can be very awkward, especially if two or more lamps are switched into one circuit, as very often happens in a small fit-up.

A dimmer which gives a completely different performance in this respect is the induction dimmer. An induction dimmer designed to handle a 500-watt circuit will give perfectly smooth and even control whether the lamp in circuit is 500 watts or a tiny 15-watt miniature. These dimmers are usually much more compact than the resistance dimmers and considerably lighter. They are, however, more sensitive to abuse and are inclined to react badly to power surge. Availability may be a handicap. A Japanese firm had a very good line in one- and two-amp induction dimmers some years ago, and we bought several for the Little Angel Theatre. They are still giving good service but they have one peculiarity which should be noted. When they are turned on to full, they actually increase the output voltage to about 10 volts above the input. This meant that our lamps were in danger of being overloaded, which could of course shorten their lives, and we had to put stop pins in the control knobs of the dimmers to keep their output to the right maximum level.

The most popular means of lighting-control at the moment is the thyrister dimmer. Dimmer boards using this system are available now in a large variety of makes, sizes and designs. Many of them are rather costly but they give a fine range of push-button performance ability. If you have the money, try looking at Strand Electric 'Tempus' range of controls and dimmer packs or at a small 'ACT 2' low-cost dimmer. If, as is more than possible, you find these beyond your budget, look around the smarter electric lighting supply firms and you will most likely find some effective little instruments designed for controlling household lights, exhibition lighting and so on. They are mostly built in single units, so I suggest you try out one or two different makes and designs before you set about building up a whole system. Make quite sure that they do not radiate electric impulses which will interfere with gramophone or tape-recording machines. Some of the first thyrister dimmers designed were very troublesome in this respect. Be careful always to get instruments suitable for the power needed.

29   Positioning and Wiring up the Lights

As you design your lighting outfit, bear in mind some of the essential extras to be incorporated. These will include a 'working light', an ordinary naked light used when setting scenes and for general work before and after performances. This light saves you having to use your stage lights unnecessarily.

It is also important to have a few plugs on independent circuits so that extra lights can be added at will. Your production might need a light incorporated in a prop lamp or a light for a shadow screen or other effect.

If you are to use sound equipment such as record-player, tape-recorder or microphone and amplifier, it is always best not to plug these into the stage lighting circuit. It has always been proved better to plug them into a different source on the main supply.

When the lighting set-up is planned, I suggest that a diagram should be made showing the positions of the lights on the stage and the way they are linked up with the dimmer board and the switchboard. After this a wiring circuit will have to be devised. If you have no knowledge of electrical wiring, this will, of course, have to be handed on to an expert. A stage switchboard with full dimmer control can be quite complex, and even when the work of wiring is done by a knowledgeable person it should be carefully tested out with a proper testing-meter before it is connected up to the mains. If no testing-meter is available, a battery and a low-voltage lamp can be used.

With the lights, the switchboard and the dimmers carefully tested, the next thing is to place them all in the right position for maximum effective results. Easy access to switchboard and dimmers is essential but these items must not obstruct the movements of puppet-operators. Cables must be placed so as not to hamper footwork in any way, and lamps must be placed in the most advantageous positions. This is best done by trial and error, and it is a good idea to set your puppets up in the positions in which they are most likely to appear on stage and beam the appropriate lights onto them one at a time, noting the results carefully as you go along. Treat the lights allocated to the backdrops and scenery in the same way and draw up a plan showing how all lights are positioned for, as near as you can judge, the best results. This might look something like Figure 66

with the positions of lamps and the directions of effective beams of light radiating from them shown diagrammatically.

For the sake of clarity Figure 66 shows only eight lights in position, and perhaps it would be a good idea to start off with only eight and to add others as the expertise develops. To read the plan: SL and SR are small Fresnel spots lighting from outside the proscenium opening. PL and PR are floods directed down onto the playboard area from fairly high up behind the proscenium

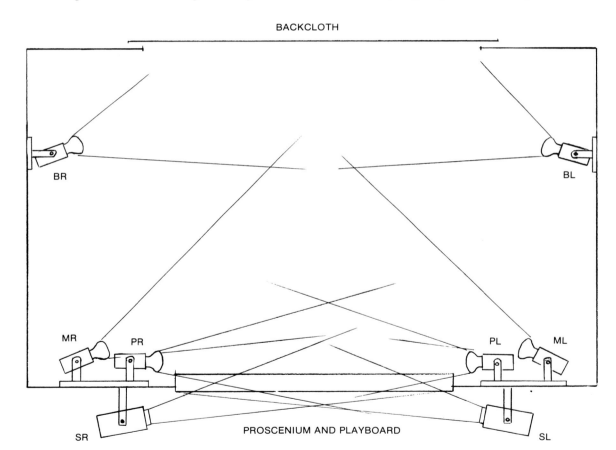

66 Plan for eight light positions for fit-up

124

opening on either side. ML and MR are similar lights from as near as possible the same positions as PL and PR but directed to the mid-stage playing area. BL and BR are floods positioned so as to give the best light onto the backdrop area. In all cases the light positions should be such that shadows of puppets are not cast on the backdrop. Having aimed and positioned all lights carefully, switch them all on to full and look at the results from the audience point of view, with an assistant moving two of the puppets into all the positions they are likely to be placed in during production.

30 Colour

When it is clear that the best results have been obtained, start to think in terms of colour. Envisage some general requirements to start off with. For instance, you might need an outdoor daylight scene followed by a night effect, with perhaps one or two strong colours for some special purpose. Experiment is needed here again, but before you start, here are some useful hints to be borne in mind:

1. Don't use too much strong colour.
2. Keep the front spots (or floods) SL and SR in Figure 66 for the clearest, brightest effects.
3. A pale blue slide (steel) gives a good daylight colour balance.
4. Plain electric light has a yellow quality which looks bad on blues. The same light dimmed to below 75 per cent begins to turn an ugly brown, which can be disastrous.
5. Don't throw amber or yellow light onto blues or blacks.

6. Don't light greens with red light or vice versa.
7. Orange and certain greens don't mix too well either, though some weird effects can be obtained.

Experiment with colour in your lamps. Refer to Figure 66 and set up the following colour slides cut from sheets of Cinemoid or Roscaline:

SL—steel blue	SR—light amber
PL—turquoise blue	PR—medium blue
ML—magenta red	MR—steel blue
BL—medium blue	BR—light turquoise blue

Set up some puppets, arranging them in fixed positions, so that there will be no complaints from arm-weary puppeteers as you experiment, and try your luck. First switch on lights one at a time, noting the effects you have achieved, then switch on all lights and try reducing them each separately to see what each light means in combination with all the others. After that try grouping the lights so as to get a pure daylight effect and then a dark night effect. Then try for a strong dramatic effect, using the magenta red from one side against the turquoise blue from the other side. Whenever a shadow comes up, see if you can 'light it out' by bringing up another light directed straight onto the shadow.

You might prefer to give your lights numbers instead of referring to them by letters, giving those on stage right even numbers and stage left odd numbers and beginning with SL and SR as numbers 1 and 2, but for a small set of lights (up to twenty circuits) letters are probably better. Whichever you choose, mark your switchboard and dimmer board accordingly.

CUE No.	CUE	LIGHT	DIMMER		NOTES
	TITLE OF PLAY		**ACT 1**		**SCENE 3**
1.	Preset	PL	10		
		PR	10		
		BR	8		
		BL	8		
2.	Curtain	SR	0 —— 10		Fast
	then.....	SL	0 —— 10		
3.	Enter Percy	MR	0 —— 7		Slow
4.	Enter Clown	MR	7 —— 3		Slow 10 sec.
		ML	0 —— 10		X fade.

Prepare a chart with columns for cues, lamps and degrees of power on the dimmers. Figure 67 gives an idea as to how such a chart could be laid out. You might use it as a starting-point but every lighting expert has his own method of setting out his work. Some people, for instance, prefer to work from a chart which shows only the dimmer and switch changes for each cue. According to this arrangement the switchboard operator will have to read only the few essential figures and letters on the chart—an obvious advantage. He should, however, keep handy complete details of lighting for each part of each scene. Only by doing this can he check up on faults and errors which may occur as rehearsals and performances proceed.

31 Sound-Equipment

The use of sound-equipment with puppets has given rise to a great deal of controversy. I do not propose to be involved but will simply set out the various options open to you and make a few comments which may help you to decide what sort of equipment you think would be good for your particular purpose.

If you and your assistant puppeteers have good voices with powers of projection sufficient for the size of audience you propose to entertain, of course no microphone or amplification device will be needed. But do bear in mind that the term 'power of projection' does not just mean the ability to make a noise. An actor with good power of voice projection is one who can appear to be speaking with a normal voice and yet be heard perfectly by several hundred people in a normal theatre. This is more than most puppeteers will need to accomplish but for those who propose to use no voice-amplification device the matter of projection must be very carefully attended to. Test out the voices to be used in your show with an audience of friends who are prepared to give true and intelligent criticism and work from there. To acquire good voice projection something more is needed than the ability to shout, and special advice and a course of training may be needed.

Microphones

If you decide to use microphones, be prepared to spend quite a considerable sum of money. Cheap microphones are worse than useless as they can only reduce the quality of your performance. In fact, the distortion caused by a bad microphone can easily lessen the effective carrying-power of a voice.

You will have to decide where to position the microphone or microphones you propose to use. Fortunately microphones of good quality can now be obtained in very small sizes so that two or three can be installed at mouth height (or just below) underneath the playboard. The danger here is, of course, that very often the microphones will be too close to the mouths of the speakers and an arrangement of microphones over the proscenium arch might be better. In any case some very careful experiment must be undertaken in order to get an even pick-up of sound.

Microphones held on brackets set on the chests of the puppet-operators can give good results technically but, if the operators are involved in much action, a routine must be carefully worked out to avoid entanglement with the microphone cables. Throat microphones can be awkward for the same reason. Throat microphones can be very costly too. A chest microphone working a small pocket radio which transmits the dialogue to an amplifier and set of speakers is also to be considered but only if you have considerable funds to spare.

Amplifiers

Whatever kind of microphone you decide to use, be sure that the amplifier you select matches up properly and is capable of handling the number of microphones decided upon with power to spare. At one time valve amplifiers were the only ones which could be relied upon to give good speech amplification but great strides have been made with solid-state equipment in recent years, and it is generally agreed that there is little to choose between the two types. On the whole, valve amplifiers are somewhat heavier and rather more fragile than the other type.

Loudspeakers

The selection of loudspeakers suitable for your requirements could be quite a problem. However good your microphones, amplifiers and tape-recorders are, the results will be unsatisfactory without good-quality speakers of a suitable kind. Many modern speakers, especially the larger ones, are rich in tone value and provide a great volume of sound. Unfortunately in most cases such speakers, though wonderful for music, are totally unsuitable for speech. For many years now I have used a pair of 8 inch (20 cm) diameter Wharfdale speakers each mounted on a thick (¾ inch)—(2cm) blockboard panel about 2 feet (60 cm) long and 16 inches (40 cm) wide. This simple arrangement has been perfectly satisfactory but I doubt whether such speakers can now be obtained as types and styles have changed often in recent years. Do look around and try at least half a dozen types and makes before you decide on the correct one for your purpose. Perhaps the most suitable built-up type is the kind often used for public address systems which has a number of small speakers mounted in a row in a narrow, shallow box. If you decide on such an arrangement, remember that the line of speakers has to be upright so as to throw out a horizontal band of sound.

Tape-recorders

At one time the puppets' voices were spoken by a selected troupe of readers who either sat in the wings and projected their voices diagonally across the stage and through the proscenium or sat in the orchestra pit in front of the proscenium watching the movements of the puppets in a long, horizontal mirror in front of them and projecting their voices over the mirror towards the ceiling of the auditorium. This is an absolutely splendid arrangement if you can afford a troupe of readers or if you are working with a large group on an amateur basis and you have proficient readers amongst them. The alternative, is, of course, for puppet operators to speak the lines for the figures they are working, using microphones if necessary, or to rehearse the play very thoroughly and then record the dialogue on tape. The advantages of using a tape-recorder are:

1. You can perfect your timing and your speech and finally edit the tape in such a way as to finish up with the best possible rendering of the play which can then be delivered through suitably placed loudspeakers at a volume to suit the size and condition of the audience and the auditorium.

2. Once the recording is made, the play can be rehearsed indefinitely with the same style and tempo.

3. Operators can be cast in certain parts and changed around without reference to their vocal abilities.

Against these arguments it can be said that a play spoken by the puppet operators has a spontaneous quality which the tape-recorded version is bound to lack.

You must decide for yourself, but if you are new to puppetry I suggest that you and your assistant puppeteers attempt to speak the lines as you perform your puppets and resort to the tape-recorder only if you honestly think it will improve your show.

Here at the Little Angel Theatre most of our plays are recorded. Actors and actresses whom we could not possibly afford to hire for every performance have gone to great pains to make good recordings for us so that our audiences listen to well-spoken dialogue with exactly the right degree of sound volume for the acoustics of the building.

As with all mechanical and electrical equipment, only the best is good enough, and this applies even more emphatically to tape-recorders than to anything else. Out of six different makes of tape-recorder used here, only the Revox has proved consistently faultless and I have no compunction in recommending it. Originally made in Switzerland, it is now also produced in Germany. We have one of each at the Little Angel Theatre and they are equally satisfactory. These tape-recorders are known as reel-to-reel machines as opposed to the cassette type which is much smaller and usually less expensive. In my experience the reel-to-reel type gives much better results in recording voices, but of course improvements are always being made.

32 Recording Speech and Sound Effects

The manual of instruction in the use of the tape-recorder you buy is absolutely essential, as it will tell you how to set about making a recording, but here are some extra notes which may help you to achieve the quality you require.

1. Use the best microphone you can possibly buy or borrow.
2. Use professional recording tape of the best quality, 'standard play' (which is normal thickness) rather than 'long play' (which is thin and flimsy).
3. For the same money a two-track stereo tape-recorder gives better results than a four-track machine.
4. Have your microphone and readers as far from the tape-recorder as possible. A good microphone will pick up noise from the tape-recorder if it is too near.
5. Test out your recording chamber for echo and sound distortion. Hard brick or concrete walls surrounding a large empty room will give a devastating echo. Round a small room they will give a hard, boxed-in quality. Space, soft materials and broken surfaces will give the best results. An old-fashioned room with carpets, small pictures, lots of padded furniture, thick wallpaper and heavy curtains will usually give good results, but beware of things that rattle or vibrate. The room should of course be soundproof and free from electronic disturbance. A vacuum cleaner, radio, even a refrigerator in the next room, can cause a murmur on the recorded tape.
6. Test out your recording set-up very fully and long before your readers are due in for recording. It sometimes takes longer than you think to get the machine working at its best.
7. Split your text into easily handled sections and number them. The reader who starts each section should mark it by stating the number of the section, and if more than one attempt is made to record that section, he should give the number of the attempts. For instance, he should say before starting to read, 'Section 1, take 1', pause for three seconds and then read. Insist on at least ten seconds of absolute silence after each take. The readers will want to listen to each attempt before going on to the next section, so run the tape back and play it through to them; if there is any doubt as to the dramatic rendering of the piece or the quality of the recording, make a second effort, calling it 'Section 1, take 2'. Do not wipe or eliminate a 'take' unless it is a total failure; you might find that, in the end, parts of it could be used.

129

It takes quite a time to record a play properly. A lot will depend on how well it is studied and rehearsed before recording begins. Be sure to call as many rehearsal sessions as may be necessary to get the work into proper shape before starting to record. When it comes to recording, allow one four-hour session for every half hour of performance time, and if possible don't work for more than one session per day. Unless the readers are very expert, the quality of their work will deteriorate after a hard four hours of recording. Bear in mind that once the recording is complete and put to use you will hear any faults or failures in it over and over again as you rehearse and then perform the play. So edit the work very carefully, first playing the whole of the recording through and noting which 'takes' are to be used and which should be eliminated and then systematically cutting out the unwanted parts. These should all be spliced together and run on to a spool marked 'off-cuts'. Never throw anything away until the editing is absolutely complete. If a few vital words are thrown into the waste-paper basket, you might never be able to find them again. Editing is something you can learn only by experience. Allow plenty of time. Absolute concentration is needed and as soon as that goes stop and relax.

You will find the Revox an excellent machine for editing, and when you get the knack you can do remarkable things with it. Use only one band of the stereo system for speech and keep the second band for background noises and effects. The most genuine background noises very often don't record properly. The noise of horses hooves for instance, can be beautifully imitated by clattering two small open wooden boxes together. (Coconut shells were used in theatres in the old days.) An electric pump can be recorded to sound like a motorboat engine, and a door slam suitably recorded sounds more like a rifle shot than a genuine rifle shot does. To make a sound like an arrow hitting an animal, try hitting a hard cushion with a cane. Dog barks and owl hoots are better done by humans than by the creatures themselves. And so on. Using a good tape-recorder can be fascinating work.

130

IV
Practice and Presentation

IV
Practice and Presentation

33 Acting with Puppets

You may have spent many months planning, designing and making puppets, props and settings. The day will inevitably come when you and your fellow workers will have to concentrate on the matter of operating and presenting the finished results of your work in the form of an entertainment.

You will have experimented with each of the puppets that you have made, naturally, but now, as you approach the period of rehearsal and presentation, you must consider very carefully the technical problems involved in making easily understood movements and gestures with characters.

As an exercise, try to evolve a ten-minute sketch which can be mimed and easily understood without the use of speech. Act the part out with your own body, using no facial expression, and then try to translate your movements into puppet movement. Don't be trapped into the common mistake of acting with your own body at the same time as you work your puppet. Try out your personal action first, and then, keeping your

body as still as possible, do as accurately as you can the same action with your puppet. Avoid wagging your puppet's head with every word that is spoken. This is a very unfortunate habit which many glove-puppet operators get into. Work out positive attitudes to express each sentence that is being spoken, emphasizing a word if necessary with the sweep of an arm or a slight stiffening of the stance.

Keep your puppet still when another puppet is speaking. This is one of the golden rules of acting, and it should be strictly observed when working with puppets.

Glove puppets can play out to the audience with great advantage but be careful of your stance. If a puppet leans out too far over the playboard, he might miss the light or appear to be looking down at the floor in front of the stage instead of at the audience. When a puppet addresses the audience, he should look straight out to the centre of the auditorium. If he has to turn a little, he should look to one side and then the other, never with a bias to right or left. If he is addressing another puppet on stage, he

133

should turn at an angle of 45 degrees towards the other puppet, presenting his profile as little as possible to the audience.

One of the most difficult things about working with glove or rod puppets is the matter of height in relation to the playboard. As the puppeteer's arm wearies and begins to flag, the puppet sinks down until he is seen only from the waist up by the audience; obviously the puppet-operator must be resolute and strong. The rod puppet, although he may be heavier, suffers less in this way because his point of support is lower than with a glove puppet and the operator's arm does not need to be stretched to quite such agonizing limits. Exercise and much persistent practice will build up the necessary muscular strength to keep the puppet always in full view without effort. Puppeteers not only need good arm, shoulder and back muscles but must be surefooted and capable of supple action in order to move their puppets around a small and possibly crowded stage in a dance or a chase. So keep your puppeteers nimble and strong for the happiest results.

Study your puppets carefully and work out not only significant movement for them but movements which will accentuate personal character as well. Young Percy will obviously be full of exuberant movement. He jumps with excitement, turns quickly and runs where others wallk. The Wizard Wonderful has dignity and wide, sweeping, melodramatic gestures, sometimes emphasizing a sentence with a quick look to right and left as if to make sure that everyone is listening. At the end of the play, or course, he goes right out of character and all dignity is lost. Mr Ninepence with his heavy clowning is clumsy and plodding, often looking in the wrong direction and bumping into things and getting into a terrible frenzy when two butterflies torment him by whirling round his head and refusing to be caught. Female characters usually move in a more restrained way, practising little tricks like straightening out a lock of hair, smoothing down a dress. The voice, of course, is all-important but do not depend on it any more than you can help.

34 Directing and Rehearsing a Production

Although a puppet should be able to express character and theme through action and mime, the voice is, of course, important. There will be obvious problems with small companies. Not many people can present a very great range of voices convincingly, and the falsetto squawk of a man speaking the part of a woman can be tiresome to an audience unless the part is meant to be a humorous one. There are, nevertheless, single performers who are able to produce four or five different character voices very convincingly. It is all a matter of training and ability, and I recommend that anyone who is prepared to take his work with puppet theatre seriously should sign up for a course in voice production and speech training with special emphasis on voice characterization without harmful distortion and voice production without strain. A voice which is overstressed without proper training can be damaged without hope of recovery.

When voice rehearsals are started, it is

always best to read the script through with the cast using perfectly normal voices. After the first reading a discussion should take place and various character voices should be experimentally tried out. A director might miss some good opportunities here if he lays down hard-and-fast rules; his readers might well come up with some extraordinary and very colourful ideas. If you are not tape-recording your voices, you should rehearse your operators up to a point where they can speak their lines without much reference to the script before you start working on the stage but it is quite a good idea if each operator has his puppet in position on his hand as he sits and reads and learns his part.

When the puppeteers have got the hang of the words and the characterization, the positioning of characters on stage must be settled. A director might like to work with a series of diagrams and charts but I believe that such an approach, though undoubtedly valuable, must be regarded as very tentative. However carefully a scene is planned in the mind, when it comes to acting it out on the stage improvements can always be found. It need hardly be said that it is a great advantage to have someone 'out front' watching and working on every movement and gesture during rehearsal. Sometimes, of course, this is not possible but the difference is very marked between a play that is properly directed from out front and one that is simply worked out by the puppet-operators behind the playboard.

The director should build up a pattern of movement and position which varies constantly in keeping with the mood of the play. The relative positions of puppets each to the other can be fraught with meaning: the distant, cool conversation, the threatening sentence, the endearing words of praise—all these will have a different emphaisis depending upon the relative positions of the figures taking part, and it is up to the director to work out a pattern of movement which will bring the characters to the right places for the things they are assumed to be saying. The tempo of the play will naturally be varied, and this variation will act as a stimulation to audience reaction. The slow movements of sorrow or despair, the quick, sharp movements of excitement or uncertainty, the clear, precise progress of the character who knows exactly what he is doing, the frenzied movements of the exasperated or semi-lunatic and hundreds more can be studied and used to give colour and interest to your play. Watch also the patterns caused by the figures when they reach a static moment. Four figures equally spaced across a playboard can mean one thing, three together and one separate might give a totally different impression. These matters make a director's task infinitely fascinating.

As you rehearse your play, the theme of the work will develop almost without your being aware of it. There must be stimulating moments in every part of your work but don't try to sustain the excitement without variation. Dramatic works can follow many patterns of development but it is always essential to engage the full attention of the audience within the first few minutes. The establishment of the plot can follow, and the introduction of characters, each with sufficient emphasis to be clearly imprinted on the minds of the audience, should not be too hurried or lightly dealt with. Different

135

patterns of action can then be interwoven, and minor crises should build up at varying intervals, leading to the final climax which should top them all a few minutes before the end of the work. This sounds like a very stereotyped pattern, but if you study play-construction you will be surprised to find how many dramatists more or less follow these rules.

There are, as I say, variations to ways in which interest is built up and maintained. A director will always study the intent of his playwright work according to his interpretation of all that lies behind the purpose of the writing.

35   Stage Management

To get back to more practical things: as your rehearsals proceed, you will begin to think in terms of the lighting requirements, and you will, I hope, start off by referring back to the chapter dealing with the application and positioning of lighting-equipment and lighting with colour. You might prefer to leave this until rehearsals have reached a final stage but it is recommended rather that you start with the lighting quite early on so that the activities which come under the heading of stage management can be fully integrated with puppet-operating. So light each scene carefully, giving full attention to mood and to visibility, setting down every arrangement of lights and colour slides and scene by scene switching arrangements and the degree of light as allowed by the arrangement of each dimmer. You might be able to have an expert devoted solely to this task of controlling the lights or you may have to

split the work up amongst the puppet-operators. Whichever way it goes, have the lighting chart carefully adhered to. Indifferent lighting can ruin a performance.

You might find it an advantage to have a stage management chart as well as a lighting chart but this will be necessary only if it is a really complicated production with many changes of setting and a big list of props.

36   Administration and Planning

Starting from scratch, you will probably evolve your own planning and management policy, but I include here nevertheless some notes on these aspects of work based on a twenty-year experience of running a permanent theatre plus a touring company.

We have found it best to divide the work very clearly into two main categories: (i) administration, which includes secretarial and financial matters and (ii) artistic direction, which deals with all other matters. Some duties are, of course, shared between these two departments. Publicity is one of them as it is most important that the publicity should relate closely to the artistic policy of the theatre and yet be ultimately controlled by the secretarial machine. It is an advantage if the designer who produces settings and costumes can also make drawings for brochures and posters. A sense of compatible design is also required when it comes to type-face selection, layout and printing of publicity material, but it is the administrator who will decide when the publicity material is to be formulated, printed and distributed. Planning of the repertoire should be a matter for the artistic director, as should the selection of puppet-operators and voices, but there should always be close co-operation with all members of the company on these points. The policy should always include a strong tendency towards work on new productions and different techniques. Changes made should not be too radical, unless, of course, the current policy has failed. Too strong a variation in style will lose audiences; too mild a variation will be regarded as boring.

If you run a repertoire, you must hit on the right cycle of change. If a once-popular play seems to lose its charm, do not scrap it but put it to rest for a year or two and you might find that it will come right back into full popularity. Likewise, if a play in which you have great faith proves a failure on first presentation, keep it for a couple of years, then look at it with a more practised eye and try it again. Production costs can sometimes be regained and the whole venture turned to profit.

Be very careful about insurance. Not only must you and your building, your vehicles and your puppets be insured but your puppeteers and your public must be insured as well. If a puppeteer employed by you trips over a cable, falls and injures himself or pulls a lamp down onto his head, you may be held responsible even though the accident was not your fault. If you have a workshop and your company helps with making puppets, props or scenery, they will need protection, especially if power tools are used.

You also need to be insured against claims from your audiences. A member of the audience can trip over nothing and fall and injure himself or he could have his coat stolen or claim to have suffered as a result of drinking the coffee he bought during the interval. We once had a child in the foyer who bit a chunk out of a glass containing orange juice which he had paid for. (Since then plastic tumblers only have been used.) Select a good insurance broker and have all these points carefully considered.

If you give free performances or run your theatre as a club, the circumstances change but investigate the matter fully before you open your doors and don't take chances. Your puppets and your stage equipment will also have to be insured, especialy if you tour at all widely.

37 Rules and Regulations

As soon as you admit a paying audience, your premises will be regarded as a place of public entertainment by the authorities, and again you should seek advice as to the conditions under which you may operate. The main concern will be the risk of fire and public safety. Certain rules will have been laid down by the Council of the area in which you operate, and these rules must be adhered to. They may ask for special exit doors, rows of seats to be fastened down to the floor, aisles of a certain minimum width and fire-fighting appliances and exit lights of various kinds and in various positions. In London the GLC will supply on request a booklet dealing with all the rules and regulations which apply to places of public entertainment and no doubt other urban authorities do the same.

To ignore these regulations would be to risk immediate closure. Toilets must be of a certain number according to the size of the auditorium, and the health department will inspect your premises for cleanliness, especially if you propose to serve refreshments, however light. Study the regulations. They all make good sense and many of them will add to the comfort and safety of everyone in the theatre.

This bring us to one final point, and that is the handling of your audience. The people who come to see your show come in search of pleasure and enlightenment. It is up to you and your staff to augment this in any way you can. They may be late—they may be flustered after a difficult journey or exhausted by some disruption of family behaviour. They may be—they very often are—very peculiar people, but a calm, easy approach on the part of the box-office and front-of-house staff will nearly always help them to settle in and enjoy the show. And if they can do that, the full purpose of this book, together with your own fine efforts, will not be wasted.

Shadow Theatre

The shadow puppet is a type of rod puppet and therefore deserves a place here, though it differs vastly in style and presentation from the puppets we have discussed up to now.

A broad definition of a shadow puppet would be: a two-dimensional figure shown against a semi-translucent screen and lit so that an audience on the opposite side of the screen can see the shadow of the figure only.

A shadow puppet can be made of any rigid sheet material. Cardboard, three-ply and the specially prepared hides of animals are the most commonly used, but they can be of sheet metal or plastic in one of its many forms. Quite thick material can be used; I saw recently two Javanese shadow figures made of wood, beautifully cut and carved, but such figures are very rare.

Plate 27 shows three figures made for *The Pearl Diver* a story by Oliver Goldsmith shown as a ten-minute shadow show at the Little Angel Theatre. In the photograph parts that appear black are made of plywood except for the hands of the two outer figures, which are of Celastic. The open

parts of the plywood frames are filled in with Cinemoid or Roscaline (see material used for giving colour in section on lighting). The overlapping joints are drilled and loosely fastened with short lengths of cord knotted at the back of the figure and frayed, flattened and glued in front so as to present a flat surface to the screen. (A knot pressing against the screen would be unsightly.) Hair and costume are suggested by string and pieces of flimsy net or cloth. The old woman in the middle is more solid in appearance than the other two. Her hands are cut out of pieces of plywood which slide across open parts in the main bulk of the body, giving some unexpected and rather comical movements.

These three figures could be equally well made out of strong cardboard or Celastic or a combination of both, and for colouring experiments could be made with tinted tissue paper, cellophane or polythene. The main thing is that they should be robust and the moving parts should work freely.

Each puppet can be worked by three rods. The main support rod should be a wooden

Pl. 27. THREE LADIES involved in a
shadow show called *The Pearl Diver* by
Oliver Goldsmith. The two daughters have
string wigs and diaphanous garments of
muslin and net. Their mother with her
three-ply body gives a feeling of greater
substance.

140

dowel stick about ¼ inch (7mm) diameter glued into a small wedge-shaped block of wood which in turn is fastened by a light brass hinge to a similar piece which is glued to a solid part of the figure. Figure 68 gives a side view of such an arrangement. Figure 69 shows a method easier to make, though a little more fragile. It shows the rod as a thick wire with the end bent to form a triangle which is fastened to the back of the puppet with a strip of tough canvas or webbing. The latter could beneficially be strengthened by glueing a few strands of strong string over it or threaded through holes and flattened and glued on the front surface of the puppet. The arms are worked by thin wire rods with small loops which are tied through holes to the hands with nylon thread or thick strong linen thread. Friction at these points is considerable, and the thread should be renewed at the first signs of wear.

The girl's legs are jointed at the hips and knees but they are not directly controlled, some rather vague movement being obtained by touching the feet down on a narrow shelf of wood which runs along the base of the screen. The puppets are usually worked lightly held against the screen with the support rod at an angle of 45 degrees to the vertical. The operator's head is thus at a low level, and a source of light coming from

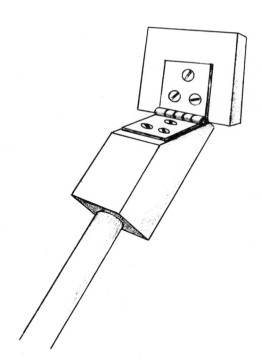

68 Device for fixing control rod to shadow puppet

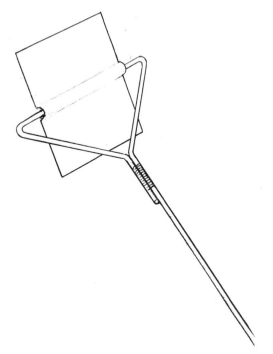

69 Wire control rod hinge for shadow puppet

behind and above does not throw the shadow of the head or hands of the puppeteer on the screen. (Greek puppeteers use a different arrangement which will be described later.)

Plate 28 shows a photograph of two dancing figures about 36 inches (90 cm) high made for a performance of Debussy's *La Boîte à Joujoux* at the Queen Elizabeth Hall in 1968. They are now part of a troupe of sixteen figures used in a piece called *Shadow Fantasy* shown at the Little Angel Theatre. The figures in Plate 28 differ from the *Pearl Diver* girls (in Plate 27) inasmuch as their arms, which are made of stiff rubber tubing, are not directly controlled and have only a slight swinging or bouncing movement. However, their legs are jointed at hips and knees and can be controlled by threads joined to points just above the knees. There are loops at the ends of wire antennae sprouting from the shoulders, and the threads run through these and down to wooden bars which can be pulled or worked with a seasaw action by the operators. When not in action the bars are fastened into clips at the lower ends of the main support rods.

With a little practice some simple but charming balletic effect can be obtained: the girl has a saucy, bouncing step while her elegant partner, relying much on carefully draped muslin, displays his skill with airy, drifting movements across the screen.

Included in the same troupe are some comical sheep with flapping ears of thin rubber (old bicycle tube) and woollen coats made of thick, soft string. They are hinged to a single rod at the spine so that they can be flicked over and made to run in either direction.

Pl. 28. *Right:* SHADOW PUPPETS made originally for a production at the Queen Elizabeth Hall and now a part of a balletic piece called *Shadow Fantasy*. The figures have plywood frames filled in with Cinemoid and are operated by rods from below.

A single, perfectly straightforward light is all that is needed for this show. We use a 150 watt mushroom reflector bulb mounted in a large beer can. Sheets of Cinemoid mounted in three-ply frames are used for occasional colour effects.

Another important item in our repertoire; known as *Crystal Shadows*, uses colour and what might be called projected effects in a way which was discovered only after much careful planning and experiment. The figures used are strange creatures made from drawings and designs by Michael Marks (Plate 29). They are part human, part bird, flower or fish, and their particular magic demands that they should be lit by colours mixed and sometimes blended into strange watery or floral or abstract patterns. To do this we set up, about two feet (60 cm) apart, two metal cans with quartz iodine lamps mounted in them. No lenses were used. In front of the lamps we placed a wooden rack which held interchangeable Cinemoid slides for colour and Cabrolite or other clear plastic sheets painted with the chosen designs in a translucent paint known as French Enamel Varnish. The lights were independently controlled by Variac-type dimmers.

If a shadow figure is held away from the screen, an ordinary filament lamp such as the mushroom reflector bulb used for *Shadow Fantasy* will give a soft, diffused

142

144

Pl. 29. *Left: CRYSTAL SHADOWS*, a production based on imaginative designs by Michael Marks. The original drawings were enlarged and traced onto a clear plastic material about the thickness and consistency of strong cardboard. They were then painted with coloured transparent vanish.

shadow. On the other hand a quartz-iodine lamp, providing a very fine point of light, casts a sharp shadow, even from some distance behind a screen, so that a water pattern painted on a square foot of Cabrolite or acetate can be made to cast a 5 foot (1.5m) square pattern onto a screen. This can be faded in from a black-out or mixed in with colour from another lamp at will. Some careful masking of lights must be done, and it will be necessary to determine the correct relative distance between lamp and colour slide and from colour slide to screen by trial and error. Or of course, it can

70 Diagram showing size of projected image in proportion to distances between lamp, slide and screen
A = lamp   B = slide   C = screen

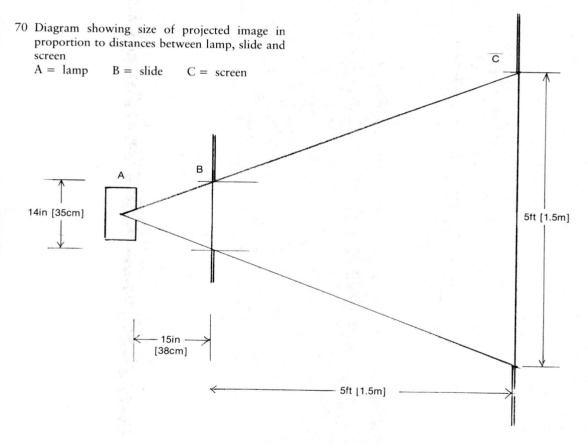

be done by making a simple scale drawing as in Figure 70, when A is a lamp mounted in a 6 inch (15cm) diameter can with a 2 inch (5cm) slot cut in one side. The light passing through this slot and a 14 inch (35cm) square painted slide B casts a 5 foot (1.5m) square image on the screen C. The distance between the slide and the screen is 5 feet (1.5m) and from slide to lamp about 15 inches (38cm).

The wonderful effects obtained when a figure can be made to change colour and appear against changing background patterns will astonish you and make all your efforts well worthwhile.

Quartz-iodine and quartz-halogen lamps can be quite difficult to set up and to handle. We have found recently that a Minuette lamp (see section on stage lighting equipment, page 115) with its lens removed makes an excellent projection lamp. This will, of course, cost a good deal more than the home-made tin-can light suggested above but it will be much safer to use and will be less likely to heat up.

If a powerful epidiascope or a specially designed slide projection is available, experiments can be made using small slides coloured with felt pens such as the special slide-projector felt pens made by Stabilo. Epidiascopes and other types of projectors are fairly common in schools and institutions nowadays, but they are expensive items and in selecting one care must be taken to ensure that it has a sufficiently wide-angle lens and enough power to be effective when used with other lights.

A warning: Without a lens, quartz-iodine and quartz-halogen lamps can cause some discomfort to the eyes and, if powerful, may

Pl. 30. *Right:* WAJANG KULIT means, in Javanese, a shadow puppet of parchment. The character shown is probably King Baladewa from one of the traditional plays about the five Pandawa. He is 24½ inches (62 cm) high and, to make the complex perforated design which goes to form his costume, his creator could have used up to as many as thirty chisels, each with a different-shaped cutting-edge. It is said that the eye is the last part of the figure to be cut and that the puppet's life begins when this is done.

even cause damage. So mask down carefully and never look into any ray of light cast by such a lamp.

There is no reason at all why shadow puppets should not be made of specially prepared leather except that it may be difficult to find and select this material. I know of only two suppliers, both merchants who prepare and provide parchment for book-binding and for drums and musical instruments. Their addresses are given in the list of suppliers at the end of this volume. There must be many more in all parts of the world; it is just a matter of tracking them down.

If you locate a supply of leather and you decide to use it, you will be following the time-honoured methods of the shadow puppeteers of the Far East, and although I do not recommend that you should imitate them too closely, a knowledge of how they work would be a help and a stimulant. The Javanese, for instance, have a very old tradition of shadow puppetry known as the Wajang Kulit, which is of the greatest interest.

They use the hide of animals (deer and buffalo) specially prepared so that it becomes semi-translucent but remains quite

146

stiff and very strong. They cut out highly elaborate figures decorated with perforated designs and coloured with dyes giving mellow tones which are exquisite as shadows. Plate 30 shows one of these figures. His main support rod is twisted and bent to fit the design of his costume. It is fastened firmly to him and is not hinged as our rods are. It has a sharp point at its base. The hands are worked by rods made of very strong, thin cane.

The puppeteer sits cross-legged behind a fairly large screen. In front of him running along the base of the screen is the soft trunk of a banana tree or palm of some sort into which the sharp ends of the puppet rods can be stabbed in order to hold them upright.

The puppeteer usually has one or two assistant's handing puppets to him from either side. He can assemble quite a crowd of characters on the screen by stabbing their control rods into the tree trunk at the base of the screen. He speaks, chants and shouts the lines of the play, whirls the characters about and at the same time beats out a loud clattering with a wooden castanet-like device fastened to one of his feet. Behind him he has an orchestra (called a Gamalan) of fifteen or more musicians with a great variety of drums, gongs, flutes and stringed instruments. Only one light is used and that is hung above and behind the puppeteer's head.

The effect of a Wajang Kulit show with full Gamalan orchestra is totally hypnotic and extremely beautiful. Audiences of Europeans unable to understand a single word of the play have been known to sit for a couple of hours quite entranced by a performance.

In Java performances are given out of doors and are said to be of great length. At one time members of audiences were segregated; men watched the show from behind the screen so that they could see the puppets, the puppeteer and the orchestra, while women were in front and could see the shadows only. I have tried both aspects and found them equally fascinating.

I cannot tell you very much about other shadows from the Far East but puppets from India and from China are to be seen in most good museum collections, and if you are interested in shadows, you should seek them out if possible. The Indian figures vary greatly. Some of them are large, colourful and of great beauty; others are effective in various ways, but few have the lace-like complexity of the Javanese figures.

Figures from China are delicately made and are usually quite exquisite. Most of those that I have seen are rather smaller than the Indian and Javanese figures, but recently I found some (in the famous puppet museum in Munich) which were quite as big as the average Javanese figure.

Nearer home are the Greek and Turkish shadows known commonly as the Karagioz (or Karagosis). Here again is a long tradition of performance, usually given by a single puppeteer (though he may have an assistant or apprentice) differing from the Javanese style of presentation inasmuch as the puppeteer stands behind the screen instead of being seated and the source of light is at the base of the screen and only a few inches away from it. This has the advantage of making the shadows of the operating rods almost invisible. It also results in the complete disappearance of the shadow of the puppet as the puppet itself is moved back away from the screen.

As in the Wajang Kulit shows, the puppeteer speaks for all the characters. In the shows I saw there was no music. Changes of scene are indicated by cut-out set pieces placed at the ends of the screen and are inter-changeable. The screen is rather wide in proportion.

The plays are witty and sometimes, especially in the case of the Turkish performances, somewhat crude. They are usually woven round the main character, Karagos, a popular figure with children and adults alike.

All in all there is plenty of traditional material to be studied before you set about making your own shadow puppets. Most museums have at least a small collection of figures, and some, such as the Stadtmuseum in Munich, have a great many very beautiful figures from the East Indies. In London the British Museum houses the Raffles Collection in which there are several hundred Javanese puppets and masks. In the Hogarth Collection (a small travelling collection to be seen only occasionally) shadows from the East are strongly represented.

Really successful contemporary shadow shows are few and far between. The most famous and completely successful is probably that of Richard Bradshaw, an Australian with a keen sense of humour and a gift of presentation which has brought him international fame. A company from Italy called Teatro Gioco Vita does a vigorous and ingenious *Story of Gilgamesh*, worth catching if ever it comes your way. In Britain, Christopher Leith does a one-hour

shadow show of great charm, but most companies limit themselves to short items in programmes of mixed media. This is probably due to a lack of confidence in the ability to hold an audience for more than a short time with shadows. There is room for exploration and experiment here, especially for those who feel drawn to a poetic style of presentation.

Some Practical Matters

In presenting shadows a great deal will depend on the quality of the screen used. For a simple shadow using one somewhat diffused light, the screen could be of thin, very finely woven linen but for the more sophisticated shows, using multiple light effects and powerful projection lamps, the plastic sheeting specially made for cinema back-projection effects is really essential. It is costly but, when you come to think of it, it is really the only expensive item necessary in putting a shadow show together. Suppliers to the cinema industry will give you prices, and there is an address in the list in the appendix. Ships' chandlers can sometimes provide a sailcloth which is also very satisfactory but it may be available in rather narrow strips, which, of course, means unsightly seams across the screen.

Setting up a small screen, up to about 4 feet (1.25m) by 6 feet (1.8m) presents no problem. It is best to use a light wooden rectangular frame firmly braced at the corners and with the screen material stapled on, or better still, fastened with strong camera tape. One of our screens has a heavy double hem all round with brass eyelets let in at 4 inch (10cm) intervals. This has advantages. Curtain cord can be threaded through the eyelets and round the frame, giving a perfect, evenly distributed tension to the screen, difficult to obtain with staples or masking tape. It does, however, add somewhat to expenses.

For a large screen a permanent frame will be unwieldy. A duralumin (aluminium alloy) tube not less than 1½ inches (4cm) diameter can be used as a roller at the top, and the bottom edge can be taped onto a wooden batten or a second duralumin roller. This together with the weight of the screen itself will probably give the working surface sufficient tension and resilience to enable the puppets to be worked against it.

If tubes and/or battens are used at the top and bottom only, the sides of the screens may tend to curl somewhat, but this can be overcome by taping the screen at a few points to the flats or whatever forms the side masking to the screen.

Screens are usually masked with a set of flats or with curtains arranged on wooden frame-work. A screen could be set in the proscenium of the fit-up described in Part III, Section 17. If shadows only are used, flats, C/D/E and F/G only will be needed as the fit-up will require no backing, but if, as is often the case, the shadows are only a part of the programme, of course the whole fit-up will be maintained. In this case it would be possible to have the screen on a roller which could be mounted on brackets above the proscenium opening and behind the proscenium curtains. It will be well out of the way when not needed, and it can be raised and lowered by means of cords fixed and operated as suggested in Section 21, Figure 55.

Positioning the light may be a problem. If it is too high, it could shine over the screen into the eyes of the audience. If it is too low, it might appear as a dazzling 'hot-spot' on the screen. If a diffused light is used, this effect can be modified by using a frosted Cinemoid or Roscaline over the lights, but if a clear projection-type light is needed, careful positioning and masking will be the only solution.

As mentioned earlier, a setting can be suggested by projecting a pattern or design or even a simple drawing onto the screen, watching the colour and the balance of light carefully to make sure that the strength of the shadow characters is not unduly diminished. Projected shadow settings can also be used very effectively as a backing for three-dimensional glove- or rod-puppet shows, though in such cases, of course, the screen will be behind the acting area. It is quite feasible to hang a shadow screen in place of a backcloth in the opening at the back of the fit-up and project light effects and designs from still further back, provided that extra space is available. Abstract and stylized designs can be most effective used in this way. Care must be taken with the stage lighting as any spill from the acting area will interfere with the projected light.

Black Theatre

'Black Theatre' is the name given to a technique of presentation in which puppets, stage furniture and props appear in shafts of brilliant light while the people handling them are in darkness and, clad in black and working against a black background, can be quite, or almost, invisible to the audience.

Plate 31 shows Angelo, a Black Theatre puppet operated by two puppeteers. For the purpose of the photograph the background has been lit so that positions of his operators can be seen working him on a tightrope. He is basically a rod puppet 30 inches (75cm) high. His head is of polystyrene covered and strengthened with paper and glue. His body and limbs are of foam plastic strengthened with wood across the shoulders and covered with a stockinette type of material for durability. His hands are of cloth sewn and stuffed, and his feet are of leather sewn or glued and stuffed. His joints are strengthened with leather or canvas webbing. His neck is in the form of a section of thick wooden rod ¾ inch (2cm) diameter which goes through his collar/shoulder piece to a fist size opening in his back. The chief operator holds this wooden rod in one hand and with the other hand controls the two hands of the puppet by means of short thin rods. A second operator holds a leather tag attached to each of the puppet's heels.

In the case of female figures in skirts, legs may be considered unnecessary, and such a puppet can very well be operated by one person alone. It is important that a Black Theatre puppet should be flexible and with good dramatic potential and above all be light in weight. The design of the operator's costume is important. It must be loose fitting and comfortable with long sleeves and plenty of overlap everywhere. Usually it is made in two parts like an old-fashioned pair of pyjamas. The best material to use is jet-black dress velvet. The operator wears a hood of the same material completely covering his head and neck. Holes for the eyes should be as small as possible and covered with black gauze. Experiments may be necessary to get the right size eye-hole and the correct density of gauze as the operator must, of course, be able to see properly under quite difficult circumstances

151

and yet not be seen. Spectacles worn by operators can cause problems as they catch light unexpectedly and glint through the gauzes. Thick black cotton gloves should be worn, preferably long ones to conceal the wrists of operators.

Plates 32 and 33 show members of Angelo's family with operators shown against a lighted background and with the light removed so that they become invisible to the audience. As you can imagine, the proper presentation of black theatre requires very special, carefully planned lighting. Banks of spotlights are needed on either side of the stage positioned so as to throw horizontal or near-horizontal beams of light across the stage through a system of vertically slotted masks. We use Strand Electric Pattern 23 spots with 500 watt lamps and lenses masked down to a ¾ inch (2cm) wide vertical slot to prevent light spreading and lighting up operators. CCT (who make the much sought-after Minuette lamps) have a profile spot which could be used in place of the Pattern 23s. We also use Minuettes carefully masked down but these are not totally satisfactory as they are Fresnel type (soft focus) and not designed for the sharp-focus work required for black theatre. There is always a certain amount of light spill round a soft focus beam.

Colour is important. Blues, greens and purples are effective and give no trouble but ambers and light reds tend to show up black-velvet-clad operators in a dirty brown light. If white light is required, it is advisable to use a very pale blue colour slide (commonly known as steel) as this has the effect of filtering the yellow out of normal electric light.

Distance from light source is another important point. If the lamps are too far from the puppets, the light beams will be spread too wide. If they are narrowed down to counteract this, there will be a very detrimental loss of power. We played *Angelo* at the Purcell Room (Festival Hall Complex) with a 20 foot (6m) proscenium opening. The lighting was a disaster. Using the same puppets and the same spotlights, we put on the show with a 10 foot (3m) proscenium opening a couple of years later, and with the much shorter throw of light all problems were easily overcome. using bigger and more brilliantly costumed figures helps considerably. *The Soldier's Tale* devils in Plate 34 go up to 8 feet (2.5m) high, and with wider beams from our Pattern 23s we were able to light them quite well in a 20 foot (6m) proscenium opening. I might say that we have tried them on an open stage and again met with difficulties. One is inclined to think that Black Theatre looks best under conditions of limited space.

Obviously some special staging arrangements are needed for the presentation of Black Theatre.

A good height for the playboard, or lower edge of the proscenium, would be 4 feet (1.2m) above the surface on which the operators stand but from an audience point

153

Pl. 32. *Left:* **BLACK THEATRE GROUP** photographed against a comparatively light backing so as to show positions of operators. The Angelo family have set up their stage, and Mother is handing out costumes from a hamper for the performance which is to follow.

Pl. 33. *Below left:* **BLACK THEATRE:** The same group as in Plate 32 but with backing in total darkness so that operators become invisible. Operators' black-velvet costumes must be adjusted with care so that no part of a light-coloured collar or cuff is revealed.

of view the playboard should be not lower than 5 feet (1.5m) above auditorium floor-level. This means raising the operator's floor-level surface by one foot (30cm) from auditorium floor-level. (See Figure 71.)

It is a great advantage to have a step up for the operators of another foot or foot and a half (30cm or 45cm) about 3 feet (90cm) back. (This is also shown in Figure 71.) Whether the sightlines will be satisfactory or not will depend very much on the seating arrangements of the hall or theatre. A raked (sloping) auditorium floor is always a help.

If you have to set up on stage, the lower you can work the better. A 3 foot (90 cm) stage will send the playboard up to a minimum of 7 feet (2.15m) above auditorium floor level. (See Figure 72.) Not so bad if the auditorium is well raked but a bit of a neck-stretcher for those in the front row, unless they are set well back.

The raised step at the back is not absolutely necessary but it does enable a second line of puppeteers to show their

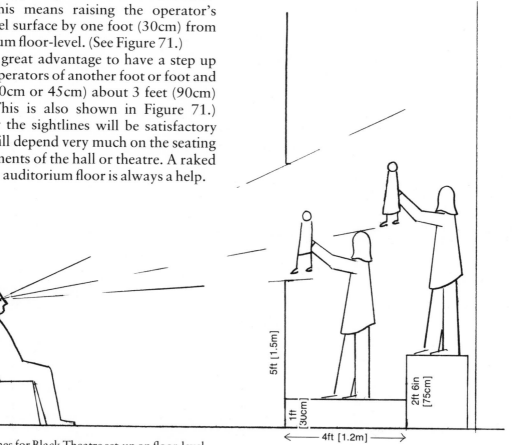

71 Sightlines for Black Theatre set-up on floor-level

155

puppets above the heads of the operators working at playboard level. Edges of platforms and steps must be clearly marked with white masking tape and lit with a carefully placed dark blue light.

To light the puppets properly, at least three spotlights, possibly four, will be needed at each side. They should be firmly clamped to a system of scaffolding so that when the beams of light are set they will not be jolted out of alignment during a performance. They will, of course, be masked by wings, which should be of the same black velvet as the operator's costumes, and a total stage backing of the same material is essential.

Props and furniture which are not set on the playboard should be mounted on movable stands which are painted black or covered with black velvet at any point visible to the audience. These stands can, of

Pl. 34. *Right:* DEVILS' HEADS: In Stravinsky's *The Soldier's Tale* the Devil appears as five different characters. Three of them are shown here in the form of large rod puppets made for a performance at the Queen Elizabeth Hall. They are, left to right: the Devil as cattle-dealer, as his diabolical self and as the butterfly-catcher.

course, be interchangeable. As rehearsals proceed, movements will be planned so that operators never pass in front of props or furniture or puppets handled by other operators. If they do, they will be seen in

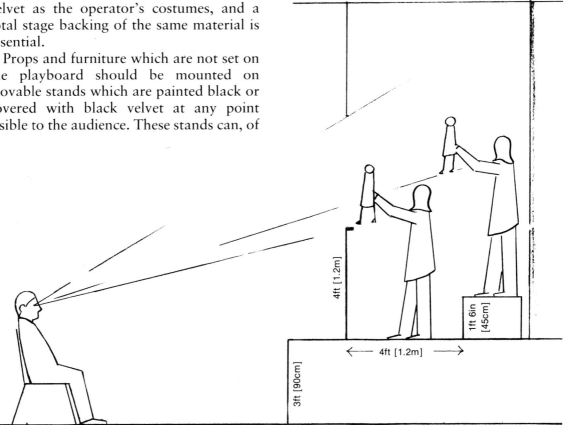

72 Sightlines for Black Theatre set-up on stage

156

silhouette by the audience. Also, operators must be careful not to move into beams of light intended for puppets.

Rehearsals for Black Theatre will probably start off with operators in normal dress and with no special lighting arrangements— but operators should learn to work in their hoods and gloves as early as possible because it takes quite a time to get used to them. Lighting should be arranged and brought into use as early as possible too, because an operator needs much practice to find a given beam of light and to work his puppet in it without being seen.

As rehearsals proceed, the operators will learn to work in with each other. Total co-ordination between all involved will become second nature but absolute maximum rehearsal time must be allowed.

During performances the auditorium needs absolute black-out. If there is to be any safety light or exit sign, this should be blue and as dark as possible.

Ultra-Violet Light

A performance lit only by ultra-violet light can also be said to be a form of Black Theatre.

Ultra-violet rays have the effect of making certain substances fluoresce while others remain totally unaffected. Ultra-violet is usually referred to by the initials UV, and for convenience we will call the materials and paints which are affected UV materials, UV paint etc.

If a puppet is coated with UV paint or clad in UV material and exposed to a source of UV light in what would otherwise be total darkness, the puppet will appear in brilliant colour. Starch, bone and certain calciums respond to UV rays, so if the puppeteer holding the figure is wearing a white starched shirt, his shirt, his fingernails and his teeth (if genuine) will also be visible in the surrounding darkness. It is customary therefore to use the same black hoods, costumes and gloves as in other forms of Black Theatre.

UV paints and materials are available in only a very limited range of colours. Their effect though brilliant can after a short time become very boring. Also a certain amount of strain is imposed upon the eyes of members of the audience watching UV. We therefore use the technique only for very limited scenes, such as our stiltwalker dance which lasts 2½ minutes and an underwater scene with fish designs painted on three-ply again only lasting three, possibly four, minutes.

Ordinary stage light, preferably low power and with fairly strong colour, can be mixed in with UV to give satisfactory results. We use this mixture to light our *Angelo* evening camp scene where the twins are practising conjuring tricks and magic. This also runs about four minutes.

The equipment needed to produce UV light is available in two forms. The first is a bulb looking like an ordinary household light in shape but fairly large and very dark purple, almost black in colour. It has a three-peg bayonet fitting instead of two, so it needs a special holder. It has to be run in conjunction with a choke to stop power surge when it is switched on. If the choke, wired in series, is not used, the lamp will blow immediately. It takes about two minutes to 'warm up'. In other words, it becomes fully effective about two minutes after it is switched on. When it is switched off, it takes a few minutes to cool off before it can be switched on again. Two bulbs are needed (wired to one choke) to cover an area of about 10 x 6 feet (3 x 1.8m).

The second type of UV light source comes in the form of a strip light or tube which looks like an ordinary fluorescent light tube. No choke is necessary and the tube, wired directly into the mains supply, can be switched on and off with immediate results.

My feeling is that power emitted by these tubes is not so strong or so rich in colour values as the more old-fashioned bulb-type lamp, but this might be just my imagination.

The tube, though more handy to use than the bulb, is more fragile, and on tour it should be packed and handled with care.

Suppliers of stage-lighting equipment usually carry UV tubes and bulbs. Brodie & Middleton, famous in London for their scenic paints, carry supplies of UV paints.

Pl. 35. ROD-GLOVE CHARACTERS: As in Plate 20, the figures shown have cast-rubber heads and hands carved in wood. These are the Wizard Wonderful and Mr Ninepence, from *Wonder Island*.

Wonder Island

A Play for rod glove puppets and three puppeteers

The characters are: Wizard Wonderful, Percy, Mr Ninepence and Tatty Cat.
The play is set on Wonder Island and the surrounding sea.

SCENE 1

WIZARD: Greetings, everybody. I am Wizard Wonderful of Wonder Island and I am fishing. I don't usually fish but today I am fishing—like mad. I must catch a fish . . . Now I'll tell you a secret. I am an inventor—a magical inventor—and I have invented something. This is a secret—you won't tell anyone, will you? I have invented a do-him-yourself flying outfit, and I have made this outfit—but so far only a small gent's do-him-yourself outfit. When you wear this do-him-yourself outfit you can fly up into the air very high, very magnificent. Would anyone like to try this outfit? No? Well then, I must continue to fish—like mad. Aha, I have a fish, a big fish—good. Now,

There is a burst of music. The curtain rises and the Wizard Wonderful is discovered stage centre with a fishing-rod, the line hanging straight down and going out of sight.

The line swings round and stretches out. A large fish is hauled up. It dangles in front of the Wizard, at first swinging out of reach as he tries to catch it.

161

with this big fish—hi—come here, big fish—here, come here. With this big fish I can get small gent for the small gent's flying-outfit. Wait and you shall see . . . Now mit mine sixteen times magnification magnifying telescope I can see—nothing—except the sea. Aha. Here comes small boat [*Reverses telescope*], very small boat. [*Reverses it again*] Now it is a bigger boat—and better boat. Small gent in boat—and friend—hmmm. No matter. Now my fish will bring this boat to me.

Fish, fish, do what I wish,

You see that boat there?

Go swim very near.

Fish, fish, do what I wish.

[*Exit Wizard. Enter Percy and Mr Nine-pence in boat*]

PERCY: It was somewhere just about here, Mr Ninepence, that I caught a very nice fish last week.

NINEPENCE: Are you sure, Percy? How do you know it's the same place?

PERCY: Well, it looks like the same place.

NINEPENCE: Without more ado let us cast in our hooks, our lines and our sinkers.

PERCY: Very well, Mr Ninepence. Ah . . . I have caught a fish, Mr Ninepence.

NINEPENCE: A blue one. And I have hooked a pink one.

PERCY: Oh What a beauty!

NINEPENCE: Rather a small one, but as you say—a perfect specimen.

PERCY: Oo . . . I have a yellow one. What luck.

NINEPENCE: And I have one with black and white stripes, a very interesting species.

The fish is caught and lowered out of sight again, and the Wizard comes up with a telescope. The telescope is supported at its centre point by a stiff vertical steel wire on which it can be spun round.

The telescope is lowered and the fish brought up onto the playboard again.

There is the sound of a motorboat off-stage. The Wizard dashes off stage right. Percy and Mr. Ninepence enter in a boat stage left. The motorboat engine noise peters out as it comes to a halt centre stage.

Percy and Mr Ninepence lower their fishing-lines and pull out fish.

Percy catches a blue fish,
Mr Ninepence a pink one.

Percy a yellow one.
Mr Ninepence a striped one.

162

PERCY: Mr Ninepence, did you see that huge one?

NINEPENCE: I did, Percy. Enormous he was and multicoloured.

PERCY: Oh, Mr Ninepence, I've got him.

NINEPENCE: Hold him, Percy. Play him. This is the catch of the year.

PERCY: I'm doing my best, Mr Ninepence.

NINEPENCE: Ho, Ho, what sport. Ha . . . Ha . . . Ho . . . Ho . . . for a life on the ocean wave. What speed. Superb.

PERCY: We're coming to an island, Mr Ninepence.

NINEPENCE: So we are.

PERCY: We are running aground.

NINEPENCE: Hold tight.
[Crunch]

PERCY: The fish has disappeared.

NINEPENCE: He's escaped, but never mind, Percy. There are plenty of other fine creatures about. *[Butterfly appears]* Take this one for example.

PERCY: Take it if you can, Mr Ninepence. I'm sure no one else wants it. *[Exit Ninepence]* I suppose I'd better go too—or he'll get lost and never come back. *[Percy exits left. Wizard enters right]*

WIZARD: Aha. So far—success. Here is small gent on the island for my flying experiment. *[Reverses telescope]* Very small gent. *[Reverses it again]* Now he is bigger—I will have to make him smaller when I catch him. I will put him in cage. But first to catch him. Where is my magic Tatty Cat? Tatty, Tatty. Puss, Puss. Kitty Kitty Kitty. Tatty Kitty.
[Enter black cat]
Titty Katty—Tatty Kit.

The Wizard Wonderful's large fish appears tantalizingly, first to the right of the boat, then to the left.

Percy's line goes suddenly taut. The big fish appears to right of boat hooked onto Percy's line and apparently dragging the boat along at great speed. Actually the boat remains stage centre, and the feeling of movement is given by two clouds on sticks which go whirling across stage from right to left several times.

Finally the boat is crashed off right, and the island comes in from the same side to centre stage half-way back.

Percy and Mr Ninepence enter cautiously from right. Boat and fishing-rods have disappeared. Mr Ninepence now carries a butterfly net.

A large butterfly settles on playboard centre.

Mr Ninepence attempts to catch it and rushes out after it stage left.

Percy exits stage left.

Wizard Wonderful appears from right, brings up his telescope from below the playboard and focuses it on Percy out left, reversing it to make the image smaller and then turning it back again. He disposes of telescope and calls his cat.

163

Help me just a little bit
Go forth and bring this boy to me.
And I will give you fish for tea.
Look. Big fish, hey? I give him to you. No.
Fetch boy here first—put him in cave.
Good Tatty. Go now.
[Exit cat]
While I am waiting, I will show you funny trick, yes?
Watch carefully.
One two, open. One two, close. Good trick, hey? I do it again.
One two, open. One two close. Iss goot, hey? Again. One two, open. One two, close. One two, open. One two, close.
[Several repeats]
Oh, oh, here he comes. One two, OPEN.
[Exit Wizard]
[Percy enters left with cat]

PERCY: Nice Kitty. What's your name? [To audience] Does anyone know what his name is? He looks very Tatty to me. Where has he gone? What were you doing in there? No. I don't think I'll go in there. Whatever are you up to? Whatever on earth goes on in there? I'd better go in and see.
[Exit Percy. Wizard enters left]

WIZARD: Aha—I have got him. Soon I shall starve him and make him small for my small gent's do-him-yourself flying machine. I am great inventor. Ha. ha. [Cat meows] Oh, Tatty Kit. Yes—here is fish for you. [Presents small fish] You don't want him? No. This is for you—big fish is for me. I am great magic inventor. Ha. Ha. Now I will go and starve the boy.
[Wizard exits through door of cave. Ninepence enters]

NINEPENCE: Oh how they torment me,

He offers the big fish to the cat as a bribe.

He bangs twice on the door of the cave in the side of the island, and the door opens. When he bangs twice again, the door shuts.

The action is repeated several times.

As cat and Percy arrive stage left, Wizard opens the door for the last time and disappears, leaving the door open.

The cat lures Percy through the cave door, which snaps shut behind him.

The Wizard springs out from behind the island. The cat appears from nowhere. Wizard offers it a very small yellow fish which hangs from a wire ring on his finger. Big fish comes up behind Wizard but he pushes it away.

Wizard goes to the cave door and, banging twice, orders it to open. He goes through and orders it to shut.

Ninepence enters left, striking out in a

164

these little flappidistric terrors. But where is Percy? You see, I am not only a great flappidoliger and fishologist but a great tracker as well. Now here I see Percy's tracks before me, and I will follow them right up to [Bump] the door of this cave. Let us try again. There are two sets of tracks this time. He must have a friend with him. And these tracks lead right up to the door of the cave. [Bump] Now there are three sets of tracks. That makes two friends if my arithmetic is not at fault. And these tracks lead right up to the door of the cave [Bump]. Oh dear, how positively despair-making. Ah. The door has opened. Success! [Exit to cave]

SCENE 2

NINEPENCE: A cave interior. Very dark, very very dark. But using my hands I can feel my way about, and by using my nose I can smell my way around. Now this smells very like a cage of some sort, with bars. And now I seem to have caught my nose in the bars of the cage. Very painful . . . very awkward.

PERCY: [In cage] Oh dear, I must have been asleep. What a funny noise. I wonder what it is. I'm so hungry. I hope the Wizard will bring me some food sometime soon. What is this? Is this something to eat perhaps? A nice big beetroot for instance or a sticky red toffee-apple? I'll take a bite out of it and see. Umph.

NINEPENCE: [Shrieks] That's not a toffee-apple or a beetroot—it's my nose.

PERCY: Mr Ninepence! Whatever is your nose doing in my cage?

NINEPENCE: It's stuck.

frenzy at two butterflies which whirl round his head and up into the air. Ninepence calms down and the butterflies exit left.

He goes over to stage right, examines the ground and traces imaginary tracks up to the door of the cave.

He collides with the door with a great crash (gong or large tin can) This manoeuvre is repeated three times.

After the last crash Ninepence in despair bangs twice on the wall next to the cave door, and the door opens immediately. He goes through the opening, and the door shuts behind him.

The island is turned about face slowly, and the lighting changes from daylight to a blue appropriate to a dark interior. Ninepence moves to the playboard and crawls along it, feeling it with his hands and sniffing it with his nose. He approaches the cage, feels it over carefully and then appears to get his nose stuck in it.

A little extra light comes up on the scene, revealing Percy in the cage.

PERCY: Well, I'd better unstick it. Shall I give it a bonk?

NINEPENCE: Yes, Percy just a tiny bonk.

PERCY: All right, just a tiny bonk. One two three—bonk.

NINEPENCE: That's no good, Percy, give it a bigger bonk.

PERCY: All right. A bigger bonk. One two three, BONK.

NINEPENCE: OW! Well done in the name of freedom, Percy. A painful measure but it is good to be free. Now in return I had better see about getting you free. I will feel around and try to find some means of escape. Aha . . . a barrel of black powder of some sort.

PERCY: How do you know it's black, Mr Ninepence?

NINEPENCE: All powder feels black in the dark, Percy. In daylight, of course, It might well be white or a blue powder but in this inky darkness it is definitely black. Moreover, it smells of fireworks.

PERCY: Look out, Mr Ninepence. It must be gunpowder.

NINEPENCE: How right you are, Percy. What luck. Now all I have to do is to light this barrel of gunpowder, and the cave will be blown to pieces and you will be free.

PERCY: I don't think you ought to do that, Mr Ninepence. We might be blown to pieces, too. [A noise is heard] Oh look out, Mr Ninepence, here comes the Wizard Wonderful. If he finds you here, he might put you in a cage and starve you too.

NINEPENCE: Very well, I shall hide behind the barrel of black powder until he has gone. [He hides]

Percy bangs Mr Ninepence's nose gently and then rather more energetically.

After the second 'bonk', Mr Ninepence howls with pain and falls backwards onto the playboard.

A small barrel has been moved in stage left. Mr Ninepence works towards this and sticks his head into it.

The Wizard is heard clearing his throat and coughing off-stage.

Mr Ninepence hides behind barrel.

166

[*Enter Wizard*]

WIZARD: Ho . . . Ho. Percy my boy. Have you starved nicely today? You are very thin, eh? Quite small.

PERCY: Oh Mr Wizard, please can I have some food? I am so hungry.

WIZARD: No.

PERCY: And I don't want to fly in your do-him-yourself flying-outfit. It's *your* do-him-yourself outfit, and so you ought to do him yourself yourself.

WIZARD: No. You shall fly in my do-him-yourself outfit. [*To audience*] I will make him do it yourself, I mean himself. Ha, why are we wasting so much time like this? Come, I will fix you up in this outfit and you will fly.

[*He exits with Percy in cage*]

NINEPENCE: Oh quick, I must save him, I must save him. I must blow the door open with this gunpowder. Quick, a fuse. Where is a fuse? There must be a fuse somewhere. Ah, here we are. Now, light fuse carefully and stand well back.

The Wizard enters and digs Percy in the ribs through the bars of the cage.

The Wizard pushes Percy's cage with Percy in it off-stage right.

Mr Ninepence dashes round the stage and finds a lighted sparkler which he applies to the barrel. Stage light fades rapidly and the cave/island is reversed to become the island again. The barrel and Mr Ninepence are removed in the near black-out.

SCENE 3

WIZARD: Ah . . . now let me see. This is not so good here. I must tighten this up a little bit. Where is my magical spanner? That is better. A little drop of oil in here. That is good. Now, when it is ready I shall say one fantastical magical poem and then I will shout you to fly. And you will wave your wings; Zo. Now. Wave your wings . . . let me see . . . No. Not like this—like this! No! Like this!

PERCY: Oh Mr Wizard, please! I'm so hungry. I feel quite weak. Please give me some food.

As light floods the stage again, the Wizard is seen dragging Percy, now equipped with do-it-yourself flying machine, in from stage right. He fusses round, applying what might be a small oil can and a cardboard spanner.

Percy listlessly flaps one wing of the machine, then the other.

167

WIZARD: No!

PERCY: Oh please, Mr Wizard, give me something to eat and then I really will try.

WIZARD: No. If you eat you will be too heavy. now waff your wings. Let me see. All right. Not very good but we will try. Now, my poem.
Creatures of the upper air,
Sitting on the clouds up there,
I send to you a little boy
To demonstrate this wonder toy.
And he will come from Wonder Isle
To flap about a little while,
And if he fall and break his neck,
I will try again next week.
Come flap, flap. Fly. Queek. Not too good. Try again. Queek. Fly. Dat is better. Bravo. I keep this rope see, so he can't fly too far. I can pull him down. Very good. Fly—flap—flap—further. GOOD!

[Explosion]

PERCY: Mr Ninepence, what a clever manœuvre.

NINEPENCE: Oh Percy, my boy! This has been a terrible experience. I'm glad you are safe and sound on terra cotta again.

PERCY: Help me out of this small gent's outfit please, Mr Ninepence, it's most uncomfortable.

NINEPENCE: Yes indeed Percy, then let us man our craft and hasten hence without more ado.

[Enter Wizard and cat.]

WIZARD: No. No. Not in there. No, not . . .

Percy flaps again forlornly.

Percy flaps more vigorously and appears to rise off the playboard. The Wizard has the white rope which goes round Percy's waist, and he makes some play of pulling Percy down and then easing up the tension so that he can rise again.

There is a terrific explosion, and a shower of rubbish (chopped up coloured cardboard) is thrown into the air in front of the cave door. Stage lights flicker. The Wizard Wonderful is whirled about. He disappears left.

The cave door bursts open and Mr Ninepence dashes out and up to Percy.

They go off right and the flying-machine is detached from Percy off-stage.

The cat chases Wizard Wonderful in from stage left, corners him against the Island and pushes him protesting through the door into the cave.

168

PERCY and NINEPENCE: Goodbye all.
Goodbye.

Curtain

Percy and Mr Ninepence enter stage right in boat. The cat joins them. Motorboat noises are heard and the boat travels across stage and out left as the curtain descends.

Appendix 1

Selection and Care of Wood-carving Tools

Teranti, Addis, Herring Bros. and Taylor are the names to look out for when buying wood-carving chisels. Of these only Taylor is still in business, but, if you come across anything secondhand made by any of the others, there is nothing wrong with a secondhand chisel provided it hasn't been allowed to get too rusty. In selecting new chisels, you will find that they are sold without handles. The chisel will have a spike which you are expected to fit into the handle of your choice. Make sure that the spike on the blade you select is straight in line with the blade, and select a handle which looks comfortable and the right size—perhaps rather too big than too small. The blades are more or less hand-made and they vary considerably. Make sure that those you select are slender and taper gracefully towards the cutting end, which should not be too thick or clumsy. Examine the inner side of a blade for pitmarks or defects—if it is unduly pitted, it will be useless to you. The outer side will appear fairly dark and rough but this need not concern you. Examine the blade for colour, as this will give some idea as to whether it has been well tempered or not. The handle end of the blade should be a purple brown. This colour should fade to clear metallic and then take on a very faint amber tint towards the cutting-end.

This amber tint is rare and is not often seen in chisels which are not very carefully tempered.

In the chapter on carving a head in wood, I suggested an assorted selection of flat chisels and gouges to start you off. As you take to the work, you will obviously need more.

When fitting new blades to handles, you may need to drill out and enlarge the holes which will receive the spikes on the blades but be careful not to make the holes too big as a loose handle puts you at a disadvantage. If you are afraid that the handle might work loose in the course of time, moisten the spike by dipping it in water before you drive it home into the handle; the rust which will form in time as a result of this will bond the metal with the wood, and the longer it lasts the firmer it will become. This is an old craftsman's tip which works well.

Figure 73 suggests a selection of twelve tools which will be about the maximum needed. All should have straight blades as curved and swan-necked blades are of little use in carving puppets. The lines in the diagram show the cutting-edges. A straight line is a flat chisel and a curved one a gouge. Only one v shape is suggested.

Don't be in too much hurry to buy. To get a good collection together needs time and patience.

73 Cutting-edges of carving-tools and angle of blade to sharpening-stone

ins		mm	ins		mm
$\frac{1}{16}$	–	2	$\frac{3}{16}$	⌣	5
$\frac{1}{4}$	—	6	$\frac{5}{16}$	⌣	8
$\frac{1}{2}$	—	13	$\frac{3}{8}$	⌣	10
1	—	25	$\frac{1}{4}$	⌄	6
$\frac{1}{4}$	⌣	6			
$\frac{3}{8}$	⌣	10			
$\frac{3}{4}$	⌣	19			
1	⌣	25			

B

20°

A

New carving-tools are sold unsharpened as fine edges would certainly be damaged in transportation and handling. Moreover, every wood-carver has his own way of putting an edge on a chisel, and for the manufacturer to do it would probably be only a waste of time. There are two phases in preparing a chisel for use. In the first it is ground, and in the second it is honed. The best way of grinding a chisel is to apply it to a wet grindstone (usually sandstone) wheel which is turned by hand or by foot treadle at a speed of about 100 to 150 revolutions per minute. Special mention is made of this because, if the stone is turned too fast, as in the case of a knife-grinder's motorized wheel, the quality and temper of the blade will be destroyed.

The chisel is held against the grindstone so as to cut away the metal at an angle of about 20 degrees to the inner surface.

The stone runs in water and is continually wet so as not to burn the metal. At the same time, the moisture prevents metal from the chisel filling the pores of the stone. If the surface of the stone were to be clogged with metal, it would lose all its abrasive power. When enough metal has been cut away from the chisel, a light fringe of steel will be seen along the edge. This should be brushed off and all moisture removed before the second phase of the sharpening begins. For this a really good oilstone is needed. A hard Arkansas sharpening-stone is one of the best.

First soak the surface of the stone with a light machine oil, then place firmly against the stone the area of the blade which is to be cut away and rub it to and fro on the stone, keeping it absolutely flat against the oiled surface. (See Figure 73B.) The oil on the Arkansas stone plays the same part as the water on the grindstone in preventing the surface of the stone from being clogged with metal.

Honing a blade is good exercise: a half-inch chisel will need ten to fifteen minutes of this treatment. When the sharp edge has developed a little light fringe again, it is almost time to stop. Turn the blade over and place it absolutely flat on the stone and rub it up and down a few times. Then test the edge on a piece of scrap carving wood.

When you have achieved as much as possible on the oilstone, you can if you wish take the job a step further by polishing the honed surface and other parts of the metal on a specially prepared leather 'strop'. This is an oblong piece of thick leather about 8 x 3 inches (20 x 8cm) with a little jeweller's grinding paste rubbed into the surface. Even without the grinding paste, the leather will give a good polish. Put a few drops of machine oil onto it, lay it on a flat surface and stroke it firmly with the chisel. The process is known as 'stropping'. It is healthy activity for fanatics with plenty of time.

Sharpening a gouge needs a little more skill as the blade must be rocked from side to side as it is applied to the grindstone and then to the sharpening stone so that the metal will be cut away as evenly as possible. Strong wrists and plenty of energy are required, and in addition quite some experience.

To finish up the process a 'slipstone' is needed. This is a wedge-shaped piece of sharpening-stone with two edges rounded to fit and rub down the inner sides of the blades. Only one or two strokes are needed.

To revert back to the appliances used, a grindstone of appropriate size might be quite difficult to find. Parry & Sons of 329 Old Street, London EC1, supplied the one which I have been using for the last thirty years but they now stock only an electrically driven wheel. It is slow running (120 revs per minute) so it would be perfectly satisfactory if you could afford such a luxury. A firm called Wouldham in Rochester, Kent, still make the hand turned variety. See list of suppliers in Appendix 4.

A number of different kinds of glue are mentioned in the course of this book. Here is a summary of their characteristics and their uses.

Carpenter's glue also referred to as **Scotch glue** and **pearl glue.** This is a good, old-fashioned glue made from the hides and bones of animals. Carpenters and joiners used it exclusively until casein and other glues became popular some years ago. Carpenter's glue comes in the form of broken slabs up to ¼ inch (.6cm) thick or in the form of small, round, light-brown beads (hence pearl glue). The slabs have to be smashed up with a hammer and put to soak overnight in cold water, just enough to cover. The glue softened in this way is then cooked in a steamer or double boiler. Special gluepots are used for this. They consist of a heavy cast-iron pot with a smaller pot suspended inside it. The larger pot is filled with water and put to boil. The smaller pot within it is filled with glue which is heated by the surrounding boiling water without ever quite reaching boiling-point.

A makeshift boiler can be made out of two tin cans (one smaller than the other) fitted with wire handles. (See Figure 74.) Be careful not to let the water boil away. If this happens, the glue will overheat and be ruined. As the glue warms up,

warm water can be added to alter the consistency. A great deal of stirring is necessary, and the glue must be kept as hot as possible while in use.

Pearl glue is treated in exactly the same way but it does need rather less time to soak in cold water before being heated than the slab glue

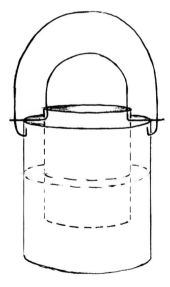

74 Home-made glue pot

does—about four hours is usually sufficient. Pearl glue is usually easier to handle and to store than slab glue. It is, however, more expensive to buy.

After using the gluepot, add a couple of drops of disinfectant as the glue cools down. This will stop it from going bad, which it does after a few days if not treated in this way.

Carpenter's glue, now seldom used by carpenters and joiners, is nevertheless of the greatest use to puppeteers and scene-painters, particularly where polystyrene is being handled, as it sticks this substance beautifully, and it is comparatively cheap. A most useful characteristic is that it can be dissolved away with hot water.

In normal climates it has a very long life but under very dry climatic conditions it crystallizes and deteriorates after a number of years, and under very wet conditions it may jellify and soften. It sticks wood, leather, polystyrene and all kinds of cloth, hair and feathers. Definitely not for rubber or metal. Fish glue and rabbit-skin glue are rare variations of carpenter's glue.

Nitro-cellulose glue, a comparatively recent invention, is usually sold in tube form ready for use. Bostick, a trade name, is one of the most common makes of nitro-cellulose glues. Its full title is Bostick 1 Clear Adhesive. Other makes are Uhu and Evo-stik (though various other glues are made under the name of Evo-stik).

This type of glue is usually used for small jobs only. It sticks wood, cloth, leather, string and hair and many other substances but not rubber or metal (although it may appear to do so for a time) and definitely not polystyrene, which it dissolves away.

It gives off inflammable fumes as it dries but it dries very quickly—a useful characteristic. It is a very good glue for quick repairs, prop-making etc. Surfaces to be joined should be clean, dry and free of oil. Once dry, it is not affected by weather conditions or moisture. It can be dissolved away easily with acetone.

N.B.: Acetone, a nitro-cellulose thinner, gives off an obnoxious gas and is highly inflammable. It should be used in a well-ventilated area.

The nitro-cellulose glues should be used by children only under supervision.

PVA (Polyvinyl Adhesive) glues have taken the place of the old-fashioned carpenter's glue in the workshops of all those who work with wood. It comes ready for use in plastic containers of all shapes and many sizes and, provided air is excluded, it keeps very well. It is opaque white and is of a creamy consistency. It can be watered down but this is not often necessary.

It won't stick polystyrene but is extremely good for wood, leather and cloth, string and feathers. It is not a 'tacky' glue, and the parts joined have to be held firmly in position during the setting process, which can take up to ten hours. The glue becomes transparent as it sets and so causes no discoloration and looks very clean. It is odourless, non-inflammable and very easy to use. Before setting, it can be dissolved away in water . Once it sets, though not generally regarded as waterproof, it is very difficult to unstick or be disposed of. Evo-stik makes a variety of PVA called Resin W, Woodwork Adhesive, and Unibond has a similar commodity called Superstrong Woodworker Adhesive.

Glue for polystyrene. There are several makes of glue which are especially suited for work with polystyrene. They form useful alternatives to carpenter's glue if you have a big polystyrene job on hand but if you need only small quantities at any one time, some wastage may occur due to the fact that these special glues are sold only in 5 litre cans and, once a can is opened, the glue deteriorates if it isn't used quickly.

The trade-name of one of the best of these

glues is Tretobond 375 Expanded Polystyrene Contact Adhesive. It should be stored carefully and kept away from children.

Rubber glue is sometimes known as rubber solution (the kind used by cyclists for mending punctures). It can be obtained in varying degrees of consistency, the thicker ones being recommended for most purposes. Try Dunlop 107 or Dunlop 888. The Pentonville Rubber Company stock it in cans but it can be obtained in tubes, and you are not likely to use all that much of it. It is needed only by those who mould heads in rubber or who use rubber for any part of their construction work. It is then absolutely necessary as nothing else will stick rubber properly.

It is inflammable and has to be kept well sealed from air when stored or it will dry out.

Copydex is a rubber-based glue but it is used only for sticking cloth or felt. It is invaluable for conditions where flexibility needs to be maintained.

Araldite is the trade name of a two-part epoxy resin. It comes in two tubes—one containing a resin and the other a hardener. The two mixed in equal quantities will stick metal, china, glass and many other hard non-absorbent materials.

It is an invaluable commodity and easy to use. Takes twelve hours to set under warm room conditions. A quick-setting variety is available but be careful not to stick your fingers together with it. Super Glue is even faster in action—it takes only seconds to set. Useful for instant repairs.

These glues should be kept away from children and clumsy or careless people.

Spray adhesives. A number of these have come into the market recently. 3M is the trade-name of one of them. They are mainly useful for glueing paper, photographs and other sheet material. Invaluable for sticking translucent and transparent materials without discoloration. Use sparingly and under well-ventilated conditons. Very dangerous in the hands of children.

Types
of Paint,
Pigment
and Dyes

For Painting:

Heads, hands and other exposed parts of puppets use oils, acrylic or emulsion paints or rubber paints

Calico or canvas backcloths, flats or drapes use dyes or scene paint in the form of dry colour (or powder colour) mixed with PVA or glue-size. OR use dyes.

Solid scenery and stage furniture use Emulsion paint, acrylics, poster paint or dyes.

Small props use acrylics, emulsion paints or designer's colours

Ultra-violet effects use ultra-violet paint or invisible ultra-violet paint

Transparencies and shadow puppets use dyes for parchment, French enamel varnish for other substances.

Acrylic Polymer is a recently developed paint based on a synthetic resin. Although the thinning solvent is water, these paints have many of the qualities and uses of artists' oil paints. Various mediums may be used with acrylic paints giving a matt, semi-matt or glossy finish to the paint. As the paint dries rapidly and is then insoluble, a retardent is useful for making the paint easy to handle. Brushes should be kept in water to prevent their hardening while work is in progress. When painting on wood, a primer is necessary. We have used glue-size and/or ordinary emulsion paint as a primer with apparent success but the correct one to use is a polymer primer (or polymer gesso).

Never use over oil paint or paint with oils over an acrylic polymer undercoat.

Best-known makes are Cryla made by George Rowney & Co Ltd and Liquitex stocked by the same company but imported from America. Also Reeves Polymer Colours—Reeves & Sons Ltd.

Emulsion paints are for the most part produced and sold for interior decoration of buildings, and they are therefore rather difficult to get in the small quantities required by puppeteers. They are excellent for anything made of wood or Celastic and in fact will take to most materials, though a metal-primer is necessary if the paint is to be applied to metal, and cracking and flaking will occur if used on rubber, calico or canvas. The colour range of any one make of emulsion paint tends to be limited to the lighter shades but Bollom & Co carry a very wide range of intense colours in a very good-quality paint. Although it contains emulsified oil, it is basically a water-soluble paint. Once dry it is quite indelible, and paint left to harden on brushes cannot easily be removed. The paint dries quickly but not as quickly as the acrylic polymer paints. It is easy to apply and has a matt finish.

Obtainable from any paint shop or hardware merchant dealing in supplies for interior decorating.

Fireproofing Mixture
Borax (crystals) 10 oz (300g)
Boracic acid (powder) 8 oz (250g)
Dissolve in 5 litres (1 gal) of water and spray or paint on.

Dry colour is a term applied to any basic pigment sold in powder form ready to be mixed with a binding or fixing medium such as glue-size or a resin of some kind.

It is the colouring matter most commonly used by scene painters as it is comparatively cheap, and mixed with a solution of glue-size or with PVA glue (in the proportion of 1 glue to 10 of water) it is easily applied to large areas of calico or canvas. Quite some skill is required, however, when it comes to selecting and mixing the paint. The strength and temperature of the glue-size are important. Some of the powdered pigments are reluctant to become absorbed into the liquid, in which case a few drops of methylated spirit can be added with immediate effect.

Most of the colours appear much deeper in tone when wet than when dry.

Brushes can be cleaned in warm water if glue-size is the binding material. Glue-size tends to putrefy, especially in warm weather. A few drops of antiseptic of almost any kind will prevent this.

Brodie & Middleton carry vast stocks of dry colour for scene-painting.

Dyes. Brodie & Middleton also carry stocks of aniline dyes which are very useful for scene painting and for colouring drapes and costumes. These dyes are not colour fast. They may fade in bright light and will rub off if too concentrated.

Dylon dyes, obtainable from any household suppliers or from the makers, are also very useful. I suggest that you apply to the makers for full details of all they have to offer as some new developments have been made recently. Dylon dyes are brilliant and are more washable and less inclined to fade than the aniline dyes but they are of course a good deal more expensive.

In handling dyes considerable experiment and practice are required. Their main advantage lies in their brilliance and the fact that they can be applied direct to almost any absorbent or semi-absorbent material without priming or under-coat and without any effect on the stiffness, flexibility or quality of the material. They can be applied over, or mixed with, other water-soluble paints.

Designer's colours. Some years ago these were produced by the main colour-manufacturers (Windsor & Newton and Reeves) as a water-colour paint of good quality and considerable brilliance but without the durable, non-fading qualities of artist's watercolours. They have proved to be very useful for colouring small props, stage furniture, for decoration on settings and in other applications where brilliance rather than large space coverage or durability happens to be necessary.

Poster paint is cheap and easy to use but usually a crude type of thick watercolour paint without much quality.

French enamel varnish. I can find no reference to this paint in my copy of *The Artist's Handbook of Materials* or in any other reference book available. All I can say is that it is an extremely useful paint for colouring slides, painting transparencies and staining woodwork. I suspect that it is a compound of dyes with an absolutely clear shellac varnish, as methylated spirit is used as a thinner, and shellac is the varnish used in what is known as French polish.

In spite of its obscure origin it is a paint well known in theatre scene-painting and prop-making studios where it is useful on account of its transparency. It can be easily obtained from the specialist paint merchants such as Brodie & Middleton. Rowneys sell it in small ink-bottle-size containers under the name of Vitrina for painting on glass.

Oil paints. The house-paint variety is of little use to puppeteers unless they happen to have a permanent theatre building which needs the usual decoration and maintenance. Artists' oil paints, however, are undoubtedly the very best for painting heads and hands and the visible parts of puppets.

The colours, as you must know, are packed in tubes so that a little at a time can be used without causing wastage. They are obtainable in a vast range of permanent colours. They are slow-drying and of a quality and texture that make them superb to handle. Glue-size or a special primer should be used as an undercoat but it should be possible for some of the oil to soak away in drying otherwise a shiny surface will result.

This tendency to dry with a glossy surface is the only disadvantage that I can see in using oils. It can be a troublesome factor when it comes to overpainting during repairs or renovations on old figures.

When overpainting with oils it might be advisable to rub down the original coating of old paint with some medium-fine sandpaper, taking the greatest care not to alter or damage in any way the original shape of the object being treated.

Turpentine is the correct thinner for oil paints.

White spirits can be used for cleaning brushes. Linseed oil is the binding agent in artist's oil colour but added linseed oil tends to make the paint undesirably shiny when dry.

Ultra-violet paints are paints which react to ultra-violet rays. There are two categories. The first is known as invisible UV paint, which is not visible in ordinary electric light or daylight but which shines out brightly when activated by ultra-violet rays. The other is reasonably visible in normal light and reacts strongly to ultra-violet light. There are very few colours available in the 'invisible' type of paint and, until recently, not very many more in the other category either. However, some new colours have now been made available, and these have added greatly to the potential of this medium which at one time could have a very boring effect when over-used in theatre.

Available from Brodie & Middleton in liquid form sold in small cans or in dry colour for more extensive use.

If bought in powder form, it should be mixed with glue size or diluted PVA of good quality as a binding agent. The invisible UV paints that I have used have tended to fade and disappear after a couple of years regardless of whether they are exposed to light or not. The others last rather longer but seem to lose some of their power with age.

Rubber paint can be specially prepared for painting heads cast in rubber by adding colouring material to vulcanized latex. Bellman and Carter are the experts in this field and can supply the commodities and all the advice needed to use them successfully. Their American counterparts are A.D.M. Tronics Inc., who apparently market a product called Pros-aide which fulfils the requirements and can, I am told, be mixed successfully with acrylics.

181

Appendix 4
List of Suppliers

Adhesives

Araldite Solvent Tele-Production Tools Ltd
la Electric Avenue
Westcliff on Sea
Essex

Beecham Proprietaries
(UHU Prods. Wholesale)
Beecham House
Brentford
Middx

Copydex Ltd (Wholesale)
Standard Works
Mount Pleasant
Alperton
Middx

Dunlop Semtex Ltd
(Thixofix Wholesale)
Chester Road
Erdington
Birmingham B35 7AL

Evode Ltd (Evostik Wholesale)
Building and Consumer Products Div
Common Road
Stafford STl6 3EH

Artist's Materials

L. Cornelissens
22 Great Queen Street
London WC2

George Rowney and Co Ltd (Wholesale)
P.O. Box 10
Bracknell
Berks

Reeves Art Shop and Dryad Craft Centre
178 Kensingston High Street
London W8

Windsor & Newton (Wholesale)
Whitefriars Avenue
Wealdstone
Harrow
Middx

Aluminium and Duralumin tubing *see* Metal

Barrels and Kegs

Hall and Ryan Ltd
20 Marshgate Lane
London E15

Beads

Ells and Farriers Ltd
5 Princes Street
Hanover Square
London W1R 8PH

Buttons and Buckles

The Button Box
44 Bedford Street
London WC2

Ashill Craft Studio
Brushford
Dulverton
Somerset (Mail Order)

Dylon International Ltd (Wholesale)
Worsley Bridge Road
London SE26

Fabrics: Canvas

Russell and Chapple Ltd
(Canvas, Hessian, Muslin)
23 Monmouth Street
London WC2

Fabrics: Dress Materials, all types

John Lewis Partnership
Oxford Street
London W1

Theatreland Ltd
14 Soho Square
London W1

Allans of Duke Street
56/58 Duke Street
Grosvenor Square
London W1M 6HS

Fabrics: Felt

B. Brown (Holborn) Ltd (Wholesale)
(Also Hessian and Suede Cloth)
32/33 Greville Street
London EC1

Feathers

E.H. Ruhle
9 Lower John Street
London W1

Louis Bund (Feathers and Flowers)
16 Ramillies Street
London W1

Fur

C. Looper and Son
3 Denman Street
London W1

Fur: Synthetic

Brimlake Ltd
Mr Vogel
38/40 Unit J5
Upper Clapton Road
London E5

Dewinter
223 Kensington Church Street
London W8

Government Surplus

Laurence Corner
62/64 Hampstead Road
London NW1

Hair: Natural and Synthetic

Delbanco Meyer and Co Ltd
Portland House
Ryland Road
London NW5

Hire: Stage Drapes

Stage Sets (London)
(Cloths, Rostra, Scenery etc)
22/24 and 42 Peto Street South
London E16

Lighting

C.G.T. Theatre Lighting Ltd
Windsor House
26 Willow Lane
Mitcham
Surrey

Donmar
Sales: 22 Shorts Gardens
          London WC2H 9AU
Hire: 39 Earlham Street
          London WC2H 9LD

Rank Strand Electric Ltd
Head Office: Sales and Hire
Great West Road
Brentford

Rosco Lab Ltd
69/71 Upper Ground
London SE1 9PQ

Theatre Projects Ltd
10 Long Acre
London WC2

Valiant Electrical Wholesale Co Ltd
20 Lettice Street
London SW6

Kenroy Electrics
Kenroy House
Dallington Street
London EC1

Metal: Fittings

Frank Romany Ltd
Ironmongers and Woodwork Supply
52 Camden High Street
London NW1

Metal: Sheet Metal Wire and Tube etc

J. Smith and Sons (Clerkenwell) Ltd
42/54 St John's Square
London EC1

Modelmaking Materials

Henry Nicholls Ltd
308 Holloway Road
London N7

Paint

Brodie and Middleton (Theatrical Suppliers)
68 Drury Lane
London WC2

Bromel
London: Depot 314/316 Old Brompton
               Road
               London SW5

               John T. Keeps & Sons Ltd
               15 Theobalds Road
               London WC1

Manchester: 40 Port Street
             Manchester

Trimite
(Flexible Rubber Paints)
Arundale Road
Uxbridge
Middx

Paper, Board and Cardboard Tubes

Wiggins Teape Ltd (Wholesale)
Chaswell Heath Mill
Mill Grove Road
Chadwell Heath

Wiggins Teape Ltd (Wholesale)
130 Long Acre
London WC2

Parchment and Vellum

William Cowley
Parchment Works
97 Caldecote Street
Newport Pagnell
Buckinghamshire
MK16 0DB

Plastics: Polystyrene

R Passmore and Co
12 Narrow Street
London E14

Sandell Perkins
Group Head Office
Cobtree House
Forstal Road
Aylesford
Maidstone
Kent

Plastics: Sheeting and P.V.C.

Grant Continental Ltd
Plastic Materials
Universale House
The Hyde
London NW9

Visjar Laboratories Ltd
(Fabrication Service)
Pegasus Road
Croydon

Rope and Cord

Arthur Beale Ltd
194 Shaftesbury Avenue
London WC2

Halls Barton Ropery Company Ltd
Virginia Works
Pennington Street
London E1

J. Shiner & Sons Hardware Merchants
(Nylon Picture Cord)
8 Windmill Street
London W1

Rubber Products: Foam Rubber

B. & M. (Latex) Sales Ltd
73 Station Road
Addlestone
Surrey

Unit 5 Supplies Ltd
111 Mortlake Road
Kew Richmond
Surrey

Pentonville Rubber Co Ltd
52 Pentonville Road
London N1

Bellman and Carter (Latex & Plaster Ltd)
358a Grand Drive
London SW20

Rubber Latex Ltd
Harling Road
Wythenshawe
Manchester

A.D.M. Tronics Inc
Northvale
New Jersey

Rubber Products: For Mouldmaking

Notcutt Ltd W.P.
44 Church Road
Teddington
Middx

Scenic: Materials and Shadow-screen material

Brodie and Middleton
(Theatrical Suppliers)
68 Drury Lane
London WC2

J. D. McDougall Ltd
(Theatre Suppliers)
4 McGrath Road
London E15

Roscolab Ltd
69/71 Upper Ground
London SE1 9PQ

Sculpture and Modelling Materials and Woodcarving Tools

The Fulham Pottery Ltd (Clay)
Burlington House
184 New Kings Road
London SW6

Henry Taylor Tools Ltd
The Forge
Lowther Road
Owlerton
Sheffield S6 2DR

Alec Tiranti Ltd
70 High Street
Theale
Reading
Berks

Alec Tiranti Ltd
21 Goodge Place
London W1

Harbutts Plasticine Ltd
High Street
Bathampton
Bath

Griffon and George
(Science & Educ Acetone)
285 Ealing Road
Alperton, Middx

Hopkins and Williams
(Acetone—for use with Samco and Celastic)
Freshwater Road
Chadwell Heath
Essex

The Luck Counter Co Ltd (Modelling materials
    and Celastic)
Spencer Street
Oadby
Leicester

Sound Equipment
(Tape Recorders and Amplifiers)

Raper and Wyman
34 Danbury Street
London N1 8JU

F.W.O. Bauch Ltd
49 Theobald Street
Boreham Wood
Herts

The Acoustical Manufacturing Co Ltd
Huntingdon
Cambridgeshire PE18 7DB

Springs

Flexal Springs Ltd
Cambridge Works Trading Estate
Montague Road
London W7

K. Rodgerson (Springs) Ltd
Menin Works
Bond Road
Mitcham
Surrey

Tools

Ashley Iles (Edge Tools) Ltd
East Kirkby
Spilsby
Lincs

Buck and Ryan Ltd
(Tools, Cutlery, Ironmongery)
101 Tottenham Court Road
London W1

S. W. Collins and Son
(Carpenters' Tools)
14 Earlham Street
London WC2

Parry and Son (Tools) Ltd
186 Main Road
Biggin Hill
Kent

Parry and Son (Tools) Ltd
329 Old Street
London EC1

Varnish (Shellac)

Ardenbite Products Ltd
57 Farringdon Road
London EC1

Wood

Moss and Co (Hammersmith) Ltd
104 King Street
London W6

Sandell Perkins
Group Head Office
Cobtree House
Forstal Road
Aylesford
Maidstone
Kent

Timberline
1a Langton Road
Tunbridge Wells
Kent

Puppet Plays

In the script cupboard at the Little Angel Theatre we have manuscripts for twenty-eight plays plus one printed play (in German), one opera and one translation of the Ramuz libretto for Stravinsky's *The Soldier's Tale* published by J. and W. Chester Ltd.

The manuscripts are mainly works derived from folk stories, (Grimm, Hans Andersen and anonymous, including two African tales) but two are derived from plays written for the human stage and several are original works written specially for us or by us. Four are derived from stories by well-known authors.

Royalties have to be paid on plays specially written for us or on works derived from stories written by living authors or to the author's estate if the author died less than 50 years ago as in the case of Ramuz's *The Soldier's Tale*.

The list of published plays which follows gives titles selected from the collection owned by The Puppet Centre, Battersea Arts Centre, Lavender Hill, London SW11. Those marked with asterisks are the ones which seem to me to be the most interesting.

Many of them have been out of print for a long time but second-hand copies might be found or they could possibly be available in libraries.

A Book of Marionette Plays by Ann Stoddard and Tony Sarg
(George Allen & Unwin)
* *Eight Plays for Hand Puppets* by A. R. Philpott
(J. Garnet Miller Ltd, London and Plays Inc, Boston)
* *Five Plays* by Garcia Lorca
(Penguin Plays)
Folktale Plays for Puppets, *Puppet Plays from Favourite Stories* and *Puppet Plays for Young Players* by Lewis Mahlmann and David Cadwalader-Jones
(Plays Inc, Boston)
* *Old England at Play* by Lynette Jeasey
(Harrap)
* *Plays for Marionettes* by Maurice Sand
(Translated by Babette and Glenn Hughes)
(Ernest Benn Ltd)
* *On Thrones of Gold* (Three Javanese Shadow Plays) by James R. Brandon
(Harvard University Press, Massachusetts)
(Oxford University Press)
Plays for Puppets by Rosalind Vallance
(Nelson)
Poor Giraffe by Marion W. Flexner and Dorothy Park Clark
Puppetry and Puppet Plays by Arthur Allen
(Allman and Son)

Puppet Plays by Dr Priestley
(Arnold)
Puppet Plays by Alfred Kreymborg
(Martin Secker)
* *St George and the Dragon* (Punch and Judy) by
Diana John
(Puffin)

With Puppets Mimes and Shadows by Soifer
(Furnow Press, New York)
Caspar and His Friends by Hans Baumann
(Phoenix House, London)

Bibliography

Adventures of a Russian Puppet Theatre by Nina Efimova
(Puppetry Imprints, Michigan)

The Art of the Puppet by Bil Baird
(Macmillan)

The Complete Book of Puppetry by David Currell
(Pitman Publishing)

Contemporary Hungarian Puppet Theatre edited by Dezso Szilagyi
(Corvina Press)

Continental Scene Printing by Vladimir Polunin
(C. W. Beaumont)

Costume Through the Ages by James Laver
(Thames and Hudson)

Dolls and Puppets by Max von Boehn
(G. Harrap and Co Ltd)
(Now re-published by Dover Publications Inc, N.Y. in 2 volumes)

Dzieje Teatru Latek by Henryk Jurkowski
(Panstwowy Insytut Wydawniczy)

The History of the English Puppet Theatre by George Speaight
(G. Harrap and Co Ltd)

Introducing Puppetry by Peter Fraser
(Batsford, London and Watson-Guptill Publications, N.Y.)

Karagoz Turkish Shadow Theatre by Metin And
(Dost Yayinlari, Ankara)

Liebens Werte Puppen Welt by Hans R. Purschke
(Marion von Schroder Verlag, Hamburg)

Masks of West Africa by Leon Underwood
(Alec Tiranti Ltd)

My Profession by Sergei Obraztsov
(Foreign Languages Publishing House, Moscow)

The Peep Show by Walter Wilkinson
(Geoffrey Bles, London)

Punch and Judy: A History by George Speaight
(Studio Vista, London)

Puppentheate, Gestern und Heute
(Staatliche Kunstsammlungen, Dresden)

The Puppet Theatre of the Modern World edited by UNIMA
(G. Harrap and Co Ltd)

Puppetry Today by Helen Binyon
(Studio Vista)

Puppets and Puppetry by Cyril W. Beaumont
(Studio Ltd)

Puppets and the Puppet Stage by Cyril W. Beaumont
(Studio Ltd)

Puppets in America 1739 to Today by Paul McFarlane
(Puppetry Imprints)

Puppets Through the Ages: An Illustrated History by Gunter Bohmer
(Macdonald, London)
Richard Teschner und Sein Figurenspiegel by R. Teschner
(Eduard Wancura Verlag, Wien, Stuttgart)
Rod and Glove Puppets by H. Fettig
(G. Harrap and Co Ltd)
Shadow Puppets by Olive Blackham
(Barrie and Rockliff)

Stage Lighting by Richard Pilbrow
(Studio Vista, London)
The Wonderful World of the Theatre by J. B. Priestley
(Macdonald, London)
The World of Puppets by Rene Simmen
(Elsevier-Phaidon)

Index

Notes